MUHAMMAD ALI
THE KING OF THE RING

CAMPFIRE®

KALYANI NAVYUG MEDIA PVT LTD

DI059891

MUHAMMAD ALI
THE KING OF THE RING

Sitting around the Campfire, telling the story, were:

WORDSMITH LEWIS HELFAND
ILLUSTRATOR LALIT KUMAR SHARMA
INKER JAGDISH KUMAR
COLORISTS VIJAY SHARMA & PRADEEP SHERAWAT
LETTERER BHAVNATH CHAUDHARY
EDITOR SUPARNA DEB
COVER ART PRINCE VARGHESE
DESIGNERS JAYAKRISHNAN K. P. & MUKESH RAWAT

www.campfire.co.in

MISSION STATEMENT

To entertain and educate young minds by creating unique illustrated books
that recount stories of human values, arouse curiosity in the world around us,
and inspire with tales of great deeds of unforgettable people.

Published by Kalyani Navyug Media Pvt Ltd
101 C, Shiv House, Hari Nagar Ashram, New Delhi 110014, India

ISBN: 978-93-80741-23-9

Copyright © 2011 Kalyani Navyug Media Pvt Ltd

All rights reserved. Published by Campfire, an imprint of Kalyani Navyug Media Pvt Ltd.

No part of this publication may be reproduced, stored in a retrieval system, or transmitted in any form or by any means,
electronic, mechanical, photocopying, recording, or otherwise, without written permission from the publisher.

Printed in India

Lewis Helfand

Lewis Helfand was born on April 27, 1978 in Philadelphia, and grew up in nearby Narberth, Pennsylvania. Although interested in cartoons and animation from a young age, Lewis turned to writing by the time he was twelve. After finishing high school, he remained in the Philadelphia area with the intention of pursuing a degree in English.

Four years later, with a degree in Political Science and a passion for comic books, Lewis began working for local publishers, proofreading books and newspaper articles. By the age of twenty-four, Lewis had been editing phone books for a year and a half, and felt no closer to his lifelong goal of writing comic books. So one day he decided to quit his job.

Lewis then spent the next two months working day and night to write and draw his first comic book, *Wasted Minute*. It tells the story of a world without crime where superheroes are forced to work regular jobs. To cover the cost of self-publishing, he began working odd jobs in offices and restaurants, and started exhibiting at local comic-book conventions. With the first issue received well, he was soon collaborating with other artists, and released four more issues over the next few years.

Outside the field of comic books, Lewis works as a freelance writer and reporter for a number of national print and online publications. He has covered everything from sports and travel to politics and culture, for magazines such as *Renaissance*, *American Health and Fitness*, and *Computer Bits*.

Lewis is one of Campfire's most prolific writers, and some of his recent titles include the award winning *Nelson Mandela: The Unconquerable Soul*, *Mother Teresa: Angel Of The Slums*, *They Changed The World: Edison-Tesla-Bell* and *World War Two: Under the Shadow of the Swastika*.

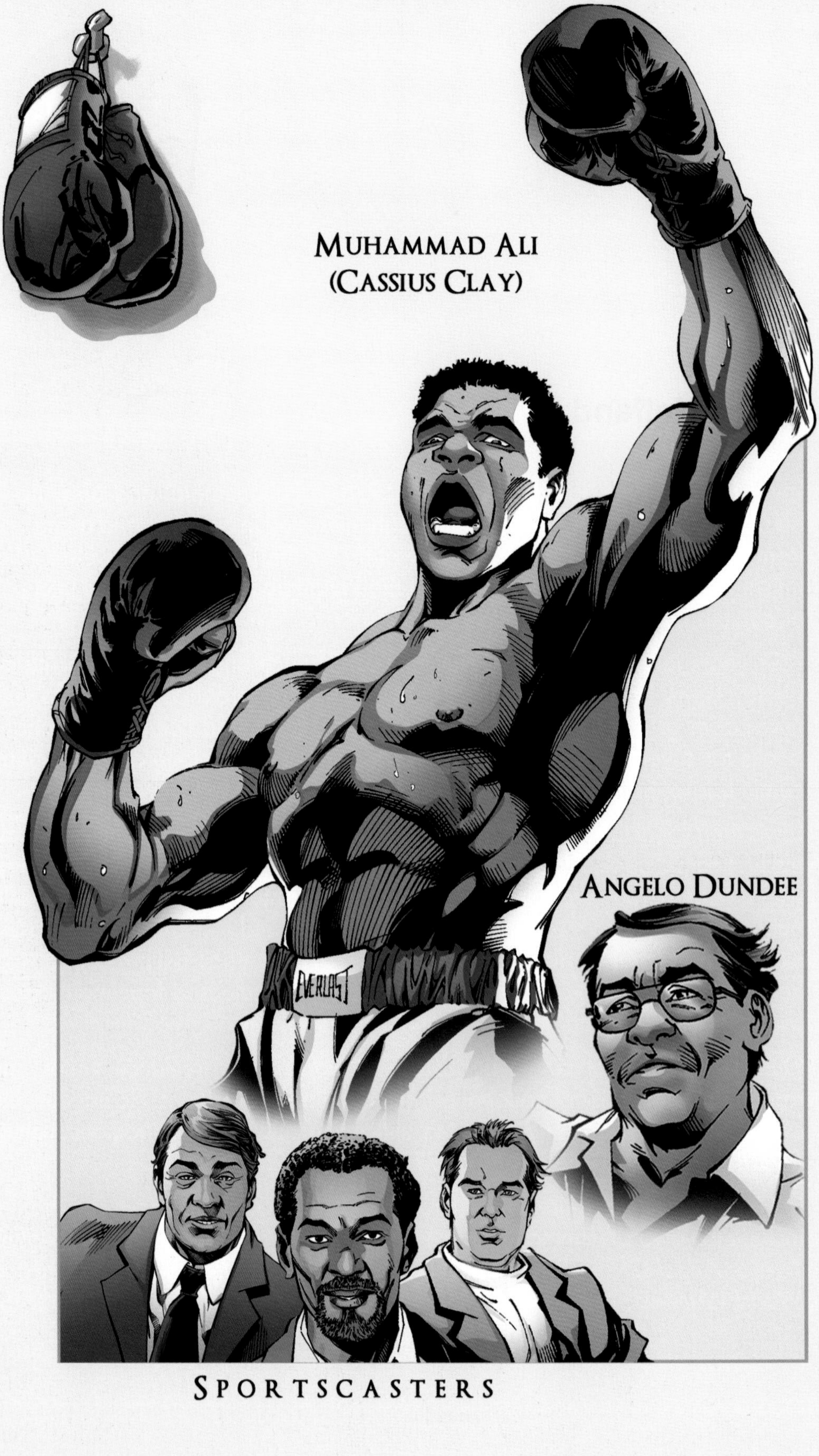
MUHAMMAD ALI
(CASSIUS CLAY)
EVERLAST
ANGELO DUNDEE
SPORTSCASTERS

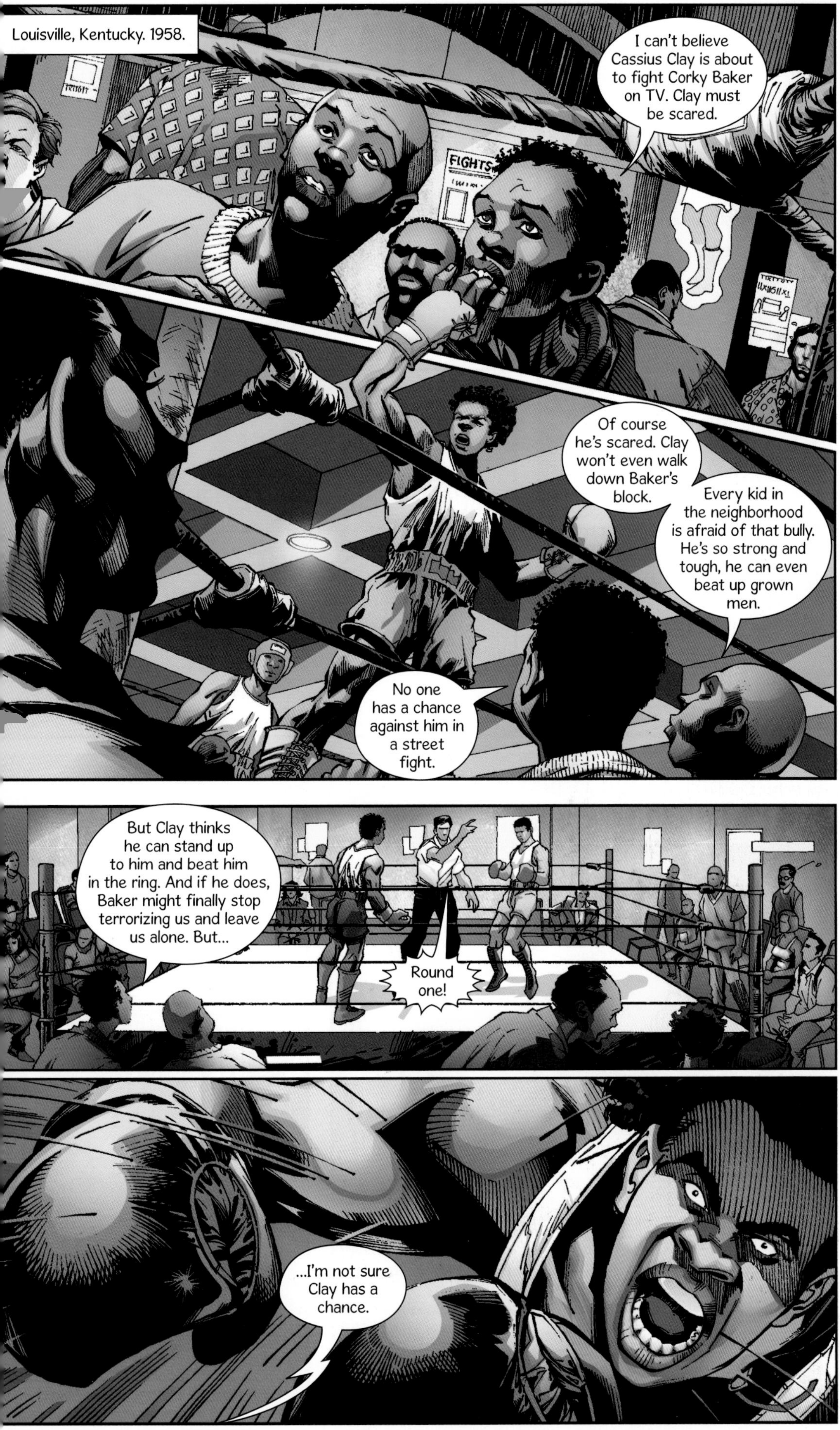

Louisville, Kentucky. 1958.
I can't believe Cassius Clay is about to fight Corky Baker on TV. Clay must be scared.
FIGHTS
Of course he's scared. Clay won't even walk down Baker's block.
Every kid in the neighborhood is afraid of that bully. He's so strong and tough, he can even beat up grown men.
No one has a chance against him in a street fight.
But Clay thinks he can stand up to him and beat him in the ring. And if he does, Baker might finally stop terrorizing us and leave us alone. But...
Round one!
...I'm not sure Clay has a chance.

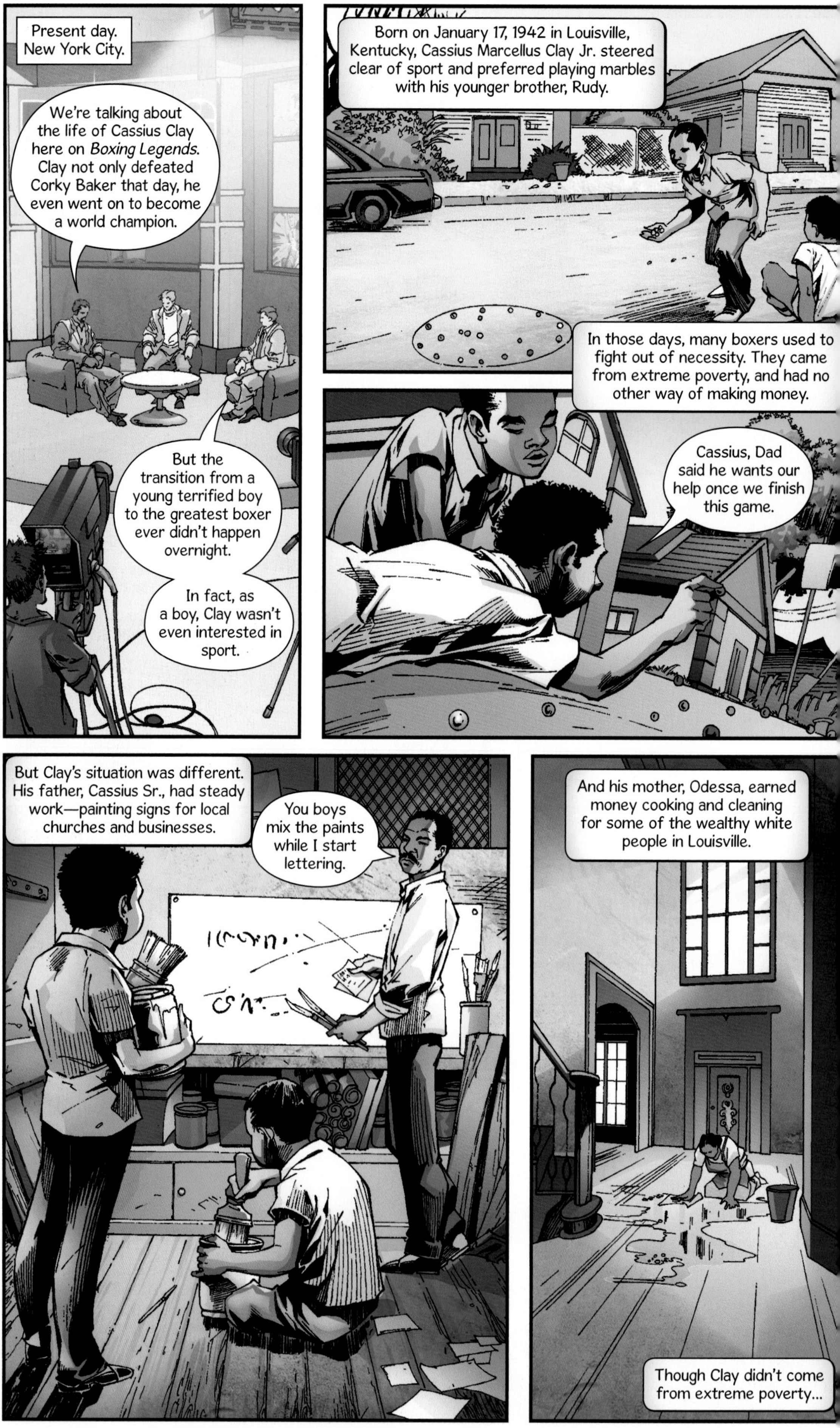

Present day. New York City.
We're talking about the life of Cassius Clay here on *Boxing Legends*. Clay not only defeated Corky Baker that day, he even went on to become a world champion.
But the transition from a young terrified boy to the greatest boxer ever didn't happen overnight.
In fact, as a boy, Clay wasn't even interested in sport.
Born on January 17, 1942 in Louisville, Kentucky, Cassius Marcellus Clay Jr. steered clear of sport and preferred playing marbles with his younger brother, Rudy.
In those days, many boxers used to fight out of necessity. They came from extreme poverty, and had no other way of making money.
Cassius, Dad said he wants our help once we finish this game.
But Clay's situation was different. His father, Cassius Sr., had steady work—painting signs for local churches and businesses.
You boys mix the paints while I start lettering.
And his mother, Odessa, earned money cooking and cleaning for some of the wealthy white people in Louisville.
Though Clay didn't come from extreme poverty...

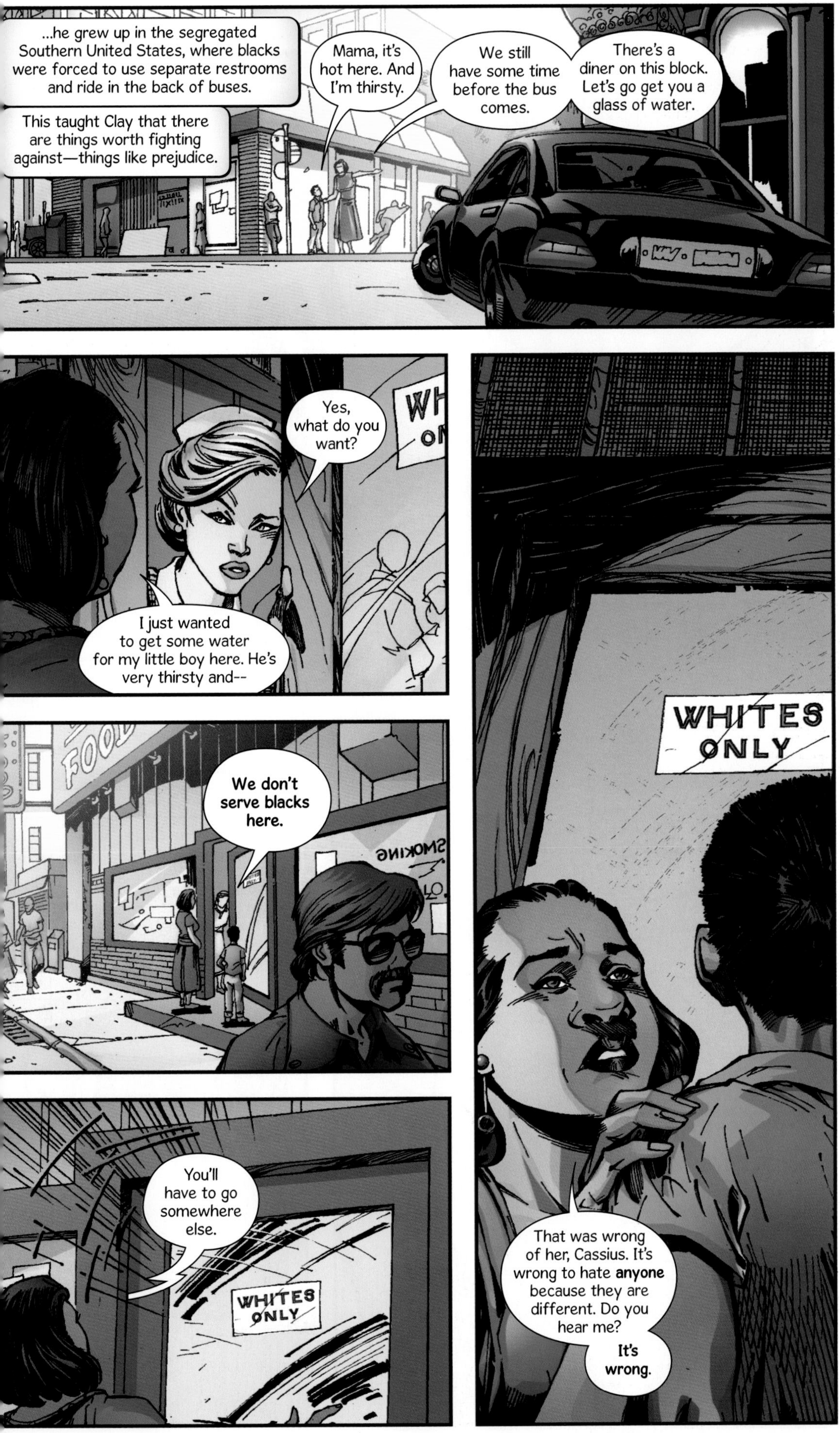
...he grew up in the segregated Southern United States, where blacks were forced to use separate restrooms and ride in the back of buses.
This taught Clay that there are things worth fighting against—things like prejudice.
Mama, it's hot here. And I'm thirsty.
We still have some time before the bus comes.
There's a diner on this block. Let's go get you a glass of water.
Yes, what do you want?
I just wanted to get some water for my little boy here. He's very thirsty and--
We don't serve blacks here.
You'll have to go somewhere else.
WHITES ONLY
WHITES ONLY
That was wrong of her, Cassius. It's wrong to hate anyone because they are different. Do you hear me?
It's wrong.

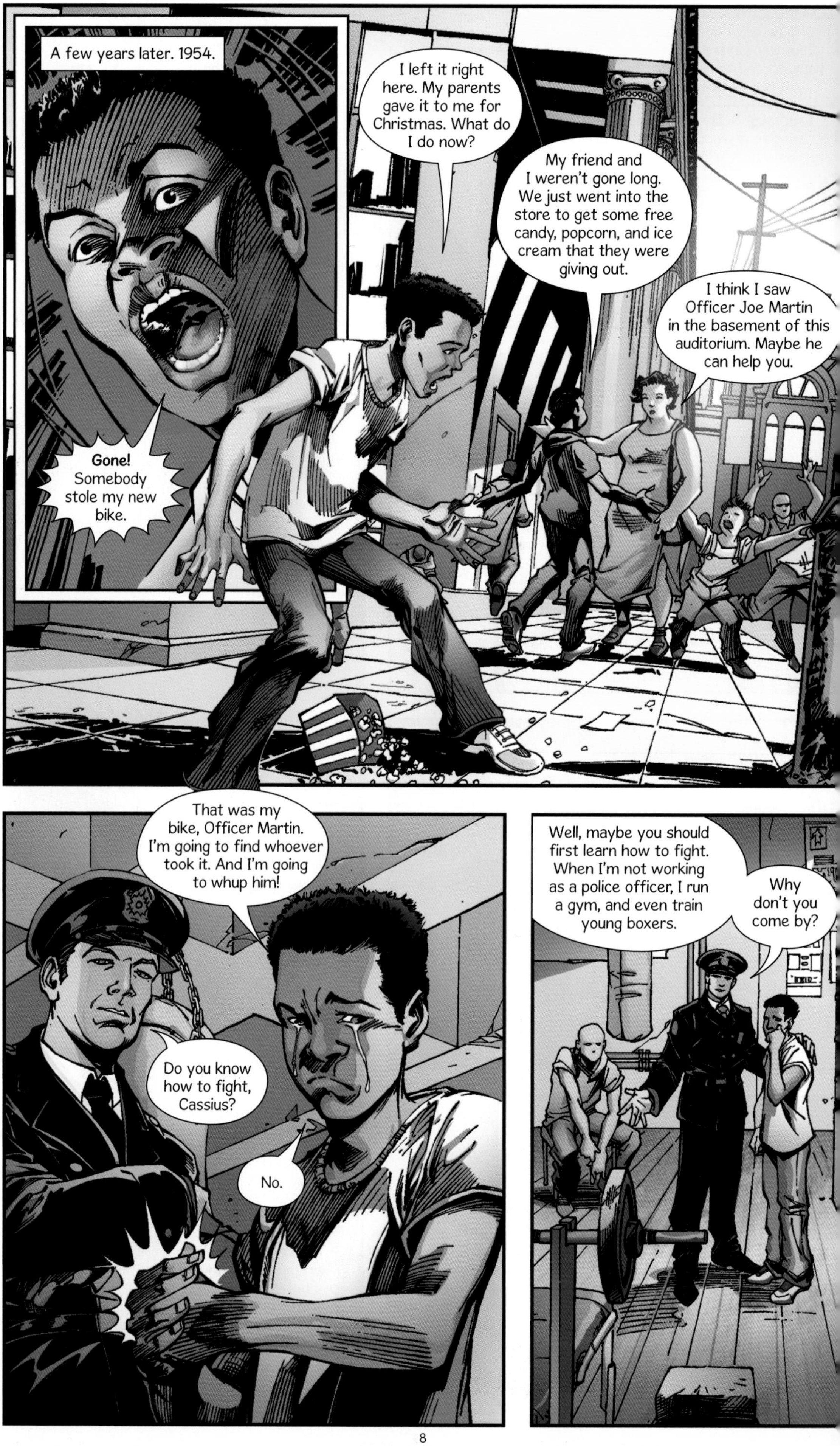

A few years later. 1954.
Gone! Somebody stole my new bike.
I left it right here. My parents gave it to me for Christmas. What do I do now?
My friend and I weren't gone long. We just went into the store to get some free candy, popcorn, and ice cream that they were giving out.
I think I saw Officer Joe Martin in the basement of this auditorium. Maybe he can help you.
That was my bike, Officer Martin. I'm going to find whoever took it. And I'm going to whup him!
Do you know how to fight, Cassius?
No.
Well, maybe you should first learn how to fight. When I'm not working as a police officer, I run a gym, and even train young boxers.
Why don't you come by?

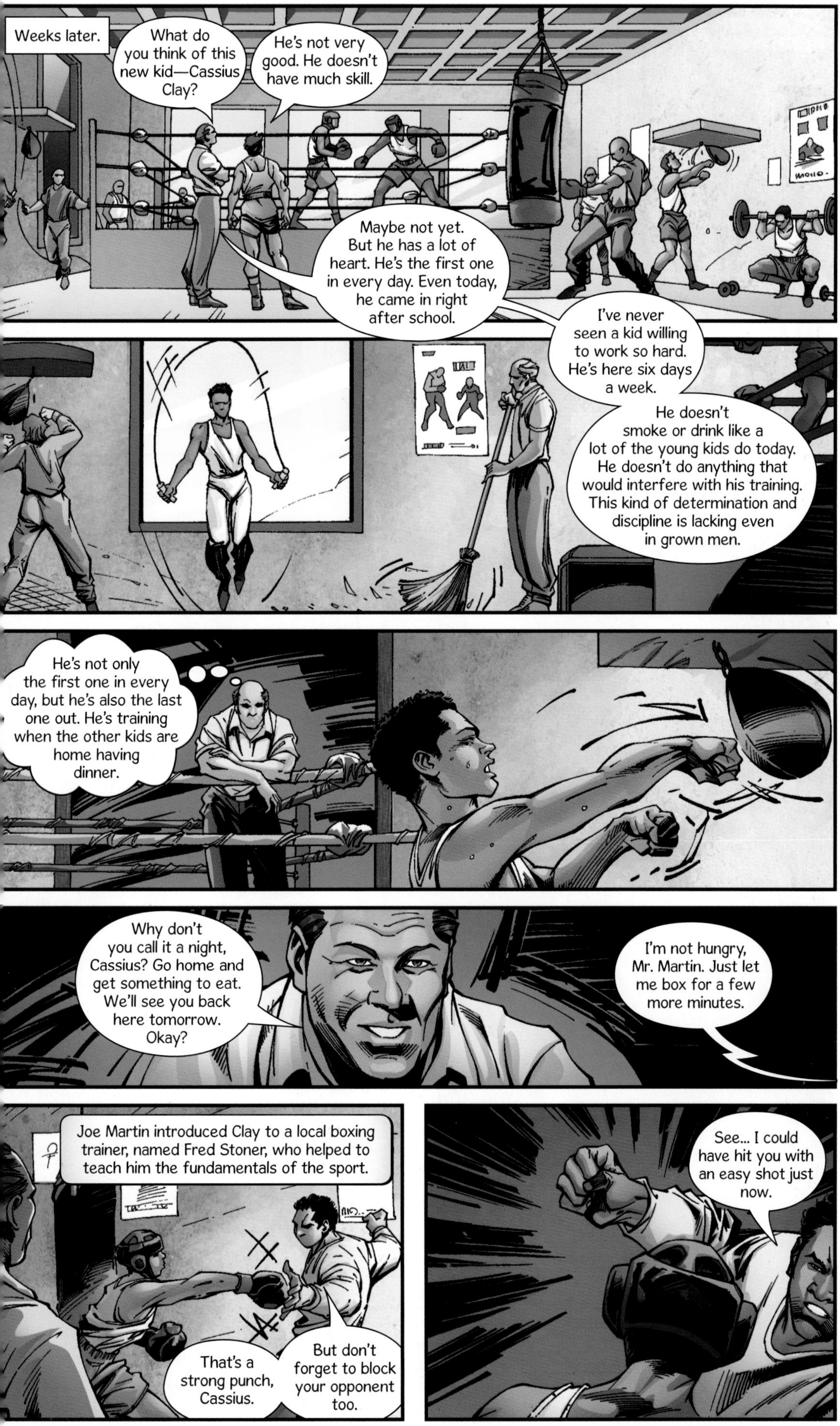

Weeks later.
What do you think of this new kid—Cassius Clay?
He's not very good. He doesn't have much skill.
Maybe not yet. But he has a lot of heart. He's the first one in every day. Even today, he came in right after school.
I've never seen a kid willing to work so hard. He's here six days a week.
He doesn't smoke or drink like a lot of the young kids do today. He doesn't do anything that would interfere with his training. This kind of determination and discipline is lacking even in grown men.
He's not only the first one in every day, but he's also the last one out. He's training when the other kids are home having dinner.
Why don't you call it a night, Cassius? Go home and get something to eat. We'll see you back here tomorrow. Okay?
I'm not hungry, Mr. Martin. Just let me box for a few more minutes.
Joe Martin introduced Clay to a local boxing trainer, named Fred Stoner, who helped to teach him the fundamentals of the sport.
That's a strong punch, Cassius.
But don't forget to block your opponent too.
See... I could have hit you with an easy shot just now.

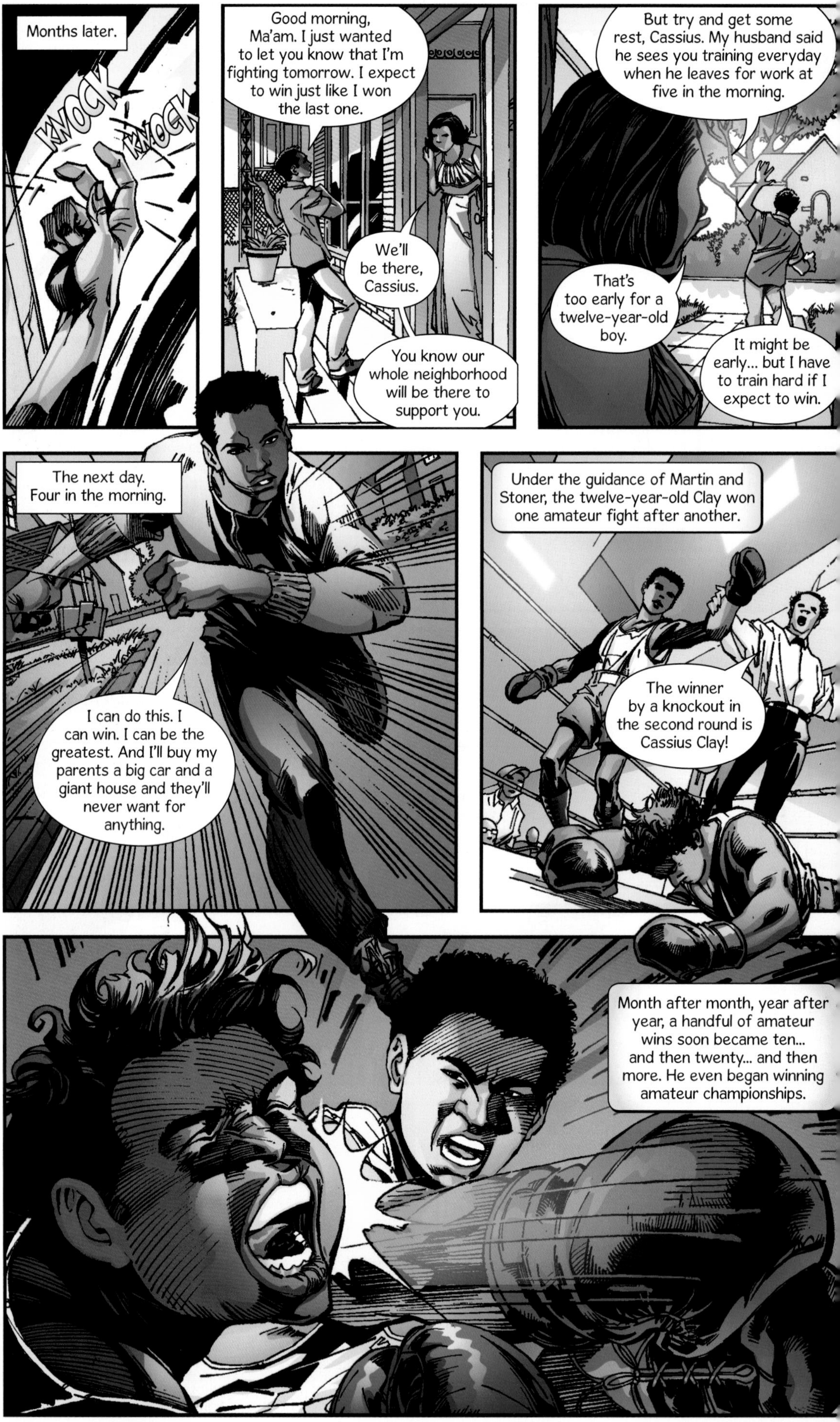
Months later.
KNOCK KNOCK
Good morning, Ma'am. I just wanted to let you know that I'm fighting tomorrow. I expect to win just like I won the last one.
We'll be there, Cassius.
You know our whole neighborhood will be there to support you.
But try and get some rest, Cassius. My husband said he sees you training everyday when he leaves for work at five in the morning.
That's too early for a twelve-year-old boy.
It might be early... but I have to train hard if I expect to win.
The next day. Four in the morning.
I can do this. I can win. I can be the greatest. And I'll buy my parents a big car and a giant house and they'll never want for anything.
Under the guidance of Martin and Stoner, the twelve-year-old Clay won one amateur fight after another.
The winner by a knockout in the second round is Cassius Clay!
Month after month, year after year, a handful of amateur wins soon became ten... and then twenty... and then more. He even began winning amateur championships.

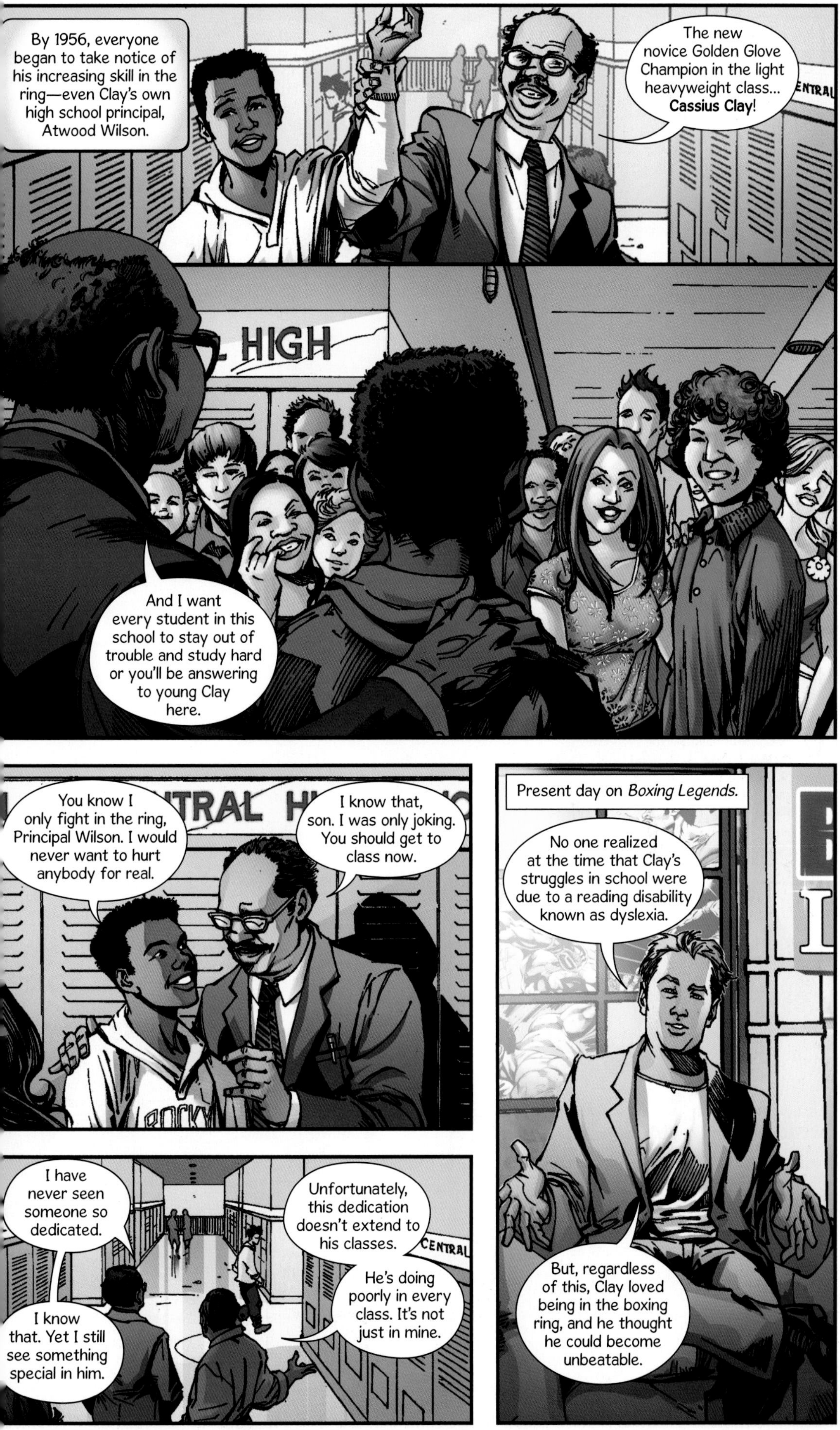

By 1956, everyone began to take notice of his increasing skill in the ring—even Clay's own high school principal, Atwood Wilson.
The new novice Golden Glove Champion in the light heavyweight class... **Cassius Clay**!
And I want every student in this school to stay out of trouble and study hard or you'll be answering to young Clay here.
You know I only fight in the ring, Principal Wilson. I would never want to hurt anybody for real.
I know that, son. I was only joking. You should get to class now.
I have never seen someone so dedicated.
I know that. Yet I still see something special in him.
Unfortunately, this dedication doesn't extend to his classes.
CENTRAL
He's doing poorly in every class. It's not just in mine.
Present day on *Boxing Legends.*
No one realized at the time that Clay's struggles in school were due to a reading disability known as dyslexia.
But, regardless of this, Clay loved being in the boxing ring, and he thought he could become unbeatable.

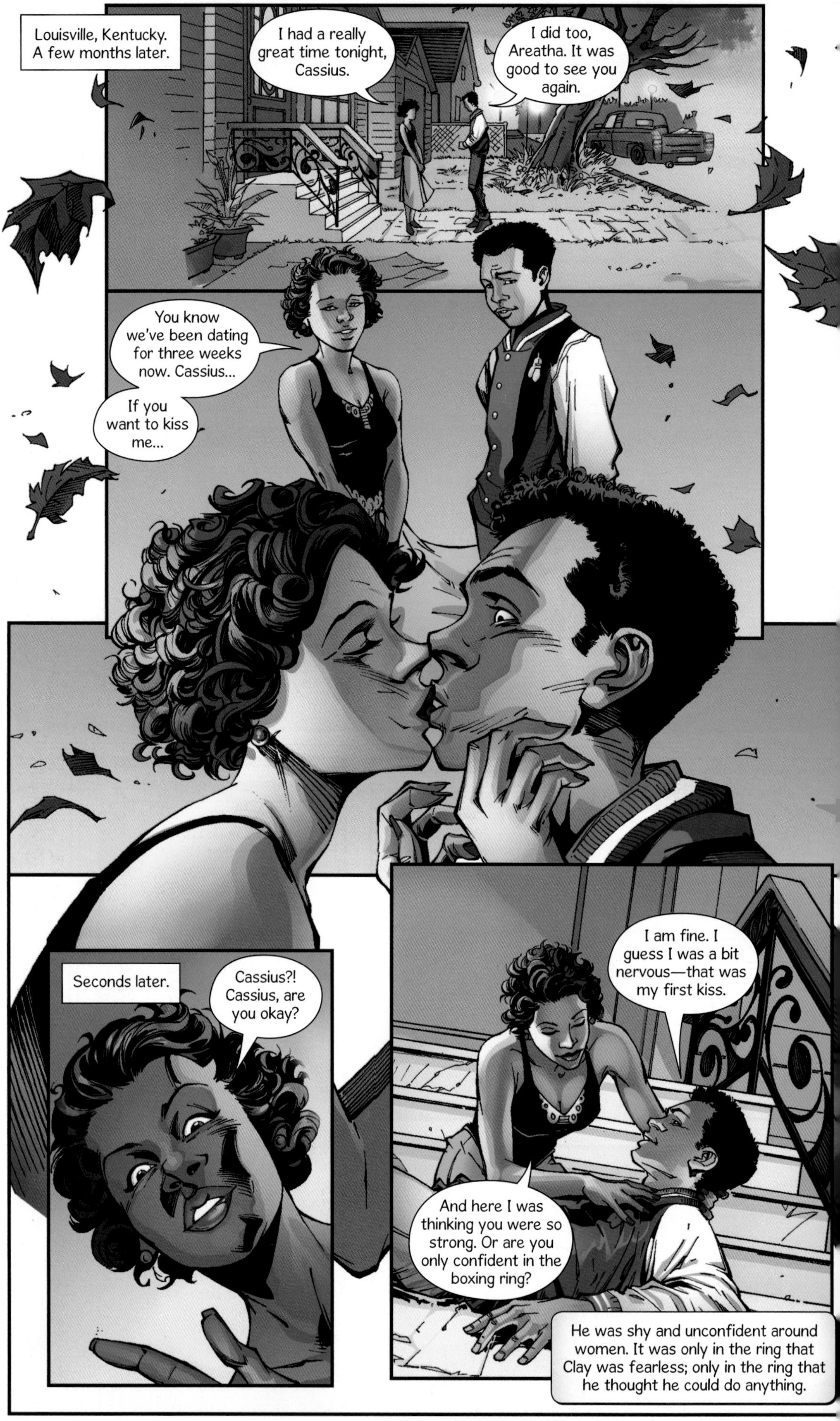
Louisville, Kentucky. A few months later.
I had a really great time tonight, Cassius.
I did too, Areatha. It was good to see you again.
You know we've been dating for three weeks now. Cassius...
If you want to kiss me...
Seconds later.
Cassius?! Cassius, are you okay?
I am fine. I guess I was a bit nervous—that was my first kiss.
And here I was thinking you were so strong. Or are you only confident in the boxing ring?
He was shy and unconfident around women. It was only in the ring that Clay was fearless; only in the ring that he thought he could do anything.

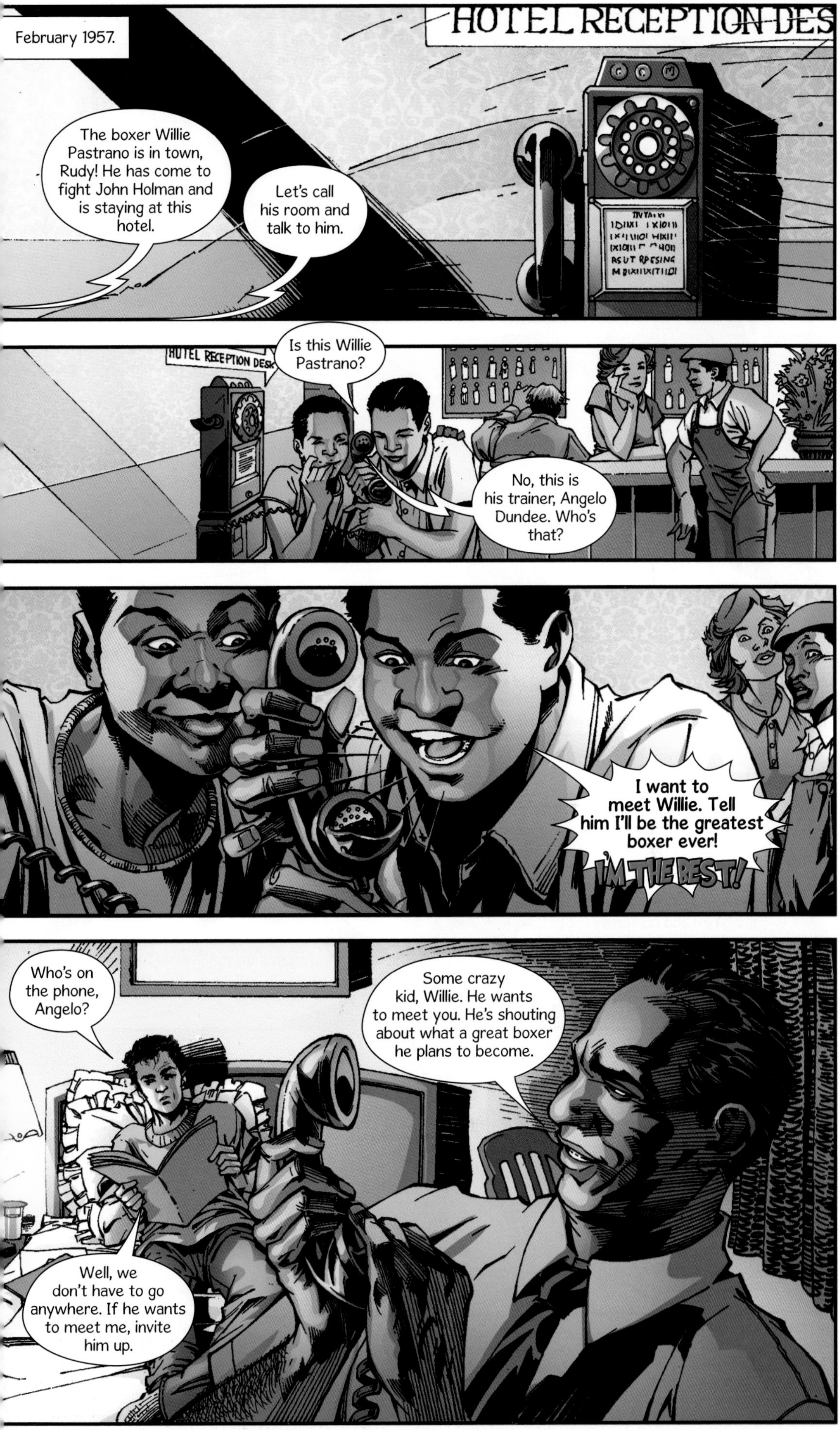
HOTEL RECEPTION DES
February 1957.
The boxer Willie Pastrano is in town, Rudy! He has come to fight John Holman and is staying at this hotel.
Let's call his room and talk to him.
HOTEL RECEPTION DESK
Is this Willie Pastrano?
No, this is his trainer, Angelo Dundee. Who's that?
I want to meet Willie. Tell him I'll be the greatest boxer ever!
I'M THE BEST!
Who's on the phone, Angelo?
Some crazy kid, Willie. He wants to meet you. He's shouting about what a great boxer he plans to become.
Well, we don't have to go anywhere. If he wants to meet me, invite him up.

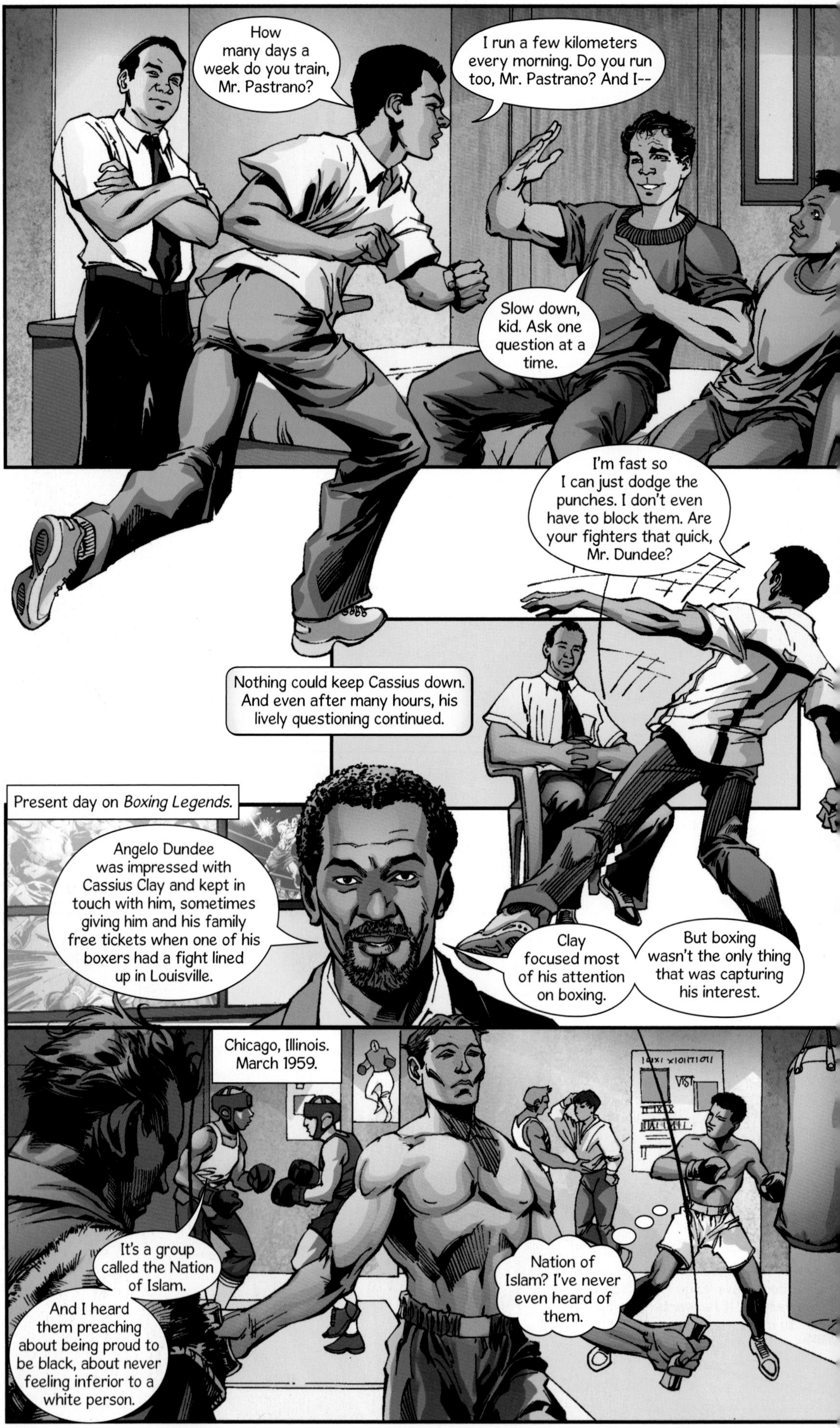
How many days a week do you train, Mr. Pastrano?
I run a few kilometers every morning. Do you run too, Mr. Pastrano? And I--
Slow down, kid. Ask one question at a time.
I'm fast so I can just dodge the punches. I don't even have to block them. Are your fighters that quick, Mr. Dundee?
Nothing could keep Cassius down. And even after many hours, his lively questioning continued.
Present day on *Boxing Legends.*
Angelo Dundee was impressed with Cassius Clay and kept in touch with him, sometimes giving him and his family free tickets when one of his boxers had a fight lined up in Louisville.
Clay focused most of his attention on boxing.
But boxing wasn't the only thing that was capturing his interest.
Chicago, Illinois. March 1959.
It's a group called the Nation of Islam.
And I heard them preaching about being proud to be black, about never feeling inferior to a white person.
Nation of Islam? I've never even heard of them.

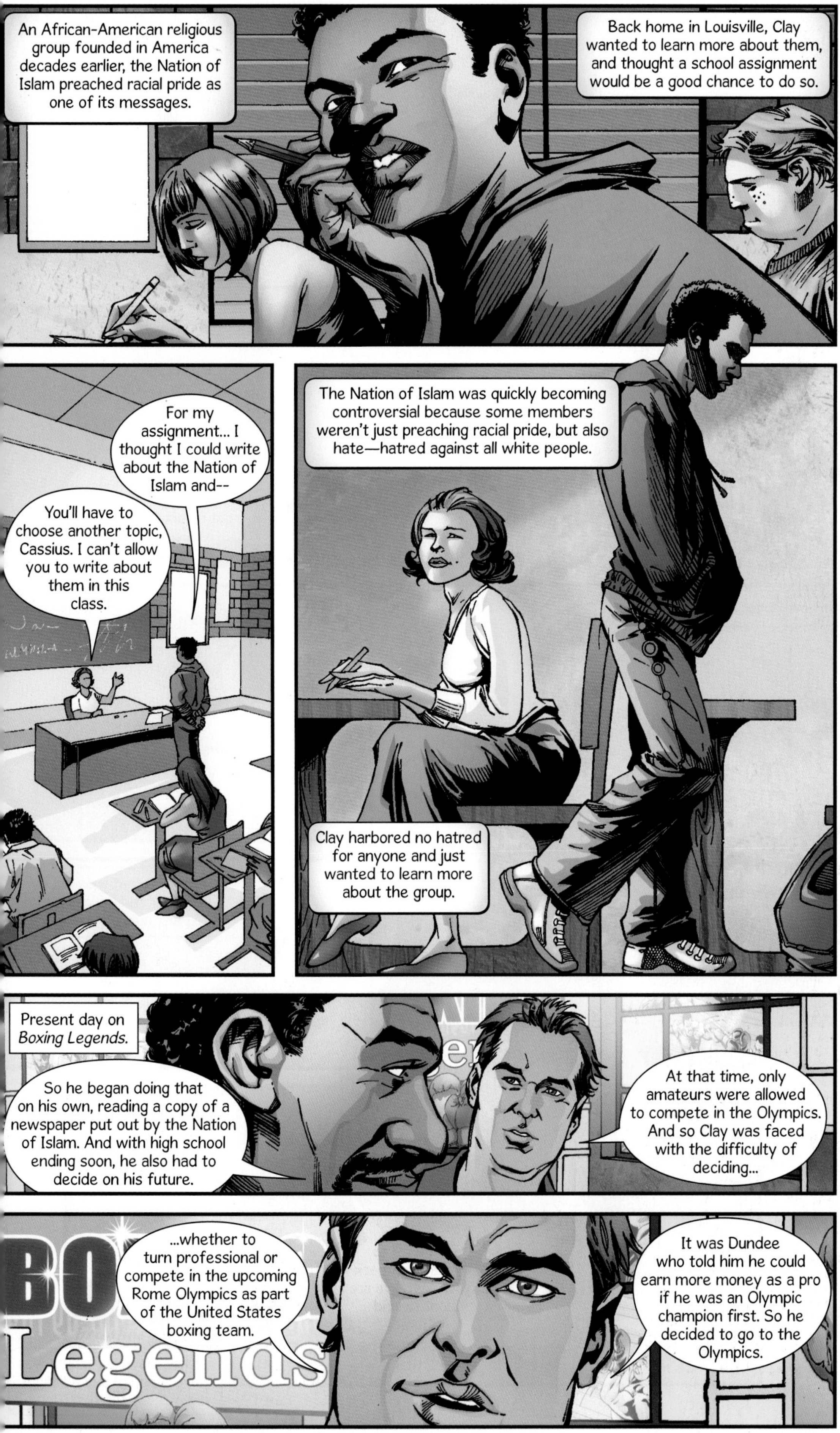
An African-American religious group founded in America decades earlier, the Nation of Islam preached racial pride as one of its messages.
Back home in Louisville, Clay wanted to learn more about them, and thought a school assignment would be a good chance to do so.
For my assignment... I thought I could write about the Nation of Islam and--
You'll have to choose another topic, Cassius. I can't allow you to write about them in this class.
The Nation of Islam was quickly becoming controversial because some members weren't just preaching racial pride, but also hate—hatred against all white people.
Clay harbored no hatred for anyone and just wanted to learn more about the group.
Present day on *Boxing Legends.*
So he began doing that on his own, reading a copy of a newspaper put out by the Nation of Islam. And with high school ending soon, he also had to decide on his future.
At that time, only amateurs were allowed to compete in the Olympics. And so Clay was faced with the difficulty of deciding...
...whether to turn professional or compete in the upcoming Rome Olympics as part of the United States boxing team.
It was Dundee who told him he could earn more money as a pro if he was an Olympic champion first. So he decided to go to the Olympics.

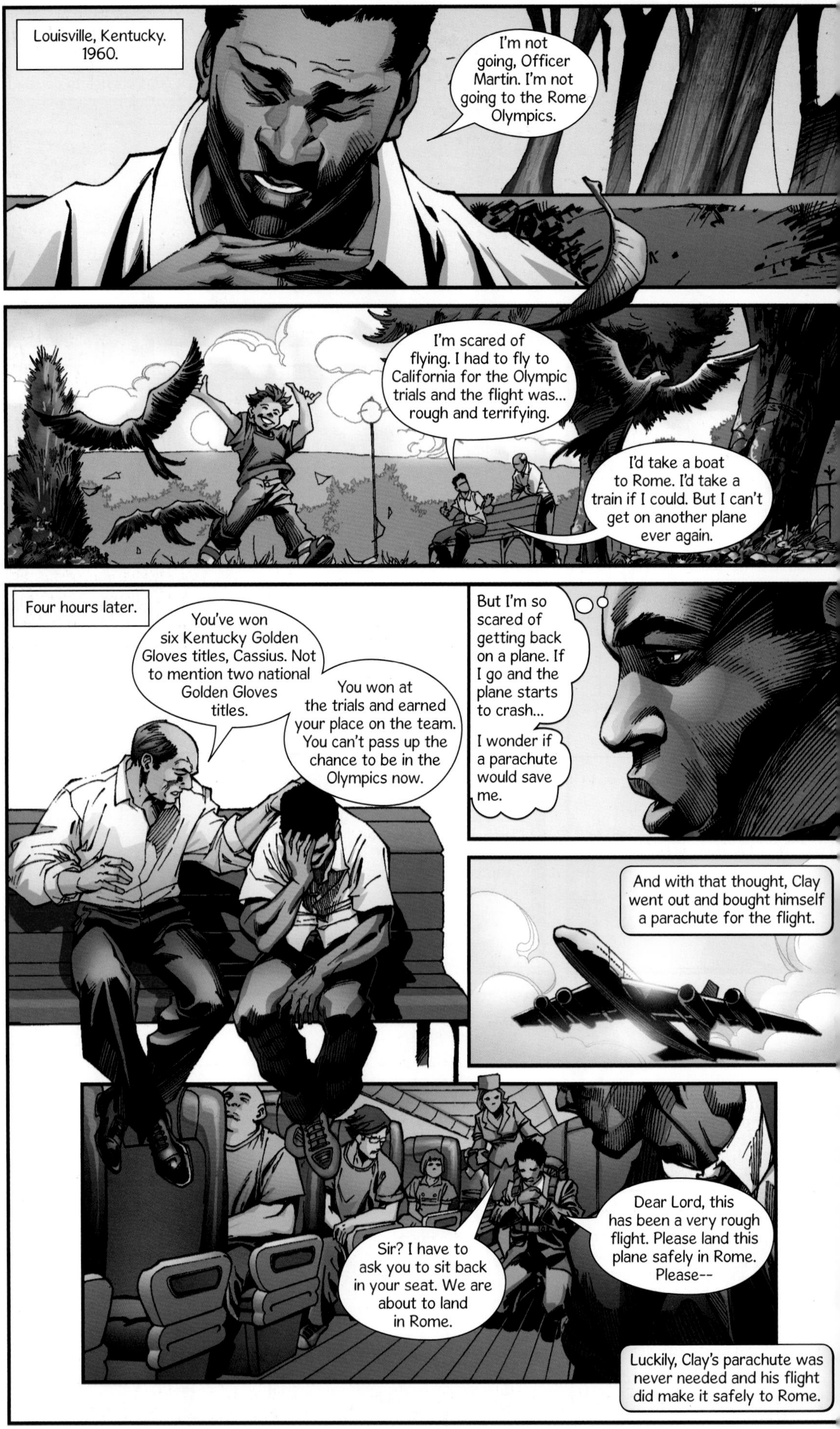
Louisville, Kentucky. 1960.
I'm not going, Officer Martin. I'm not going to the Rome Olympics.
I'm scared of flying. I had to fly to California for the Olympic trials and the flight was... rough and terrifying.
I'd take a boat to Rome. I'd take a train if I could. But I can't get on another plane ever again.
Four hours later.
You've won six Kentucky Golden Gloves titles, Cassius. Not to mention two national Golden Gloves titles.
You won at the trials and earned your place on the team. You can't pass up the chance to be in the Olympics now.
But I'm so scared of getting back on a plane. If I go and the plane starts to crash...
I wonder if a parachute would save me.
And with that thought, Clay went out and bought himself a parachute for the flight.
Dear Lord, this has been a very rough flight. Please land this plane safely in Rome. Please--
Sir? I have to ask you to sit back in your seat. We are about to land in Rome.
Luckily, Clay's parachute was never needed and his flight did make it safely to Rome.

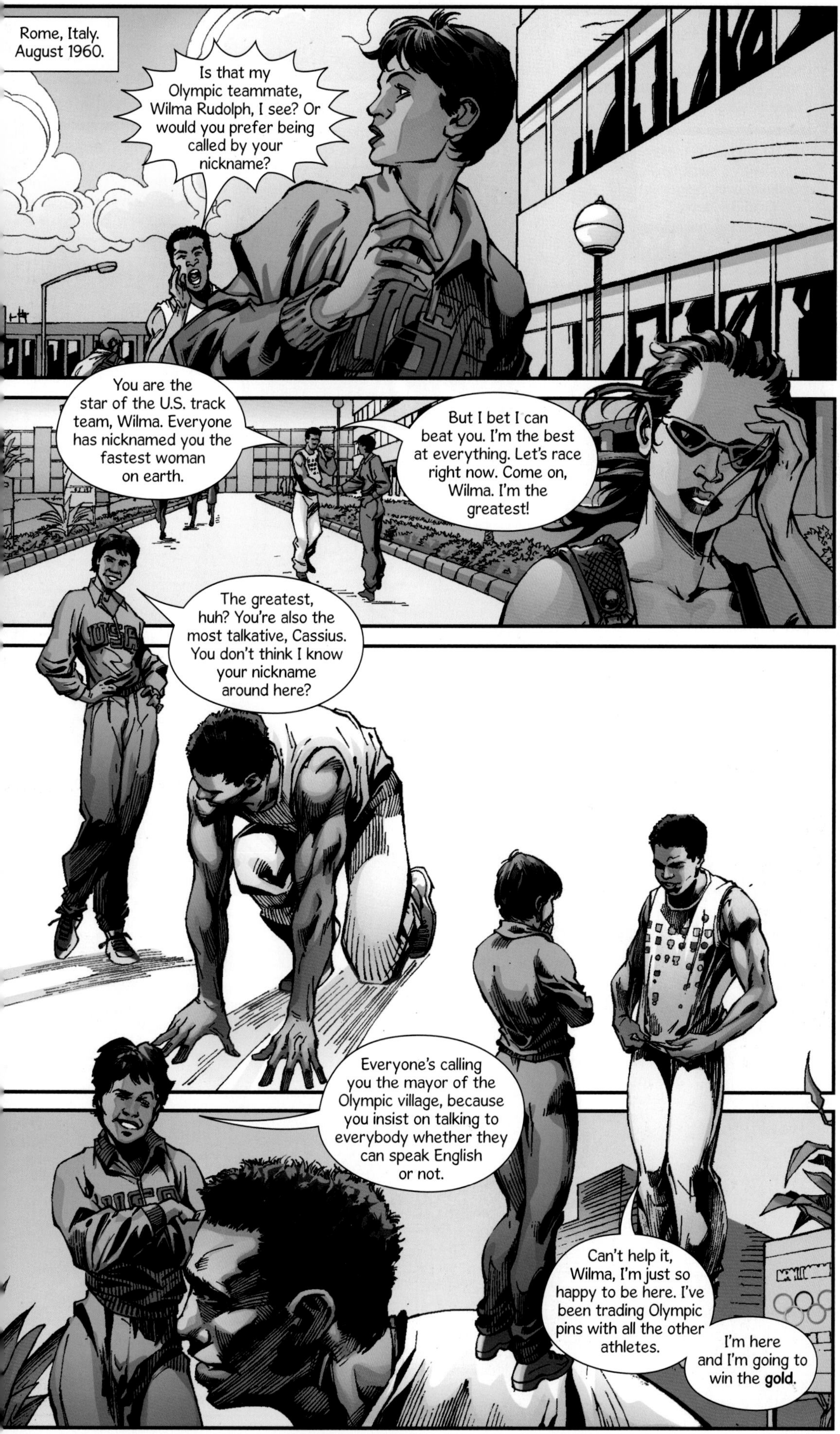

Rome, Italy.
August 1960.
Is that my Olympic teammate, Wilma Rudolph, I see? Or would you prefer being called by your nickname?
You are the star of the U.S. track team, Wilma. Everyone has nicknamed you the fastest woman on earth.
But I bet I can beat you. I'm the best at everything. Let's race right now. Come on, Wilma. I'm the greatest!
The greatest, huh? You're also the most talkative, Cassius. You don't think I know your nickname around here?
Everyone's calling you the mayor of the Olympic village, because you insist on talking to everybody whether they can speak English or not.
Can't help it, Wilma, I'm just so happy to be here. I've been trading Olympic pins with all the other athletes.
I'm here and I'm going to win the **gold**.

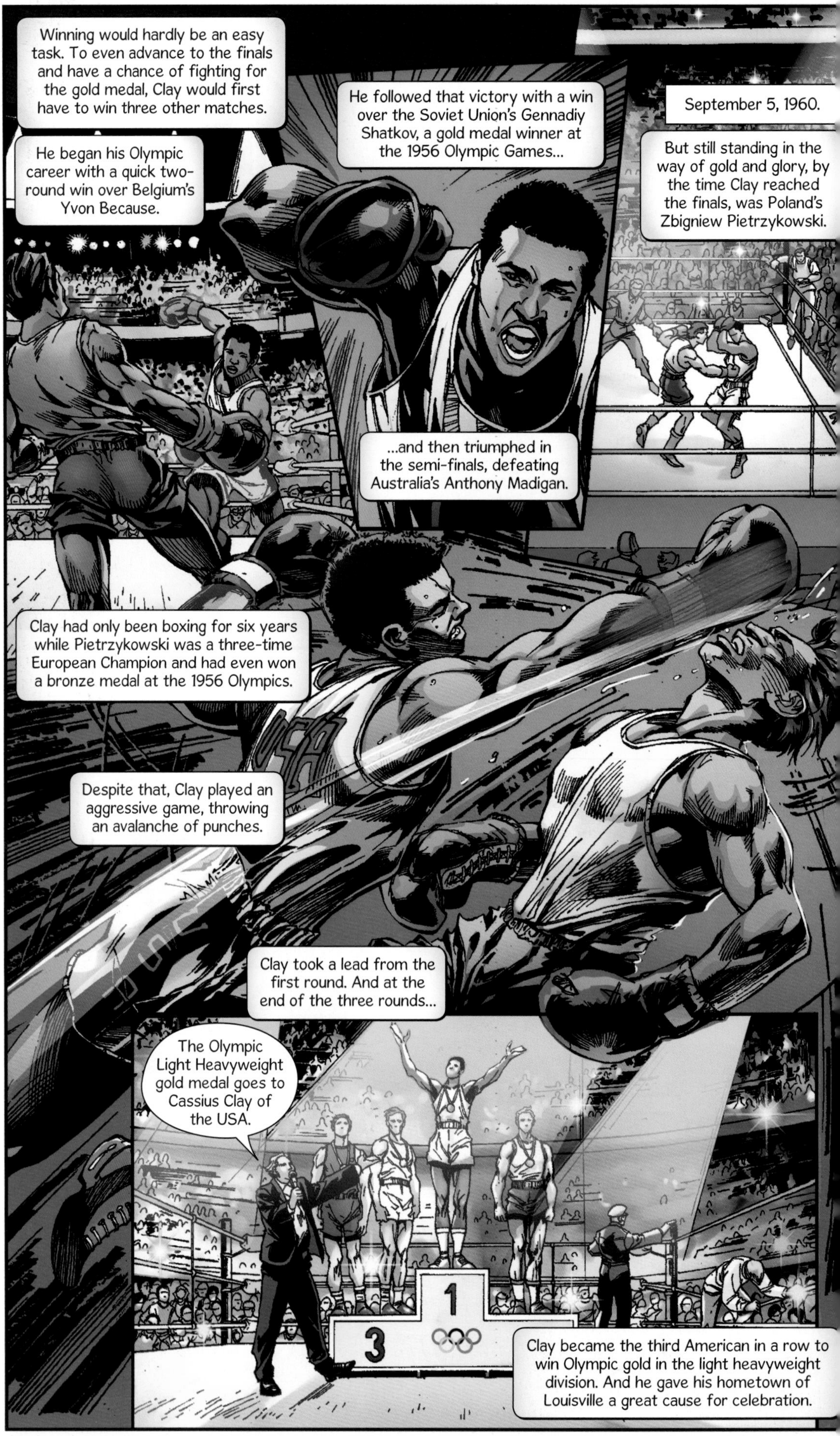

Winning would hardly be an easy task. To even advance to the finals and have a chance of fighting for the gold medal, Clay would first have to win three other matches.
He began his Olympic career with a quick two-round win over Belgium's Yvon Because.
He followed that victory with a win over the Soviet Union's Gennadiy Shatkov, a gold medal winner at the 1956 Olympic Games...
...and then triumphed in the semi-finals, defeating Australia's Anthony Madigan.
September 5, 1960.
But still standing in the way of gold and glory, by the time Clay reached the finals, was Poland's Zbigniew Pietrzykowski.
Clay had only been boxing for six years while Pietrzykowski was a three-time European Champion and had even won a bronze medal at the 1956 Olympics.
Despite that, Clay played an aggressive game, throwing an avalanche of punches.
Clay took a lead from the first round. And at the end of the three rounds...
The Olympic Light Heavyweight gold medal goes to Cassius Clay of the USA.
1
3
Clay became the third American in a row to win Olympic gold in the light heavyweight division. And he gave his hometown of Louisville a great cause for celebration.

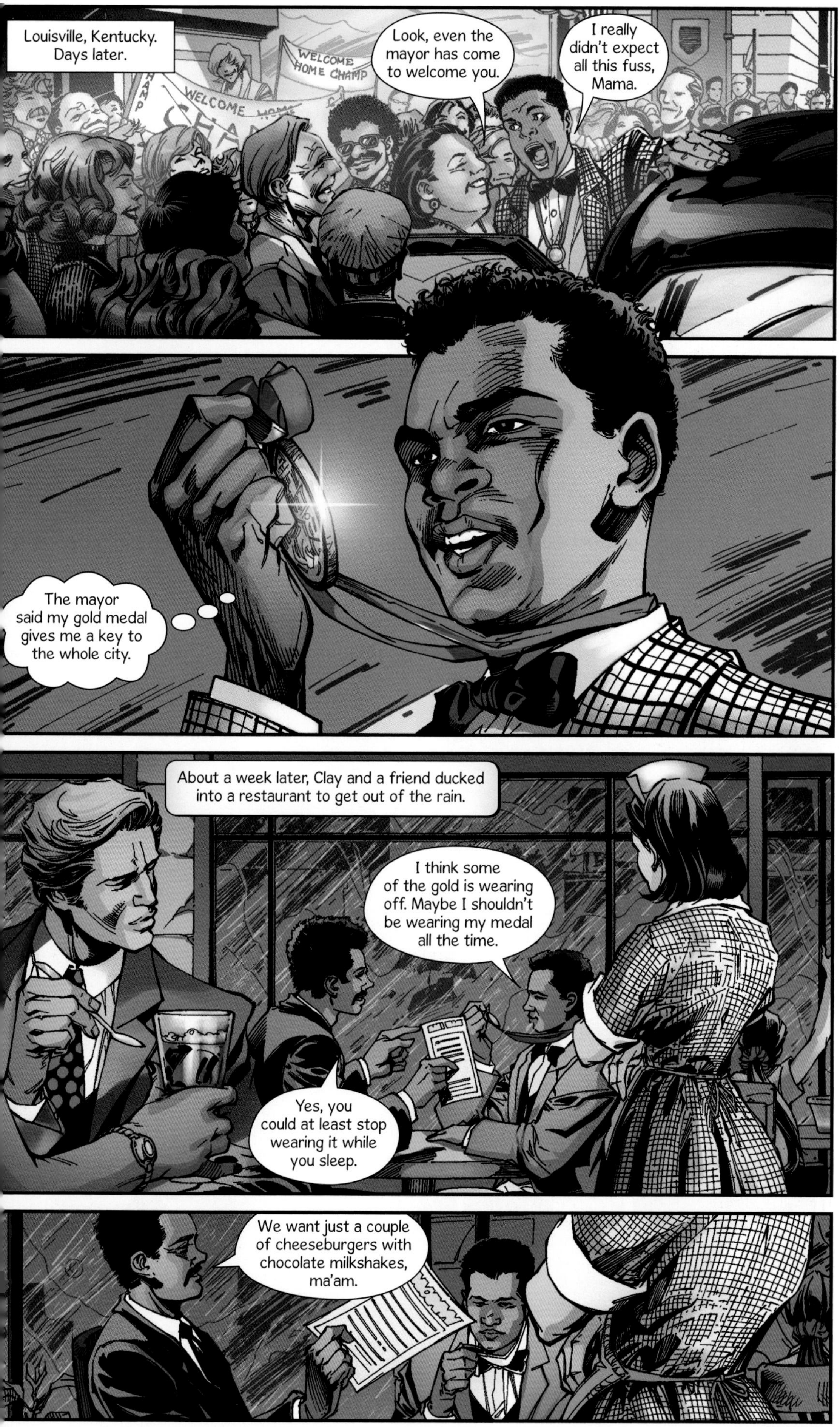

Louisville, Kentucky. Days later.
WELCOME HOME CHAMP
WELCOME HOME CHAMP
Look, even the mayor has come to welcome you.
I really didn't expect all this fuss, Mama.
The mayor said my gold medal gives me a key to the whole city.
About a week later, Clay and a friend ducked into a restaurant to get out of the rain.
I think some of the gold is wearing off. Maybe I shouldn't be wearing my medal all the time.
Yes, you could at least stop wearing it while you sleep.
We want just a couple of cheeseburgers with chocolate milkshakes, ma'am.

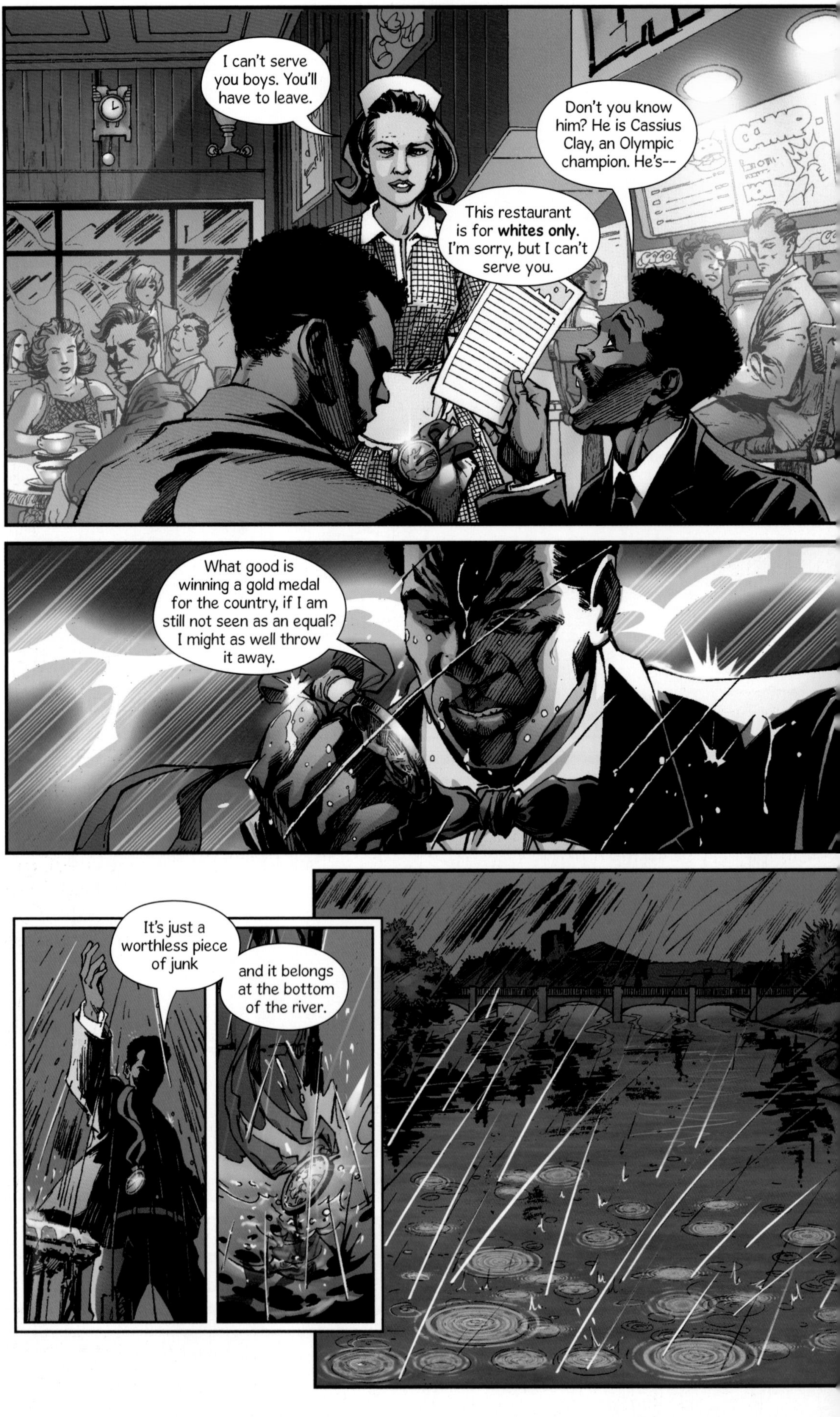
I can't serve you boys. You'll have to leave.
Don't you know him? He is Cassius Clay, an Olympic champion. He's--
This restaurant is for **whites only**. I'm sorry, but I can't serve you.
What good is winning a gold medal for the country, if I am still not seen as an equal? I might as well throw it away.
It's just a worthless piece of junk
and it belongs at the bottom of the river.

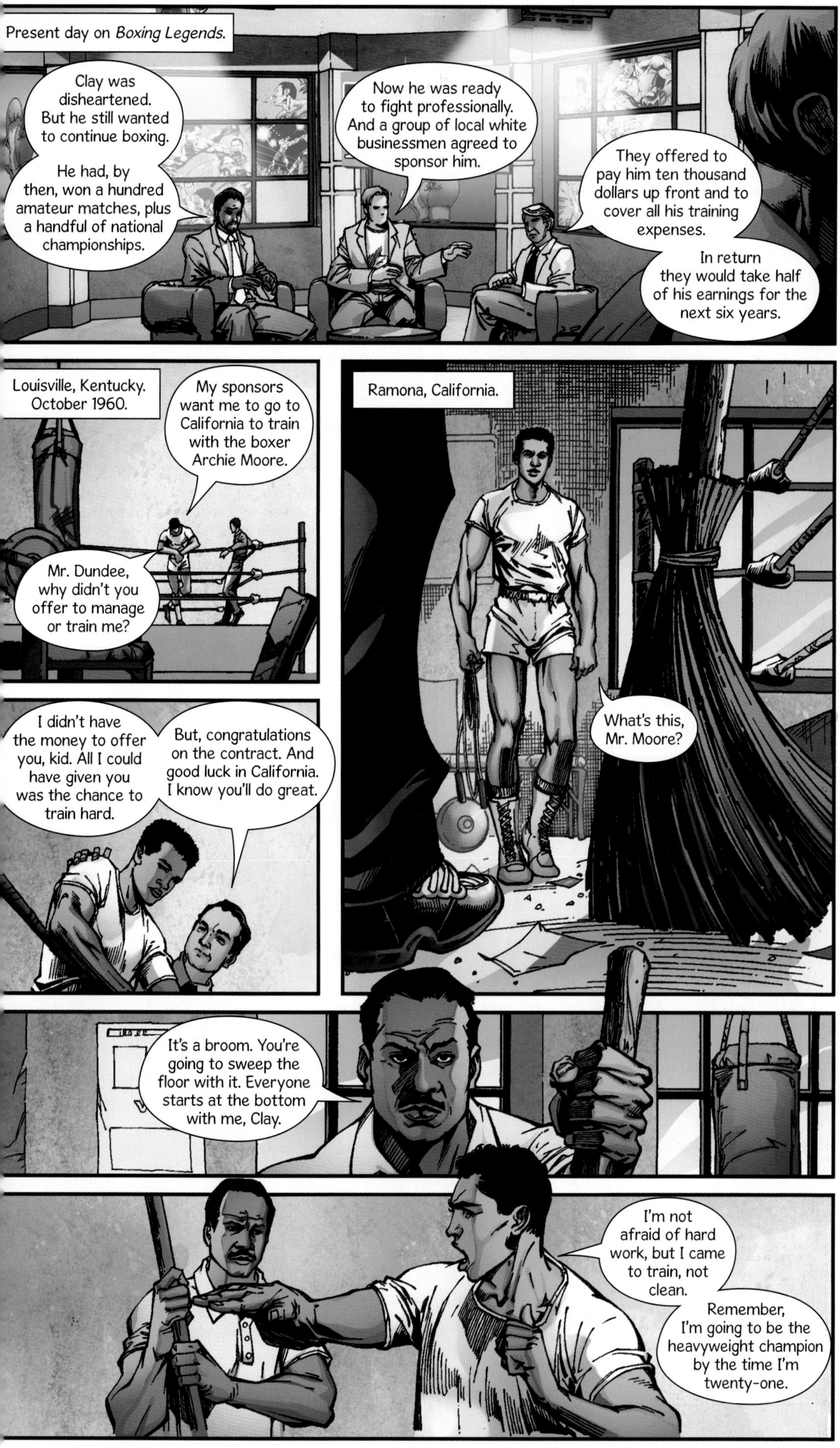

Present day on *Boxing Legends.*
Clay was disheartened. But he still wanted to continue boxing.
He had, by then, won a hundred amateur matches, plus a handful of national championships.
Now he was ready to fight professionally. And a group of local white businessmen agreed to sponsor him.
They offered to pay him ten thousand dollars up front and to cover all his training expenses.
In return they would take half of his earnings for the next six years.
Louisville, Kentucky. October 1960.
My sponsors want me to go to California to train with the boxer Archie Moore.
Mr. Dundee, why didn't you offer to manage or train me?
I didn't have the money to offer you, kid. All I could have given you was the chance to train hard.
But, congratulations on the contract. And good luck in California. I know you'll do great.
Ramona, California.
What's this, Mr. Moore?
It's a broom. You're going to sweep the floor with it. Everyone starts at the bottom with me, Clay.
I'm not afraid of hard work, but I came to train, not clean.
Remember, I'm going to be the heavyweight champion by the time I'm twenty-one.

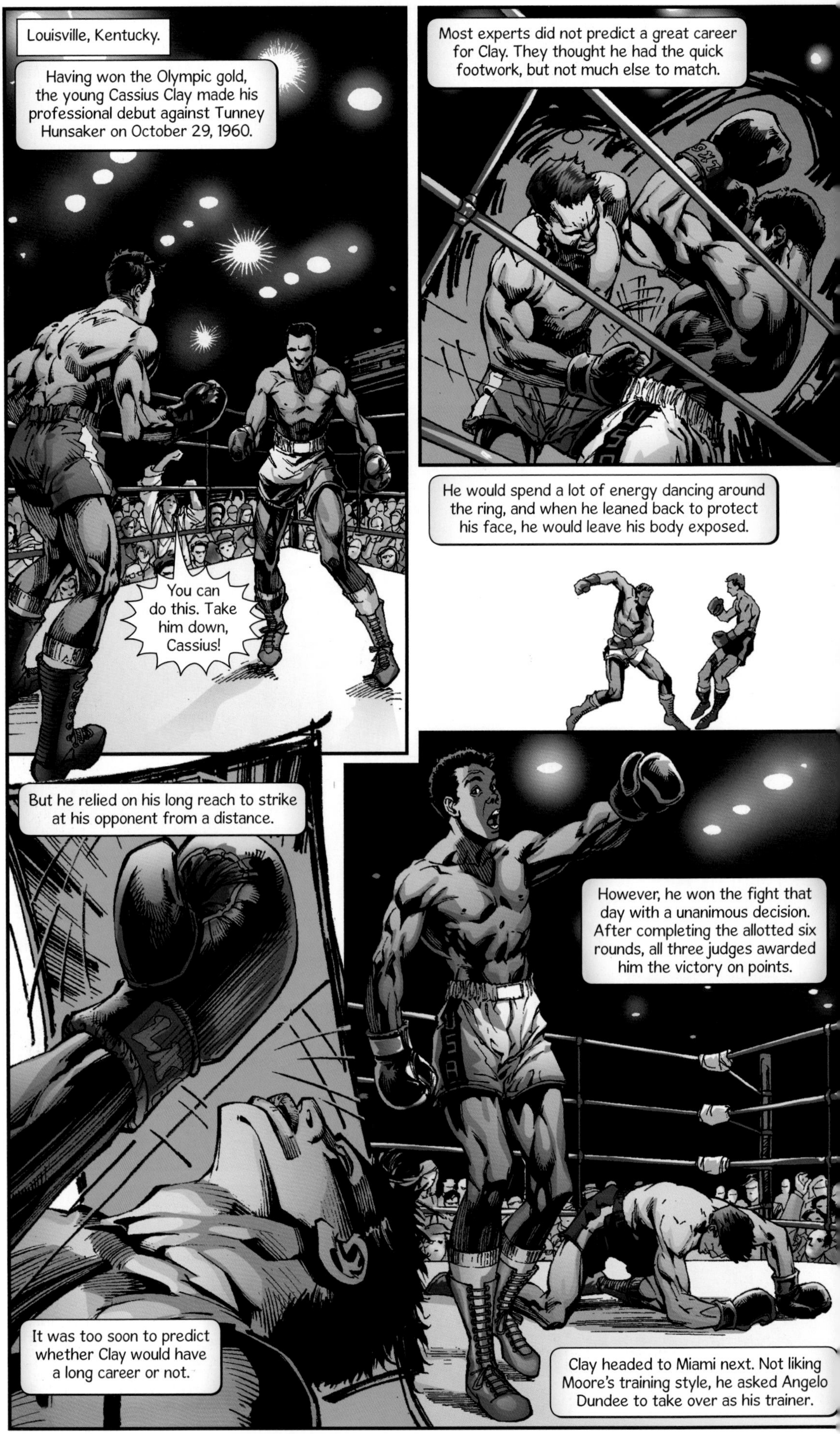
Louisville, Kentucky.
Having won the Olympic gold, the young Cassius Clay made his professional debut against Tunney Hunsaker on October 29, 1960.
You can do this. Take him down, Cassius!
Most experts did not predict a great career for Clay. They thought he had the quick footwork, but not much else to match.
He would spend a lot of energy dancing around the ring, and when he leaned back to protect his face, he would leave his body exposed.
But he relied on his long reach to strike at his opponent from a distance.
It was too soon to predict whether Clay would have a long career or not.
However, he won the fight that day with a unanimous decision. After completing the allotted six rounds, all three judges awarded him the victory on points.
Clay headed to Miami next. Not liking Moore's training style, he asked Angelo Dundee to take over as his trainer.

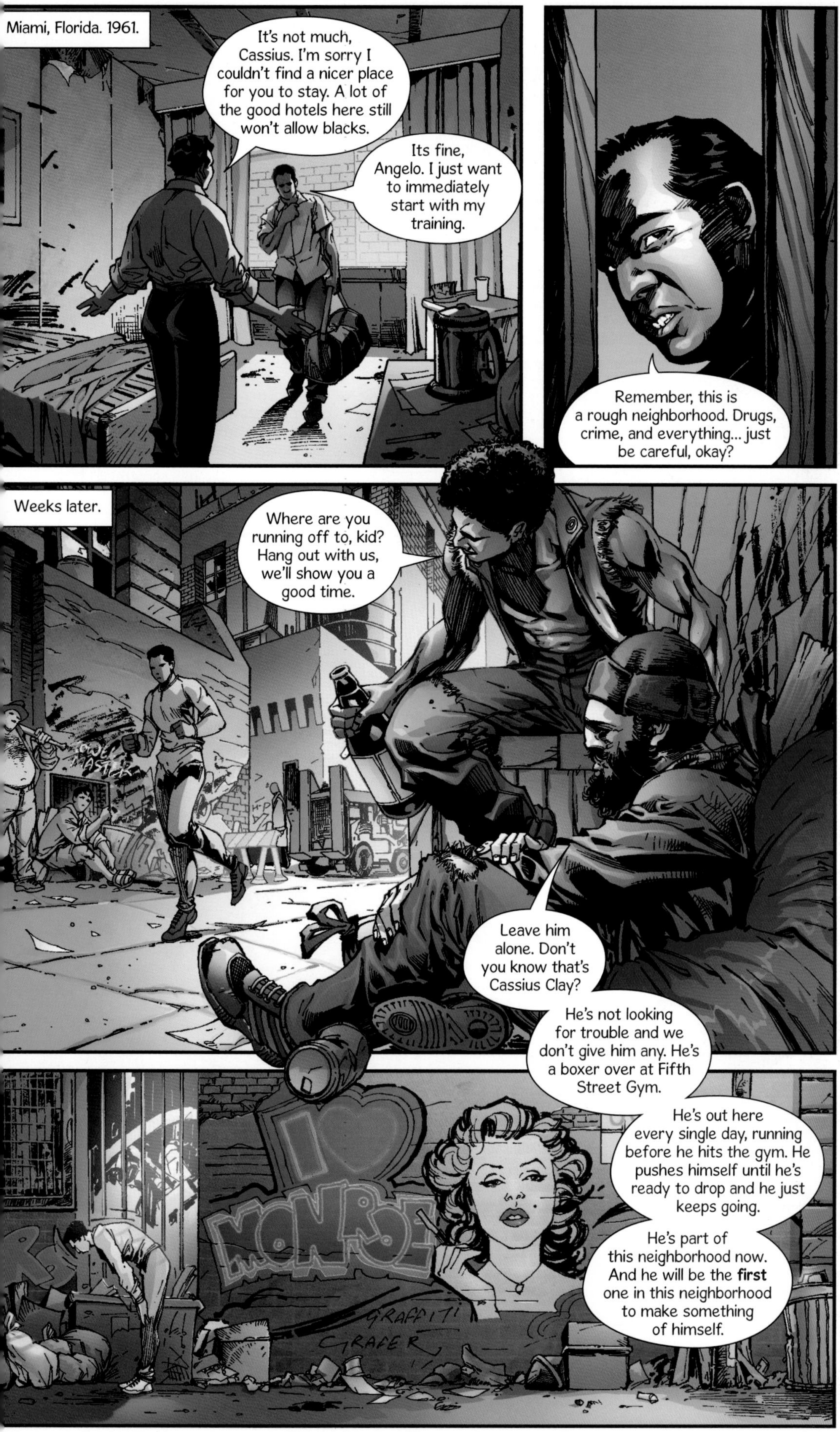
Miami, Florida. 1961.
It's not much, Cassius. I'm sorry I couldn't find a nicer place for you to stay. A lot of the good hotels here still won't allow blacks.
Its fine, Angelo. I just want to immediately start with my training.
Remember, this is a rough neighborhood. Drugs, crime, and everything... just be careful, okay?
Weeks later.
Where are you running off to, kid? Hang out with us, we'll show you a good time.
Leave him alone. Don't you know that's Cassius Clay?
He's not looking for trouble and we don't give him any. He's a boxer over at Fifth Street Gym.
He's out here every single day, running before he hits the gym. He pushes himself until he's ready to drop and he just keeps going.
He's part of this neighborhood now. And he will be the **first** one in this neighborhood to make something of himself.

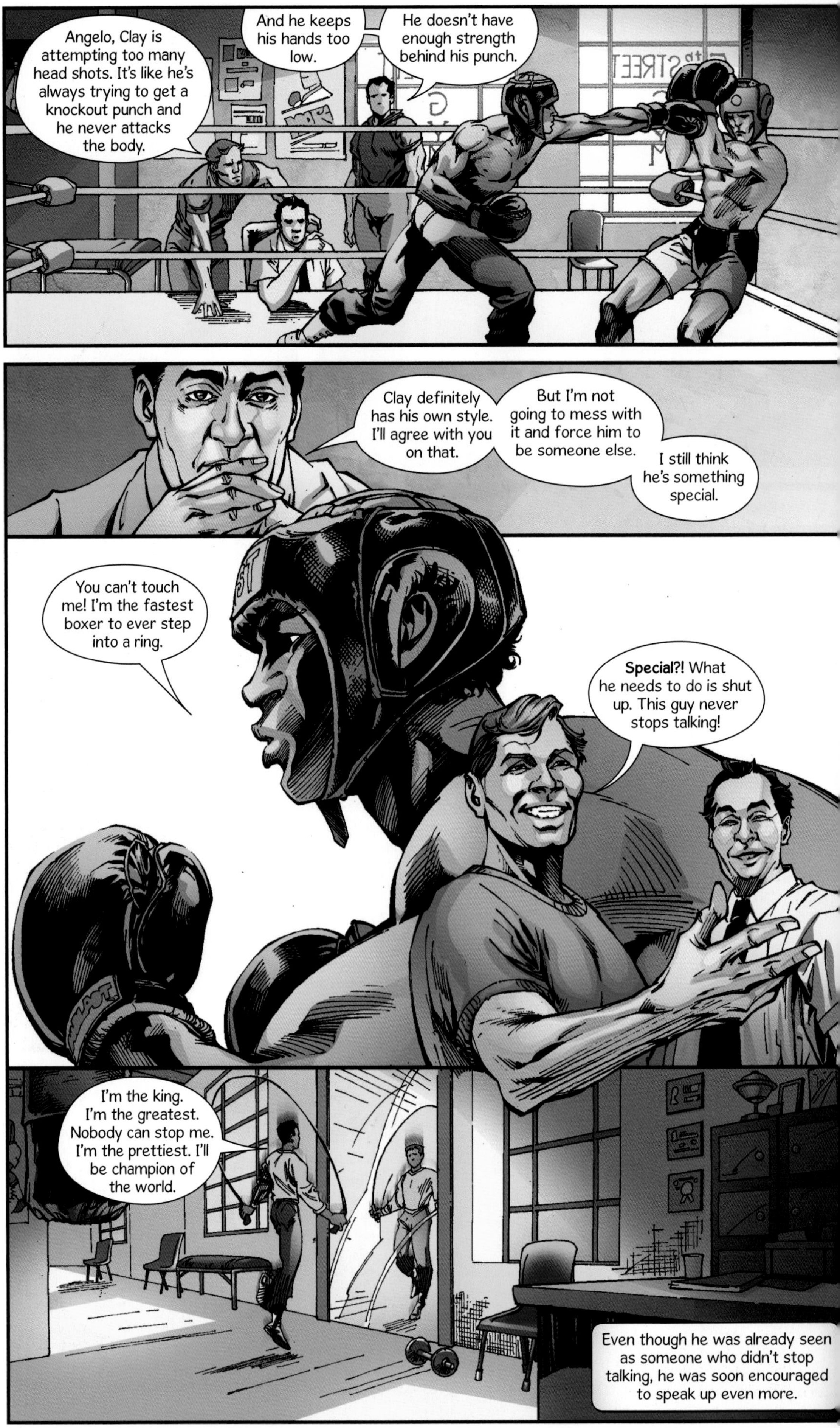
Angelo, Clay is attempting too many head shots. It's like he's always trying to get a knockout punch and he never attacks the body.
And he keeps his hands too low.
He doesn't have enough strength behind his punch.
Clay definitely has his own style. I'll agree with you on that.
But I'm not going to mess with it and force him to be someone else.
I still think he's something special.
You can't touch me! I'm the fastest boxer to ever step into a ring.
Special?! What he needs to do is shut up. This guy never stops talking!
I'm the king. I'm the greatest. Nobody can stop me. I'm the prettiest. I'll be champion of the world.
Even though he was already seen as someone who didn't stop talking, he was soon encouraged to speak up even more.

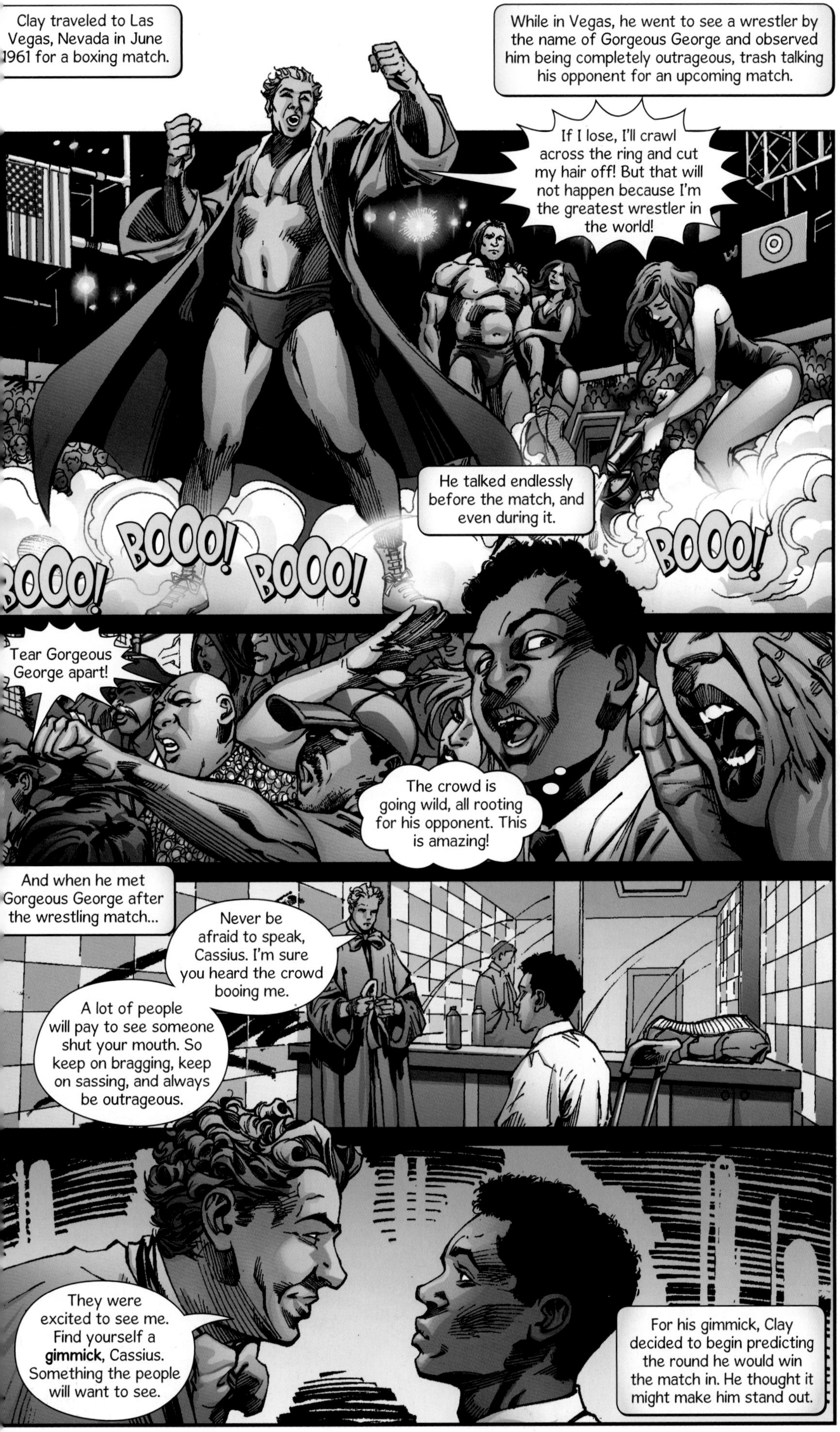
Clay traveled to Las Vegas, Nevada in June 1961 for a boxing match.
While in Vegas, he went to see a wrestler by the name of Gorgeous George and observed him being completely outrageous, trash talking his opponent for an upcoming match.
If I lose, I'll crawl across the ring and cut my hair off! But that will not happen because I'm the greatest wrestler in the world!
He talked endlessly before the match, and even during it.
BOOO!
BOOO!
BOOO!
BOOO!
Tear Gorgeous George apart!
The crowd is going wild, all rooting for his opponent. This is amazing!
And when he met Gorgeous George after the wrestling match...
Never be afraid to speak, Cassius. I'm sure you heard the crowd booing me.
A lot of people will pay to see someone shut your mouth. So keep on bragging, keep on sassing, and always be outrageous.
They were excited to see me. Find yourself a **gimmick**, Cassius. Something the people will want to see.
For his gimmick, Clay decided to begin predicting the round he would win the match in. He thought it might make him stand out.

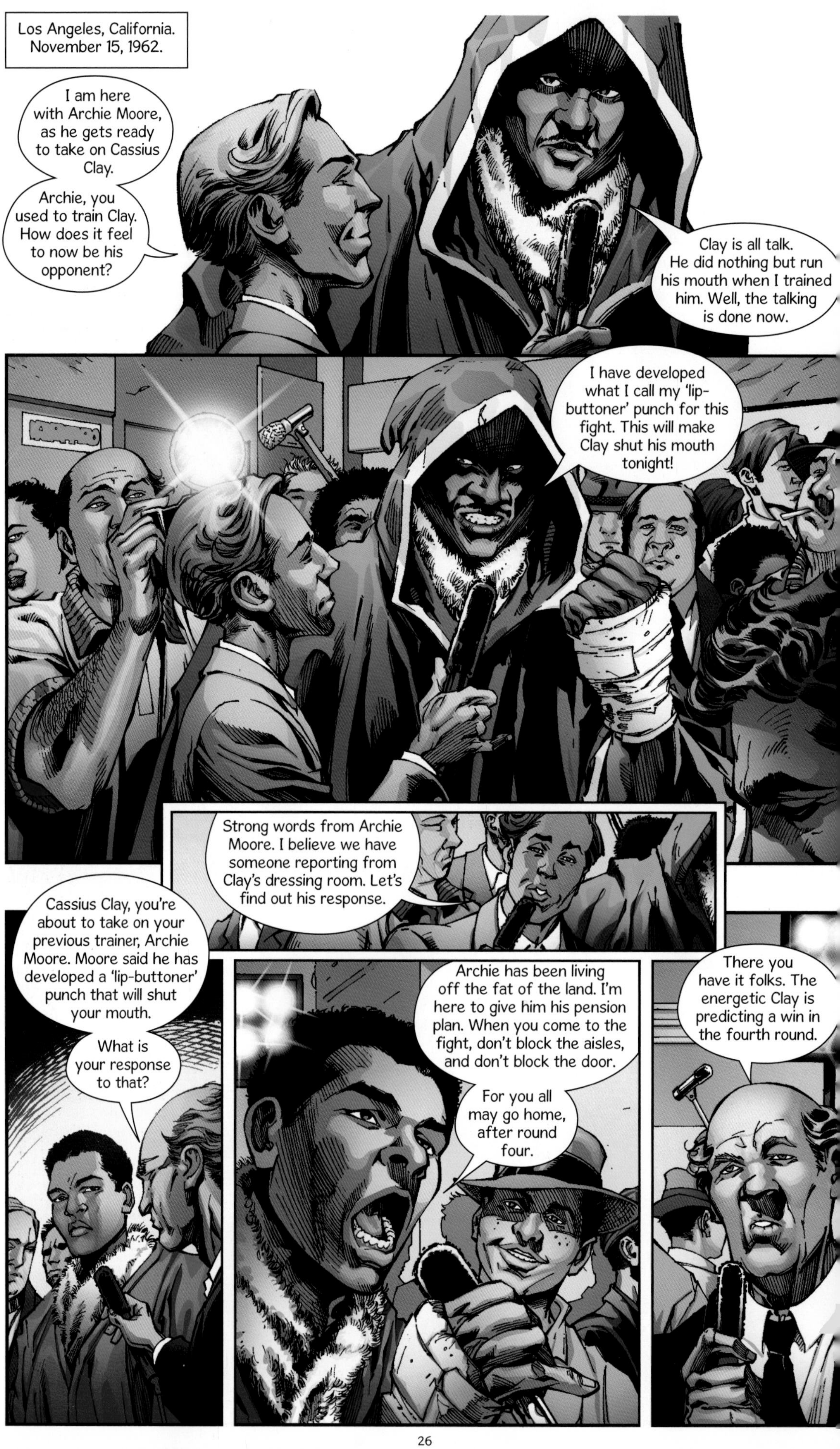
Los Angeles, California. November 15, 1962.
I am here with Archie Moore, as he gets ready to take on Cassius Clay.
Archie, you used to train Clay. How does it feel to now be his opponent?
Clay is all talk. He did nothing but run his mouth when I trained him. Well, the talking is done now.
I have developed what I call my 'lip-buttoner' punch for this fight. This will make Clay shut his mouth tonight!
Strong words from Archie Moore. I believe we have someone reporting from Clay's dressing room. Let's find out his response.
Cassius Clay, you're about to take on your previous trainer, Archie Moore. Moore said he has developed a 'lip-buttoner' punch that will shut your mouth.
What is your response to that?
Archie has been living off the fat of the land. I'm here to give him his pension plan. When you come to the fight, don't block the aisles, and don't block the door.
For you all may go home, after round four.
There you have it folks. The energetic Clay is predicting a win in the fourth round.

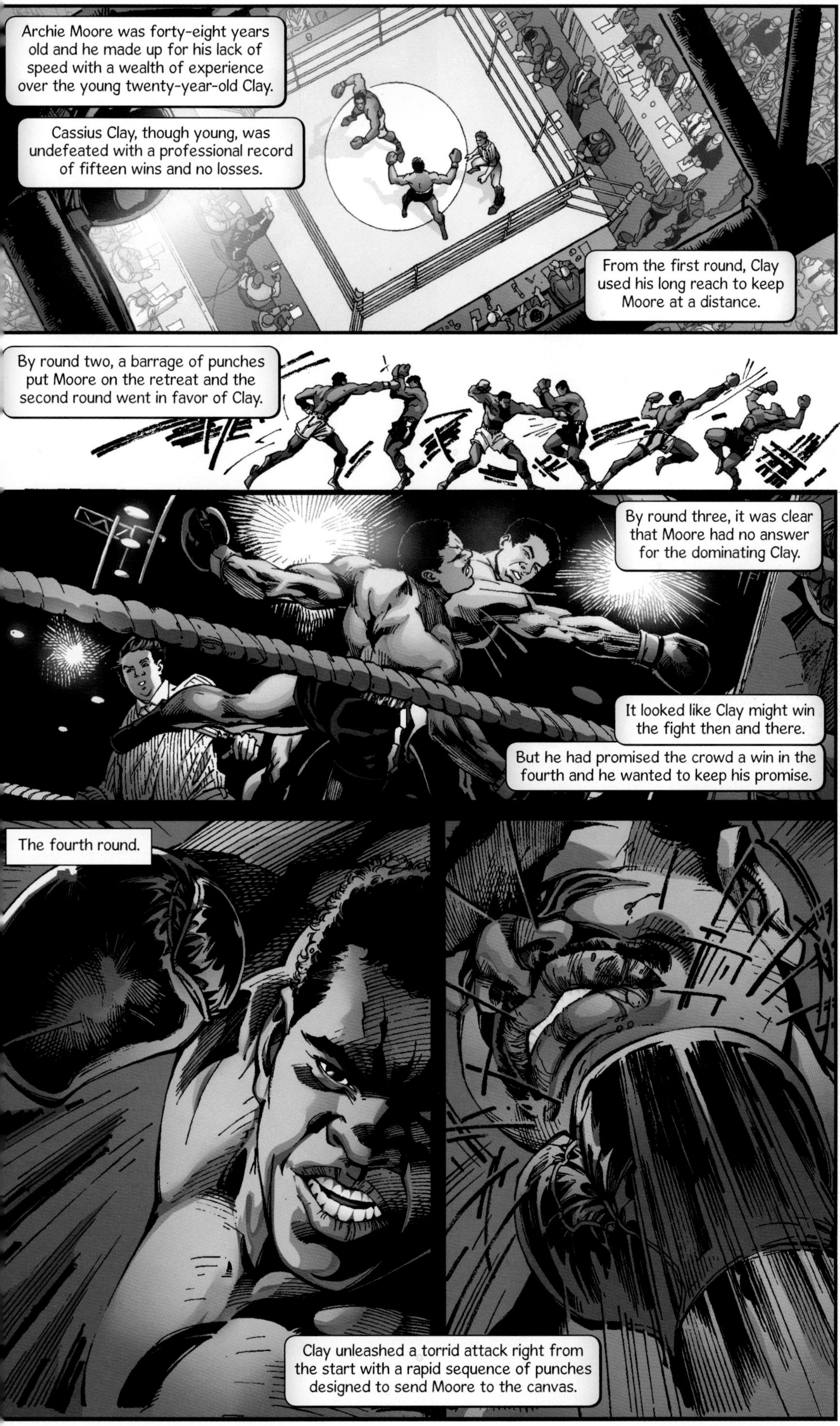
Archie Moore was forty-eight years old and he made up for his lack of speed with a wealth of experience over the young twenty-year-old Clay.
Cassius Clay, though young, was undefeated with a professional record of fifteen wins and no losses.
From the first round, Clay used his long reach to keep Moore at a distance.
By round two, a barrage of punches put Moore on the retreat and the second round went in favor of Clay.
By round three, it was clear that Moore had no answer for the dominating Clay.
It looked like Clay might win the fight then and there.
But he had promised the crowd a win in the fourth and he wanted to keep his promise.
The fourth round.
Clay unleashed a torrid attack right from the start with a rapid sequence of punches designed to send Moore to the canvas.

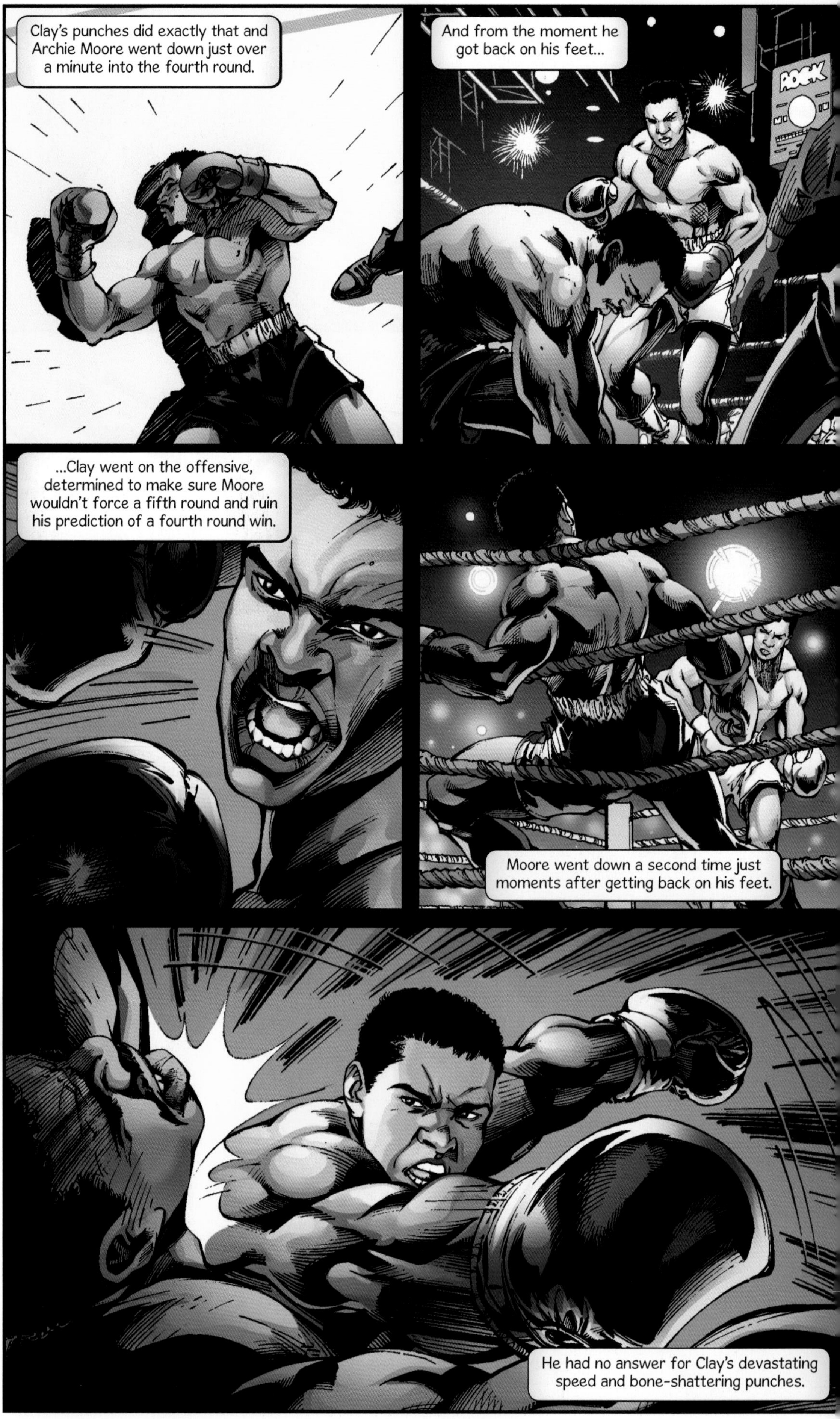

Clay's punches did exactly that and Archie Moore went down just over a minute into the fourth round.
And from the moment he got back on his feet...
ROCK
...Clay went on the offensive, determined to make sure Moore wouldn't force a fifth round and ruin his prediction of a fourth round win.
Moore went down a second time just moments after getting back on his feet.
He had no answer for Clay's devastating speed and bone-shattering punches.

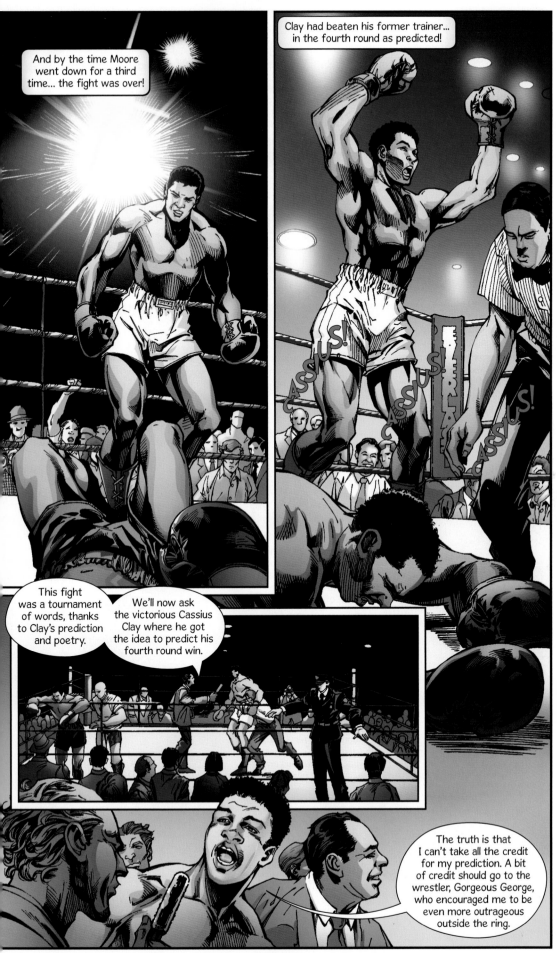

And by the time Moore went down for a third time... the fight was over!

Clay had beaten his former trainer... in the fourth round as predicted!

CASSIUS! CASSIUS! CASSIUS! CASSIUS!

This fight was a tournament of words, thanks to Clay's prediction and poetry.

We'll now ask the victorious Cassius Clay where he got the idea to predict his fourth round win.

The truth is that I can't take all the credit for my prediction. A bit of credit should go to the wrestler, Gorgeous George, who encouraged me to be even more outrageous outside the ring.

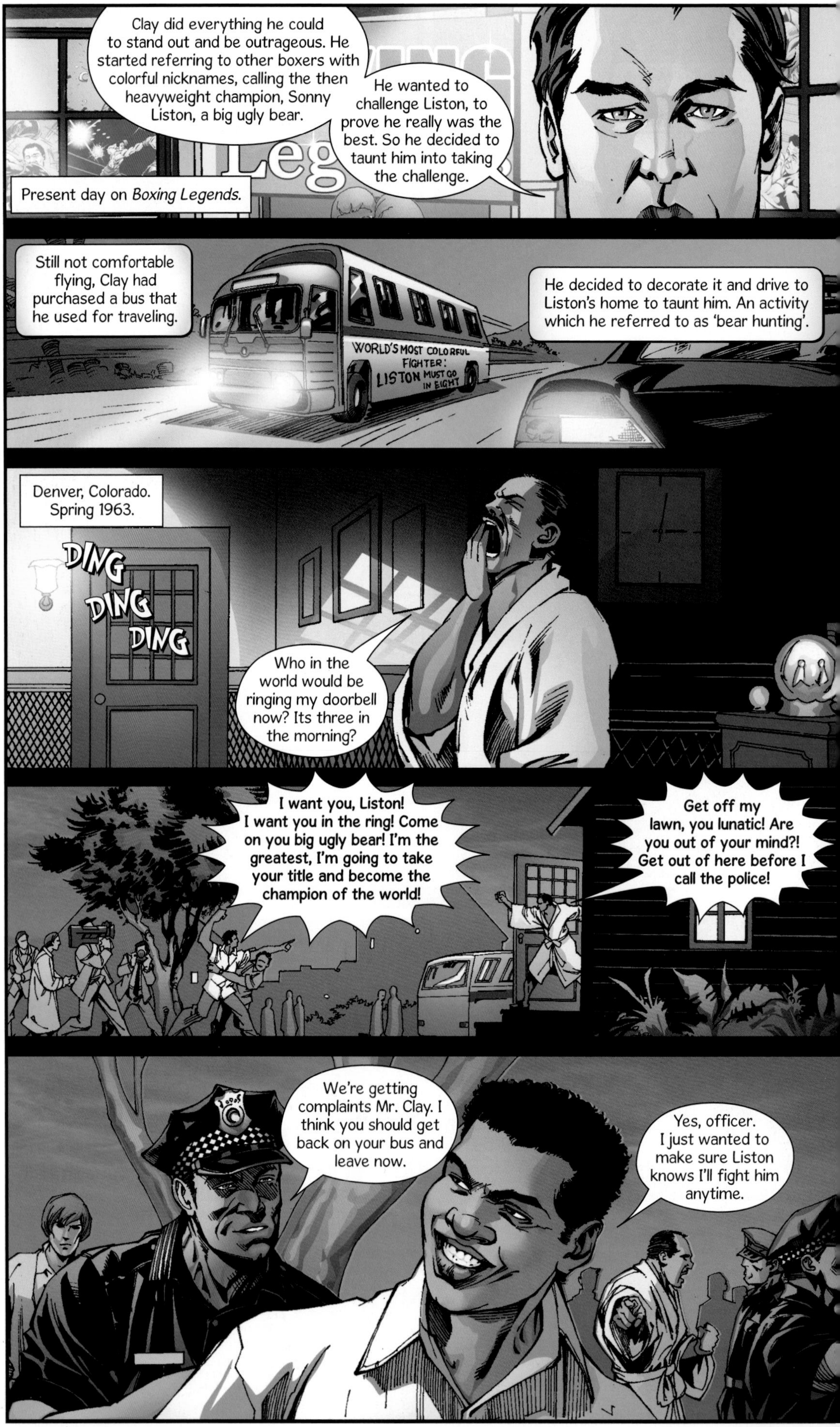
Clay did everything he could to stand out and be outrageous. He started referring to other boxers with colorful nicknames, calling the then heavyweight champion, Sonny Liston, a big ugly bear.
He wanted to challenge Liston, to prove he really was the best. So he decided to taunt him into taking the challenge.
Present day on *Boxing Legends.*
Still not comfortable flying, Clay had purchased a bus that he used for traveling.
WORLD'S MOST COLORFUL FIGHTER: LISTON MUST GO IN EIGHT
He decided to decorate it and drive to Liston's home to taunt him. An activity which he referred to as 'bear hunting'.
Denver, Colorado. Spring 1963.
DING
DING
DING
Who in the world would be ringing my doorbell now? Its three in the morning?
I want you, Liston! I want you in the ring! Come on you big ugly bear! I'm the greatest, I'm going to take your title and become the champion of the world!
Get off my lawn, you lunatic! Are you out of your mind?! Get out of here before I call the police!
We're getting complaints Mr. Clay. I think you should get back on your bus and leave now.
Yes, officer. I just wanted to make sure Liston knows I'll fight him anytime.

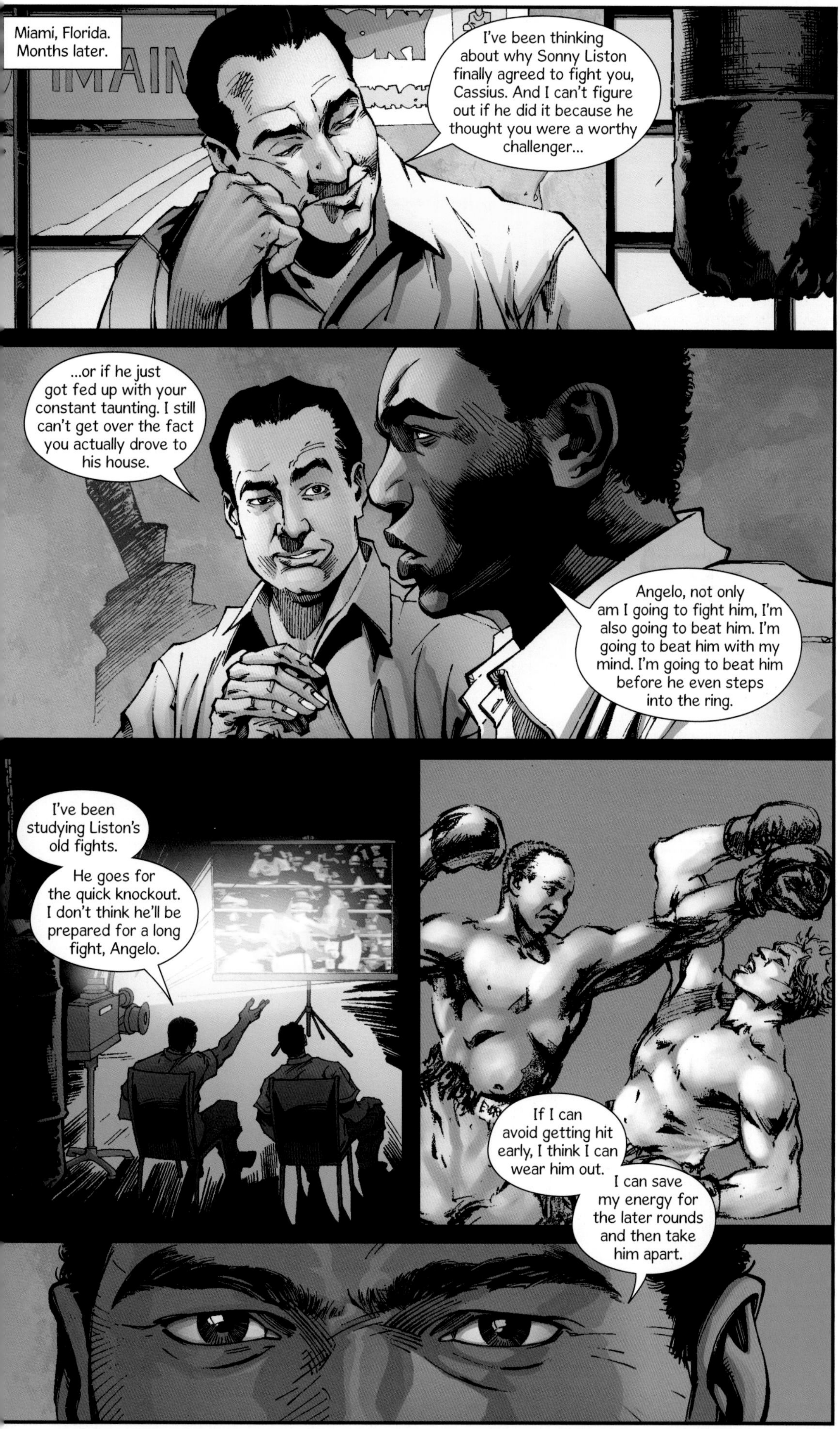
Miami, Florida. Months later.
I've been thinking about why Sonny Liston finally agreed to fight you, Cassius. And I can't figure out if he did it because he thought you were a worthy challenger...
...or if he just got fed up with your constant taunting. I still can't get over the fact you actually drove to his house.
Angelo, not only am I going to fight him, I'm also going to beat him. I'm going to beat him with my mind. I'm going to beat him before he even steps into the ring.
I've been studying Liston's old fights.
He goes for the quick knockout. I don't think he'll be prepared for a long fight, Angelo.
If I can avoid getting hit early, I think I can wear him out.
I can save my energy for the later rounds and then take him apart.

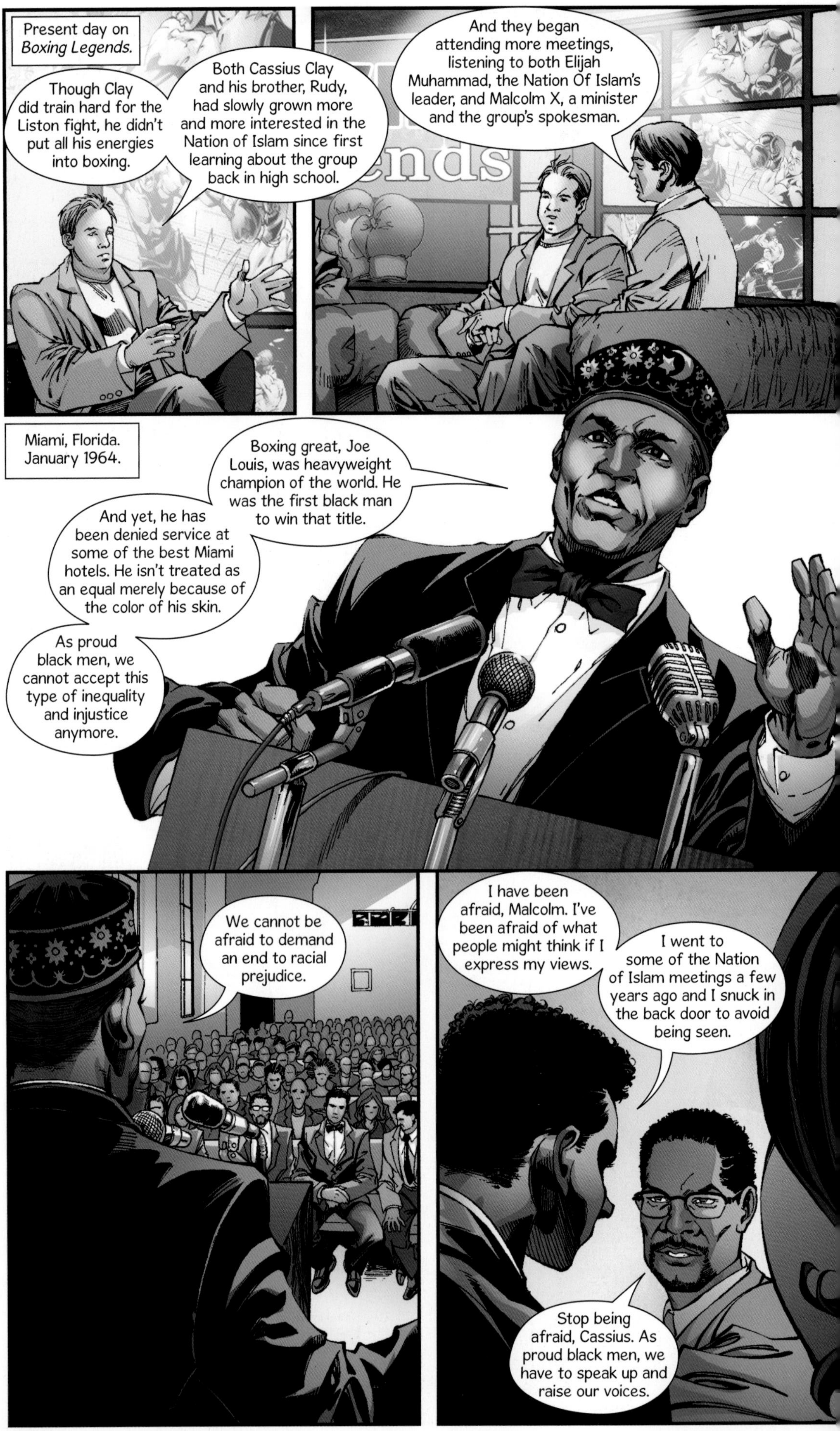
Present day on *Boxing Legends.*
Though Clay did train hard for the Liston fight, he didn't put all his energies into boxing.
Both Cassius Clay and his brother, Rudy, had slowly grown more and more interested in the Nation of Islam since first learning about the group back in high school.
And they began attending more meetings, listening to both Elijah Muhammad, the Nation Of Islam's leader, and Malcolm X, a minister and the group's spokesman.
Miami, Florida. January 1964.
Boxing great, Joe Louis, was heavyweight champion of the world. He was the first black man to win that title.
And yet, he has been denied service at some of the best Miami hotels. He isn't treated as an equal merely because of the color of his skin.
As proud black men, we cannot accept this type of inequality and injustice anymore.
We cannot be afraid to demand an end to racial prejudice.
I have been afraid, Malcolm. I've been afraid of what people might think if I express my views.
I went to some of the Nation of Islam meetings a few years ago and I snuck in the back door to avoid being seen.
Stop being afraid, Cassius. As proud black men, we have to speak up and raise our voices.

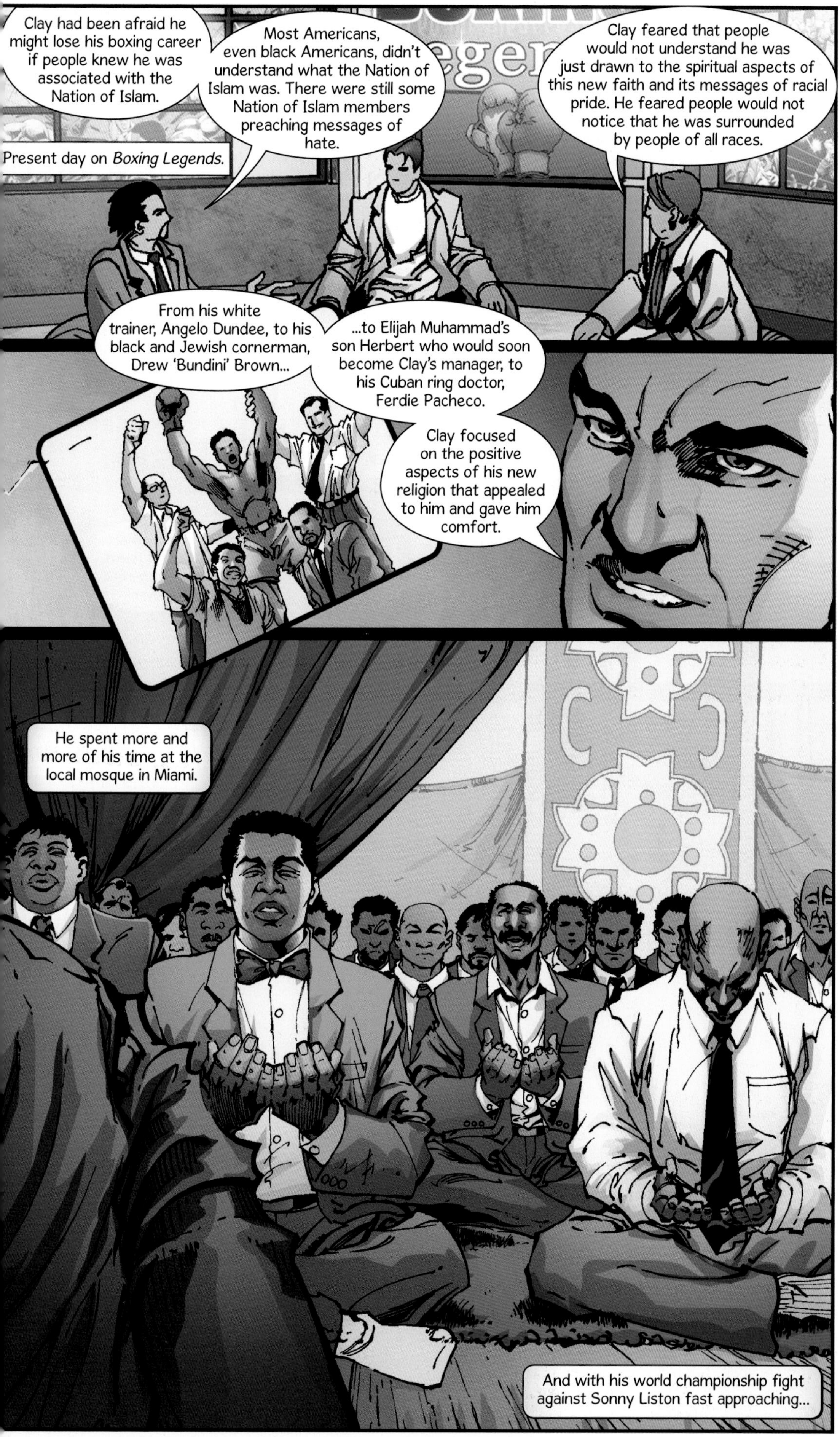

Clay had been afraid he might lose his boxing career if people knew he was associated with the Nation of Islam.
Most Americans, even black Americans, didn't understand what the Nation of Islam was. There were still some Nation of Islam members preaching messages of hate.
Clay feared that people would not understand he was just drawn to the spiritual aspects of this new faith and its messages of racial pride. He feared people would not notice that he was surrounded by people of all races.
Present day on *Boxing Legends.*
From his white trainer, Angelo Dundee, to his black and Jewish cornerman, Drew 'Bundini' Brown...
...to Elijah Muhammad's son Herbert who would soon become Clay's manager, to his Cuban ring doctor, Ferdie Pacheco.
Clay focused on the positive aspects of his new religion that appealed to him and gave him comfort.
He spent more and more of his time at the local mosque in Miami.
And with his world championship fight against Sonny Liston fast approaching...

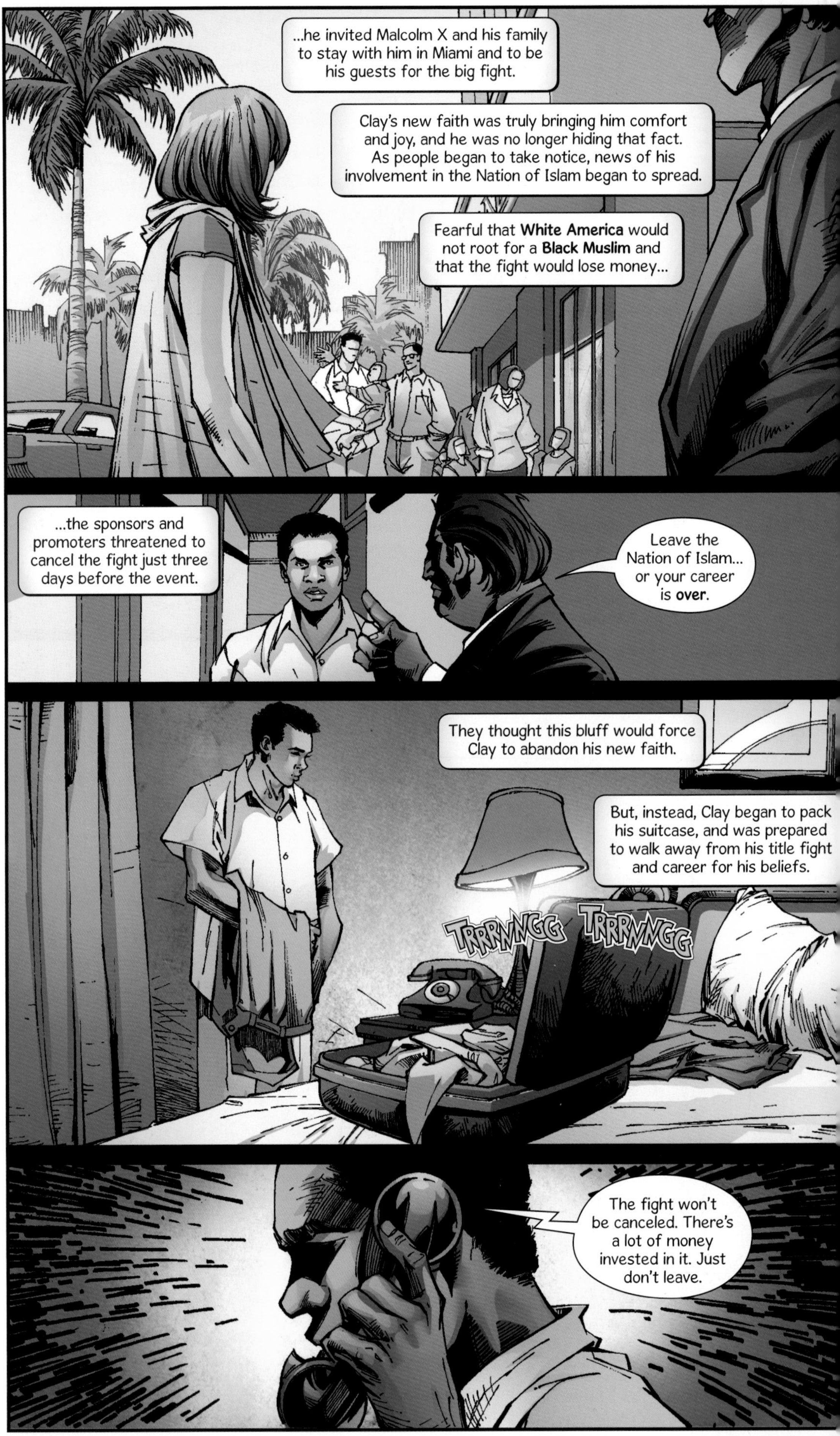
...he invited Malcolm X and his family to stay with him in Miami and to be his guests for the big fight.
Clay's new faith was truly bringing him comfort and joy, and he was no longer hiding that fact. As people began to take notice, news of his involvement in the Nation of Islam began to spread.
Fearful that **White America** would not root for a **Black Muslim** and that the fight would lose money...
...the sponsors and promoters threatened to cancel the fight just three days before the event.
Leave the Nation of Islam... or your career is **over**.
They thought this bluff would force Clay to abandon his new faith.
But, instead, Clay began to pack his suitcase, and was prepared to walk away from his title fight and career for his beliefs.
TRRRNNGG TRRRNNGG
The fight won't be canceled. There's a lot of money invested in it. Just don't leave.

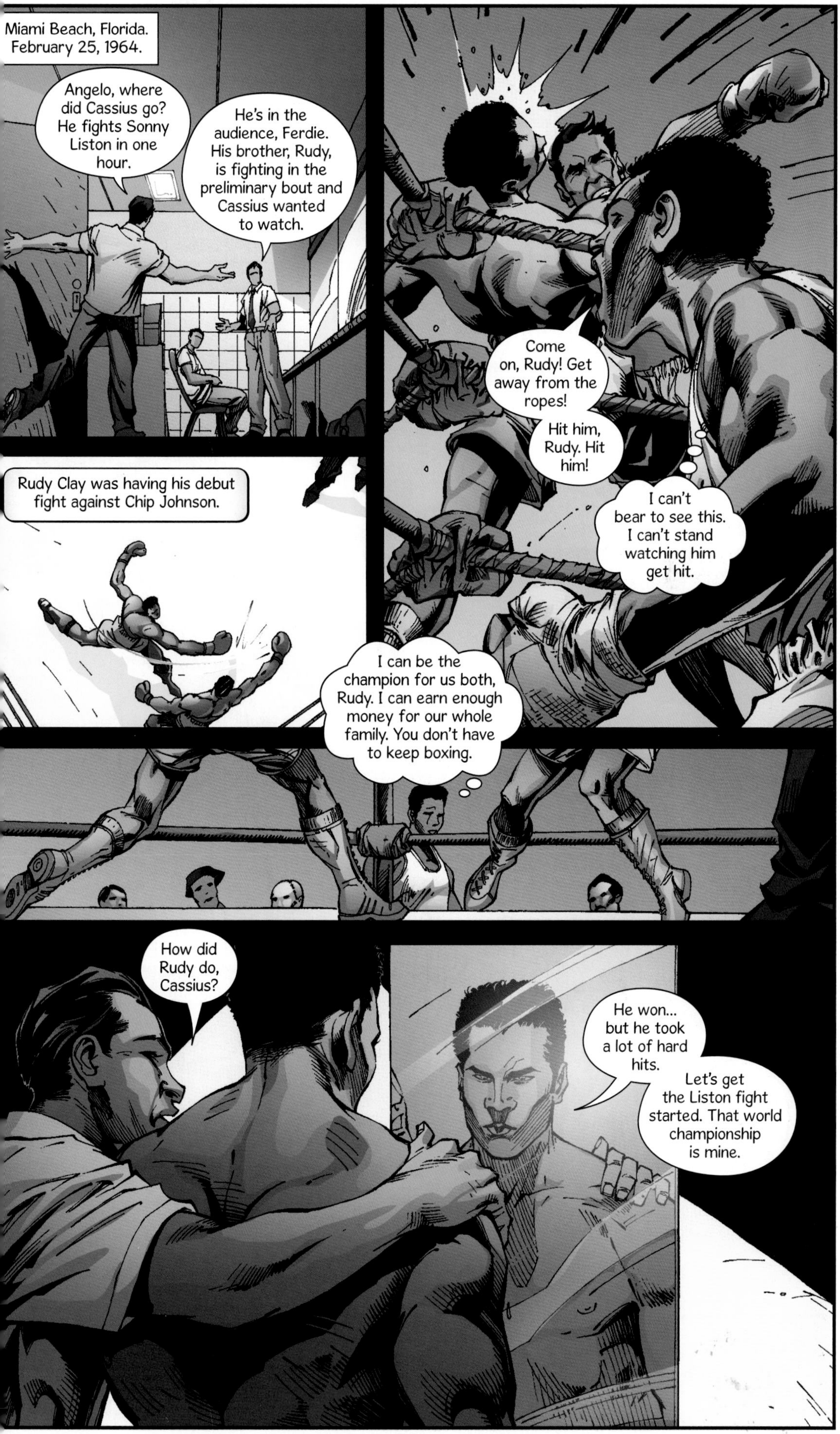
Miami Beach, Florida. February 25, 1964.
Angelo, where did Cassius go? He fights Sonny Liston in one hour.
He's in the audience, Ferdie. His brother, Rudy, is fighting in the preliminary bout and Cassius wanted to watch.
Come on, Rudy! Get away from the ropes!
Hit him, Rudy. Hit him!
I can't bear to see this. I can't stand watching him get hit.
Rudy Clay was having his debut fight against Chip Johnson.
I can be the champion for us both, Rudy. I can earn enough money for our whole family. You don't have to keep boxing.
How did Rudy do, Cassius?
He won... but he took a lot of hard hits.
Let's get the Liston fight started. That world championship is mine.

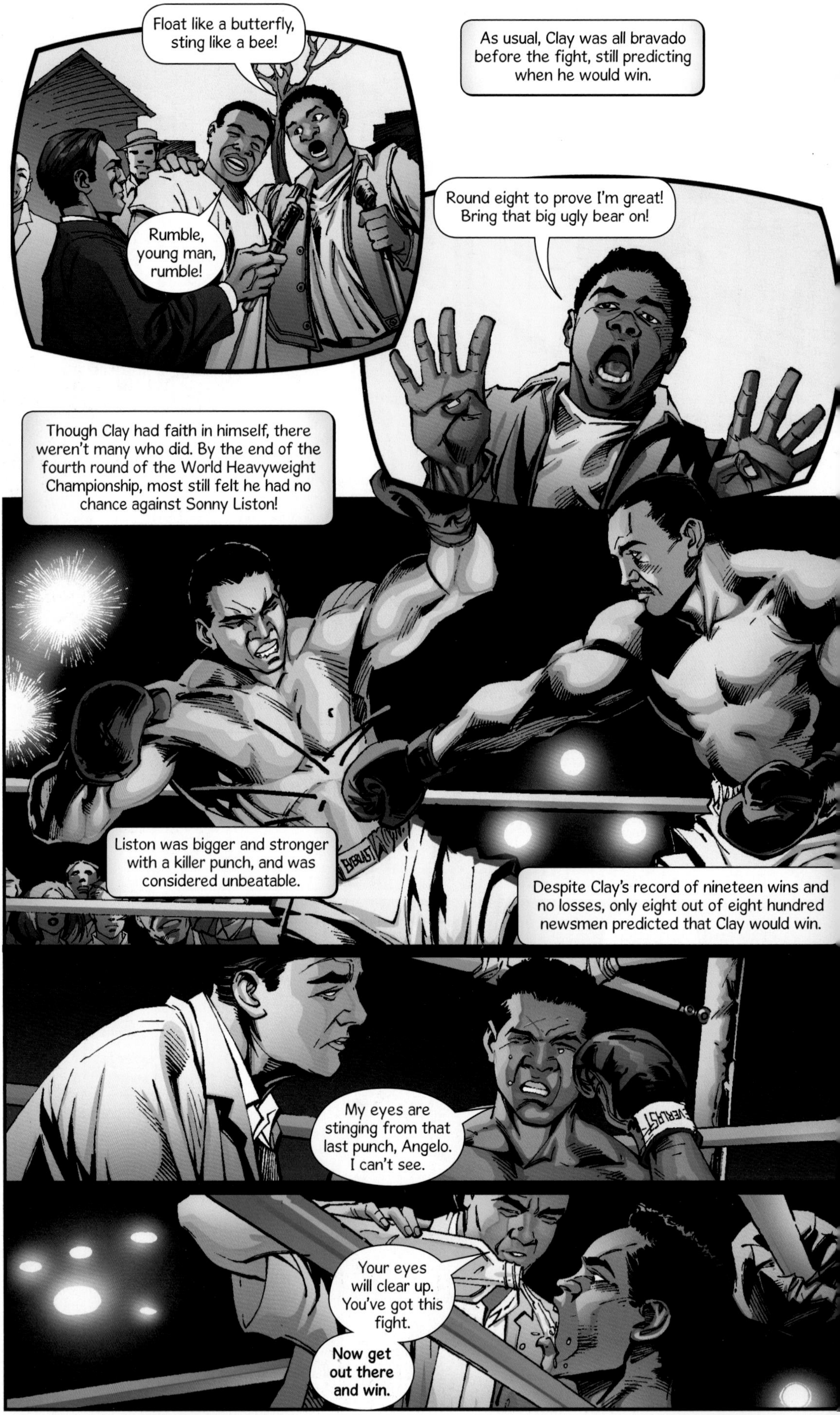
Float like a butterfly, sting like a bee!
As usual, Clay was all bravado before the fight, still predicting when he would win.
Rumble, young man, rumble!
Round eight to prove I'm great! Bring that big ugly bear on!
Though Clay had faith in himself, there weren't many who did. By the end of the fourth round of the World Heavyweight Championship, most still felt he had no chance against Sonny Liston!
Liston was bigger and stronger with a killer punch, and was considered unbeatable.
Despite Clay's record of nineteen wins and no losses, only eight out of eight hundred newsmen predicted that Clay would win.
My eyes are stinging from that last punch, Angelo. I can't see.
Your eyes will clear up. You've got this fight.
Now get out there and win.

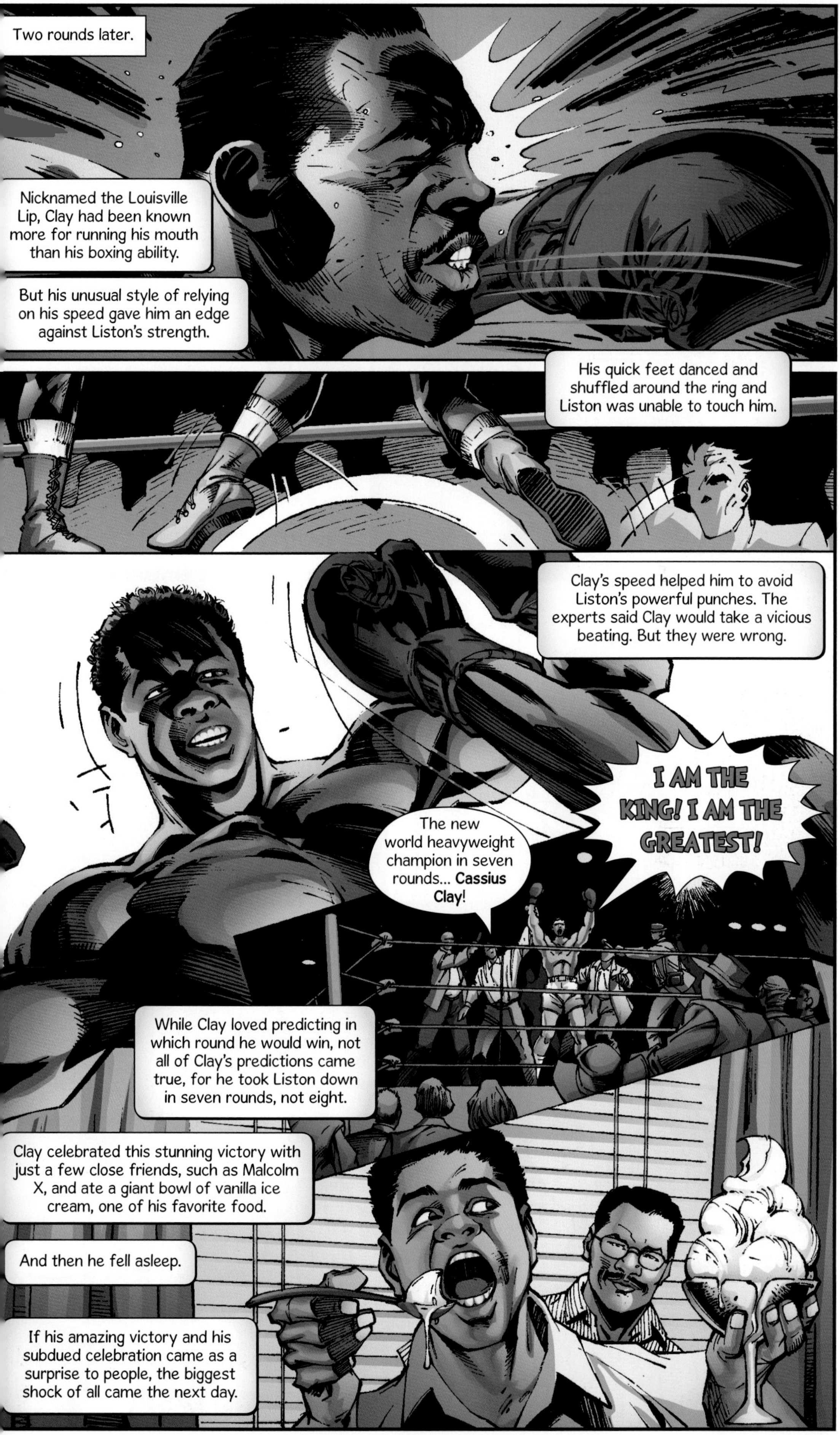

Two rounds later.
Nicknamed the Louisville Lip, Clay had been known more for running his mouth than his boxing ability.
But his unusual style of relying on his speed gave him an edge against Liston's strength.
His quick feet danced and shuffled around the ring and Liston was unable to touch him.
Clay's speed helped him to avoid Liston's powerful punches. The experts said Clay would take a vicious beating. But they were wrong.
I AM THE KING! I AM THE GREATEST!
The new world heavyweight champion in seven rounds... **Cassius Clay**!
While Clay loved predicting in which round he would win, not all of Clay's predictions came true, for he took Liston down in seven rounds, not eight.
Clay celebrated this stunning victory with just a few close friends, such as Malcolm X, and ate a giant bowl of vanilla ice cream, one of his favorite food.
And then he fell asleep.
If his amazing victory and his subdued celebration came as a surprise to people, the biggest shock of all came the next day.

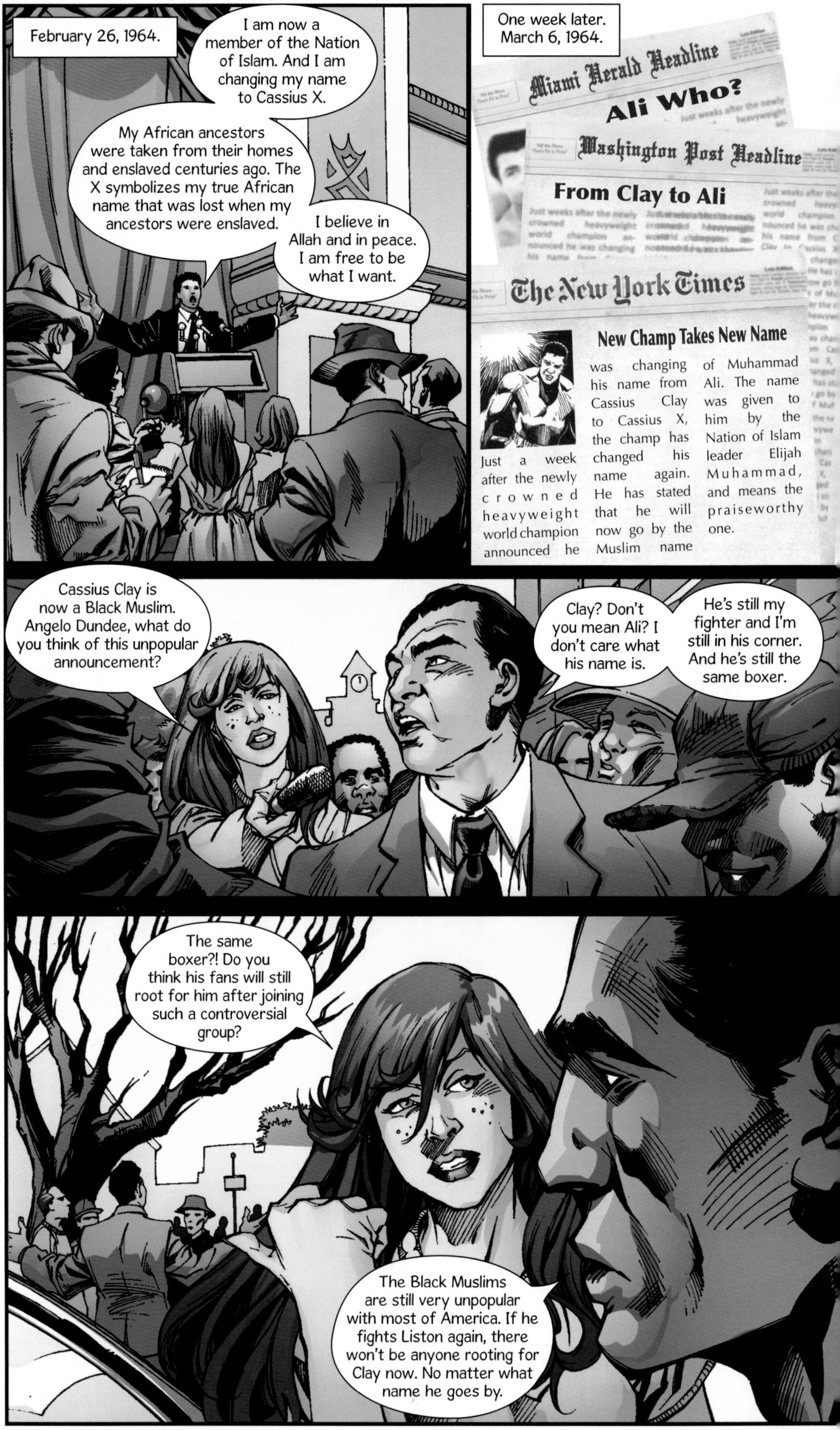
February 26, 1964.
I am now a member of the Nation of Islam. And I am changing my name to Cassius X.
My African ancestors were taken from their homes and enslaved centuries ago. The X symbolizes my true African name that was lost when my ancestors were enslaved.
I believe in Allah and in peace. I am free to be what I want.
One week later. March 6, 1964.
Miami Herald Headline
Ali Who?
Washington Post Headline
From Clay to Ali
The New York Times
New Champ Takes New Name
Just a week after the newly crowned heavyweight world champion announced he was changing his name from Cassius Clay to Cassius X, the champ has changed his name again. He has stated that he will now go by the Muslim name of Muhammad Ali. The name was given to him by the Nation of Islam leader Elijah Muhammad, and means the praiseworthy one.
Cassius Clay is now a Black Muslim. Angelo Dundee, what do you think of this unpopular announcement?
Clay? Don't you mean Ali? I don't care what his name is.
He's still my fighter and I'm still in his corner. And he's still the same boxer.
The same boxer?! Do you think his fans will still root for him after joining such a controversial group?
The Black Muslims are still very unpopular with most of America. If he fights Liston again, there won't be anyone rooting for Clay now. No matter what name he goes by.

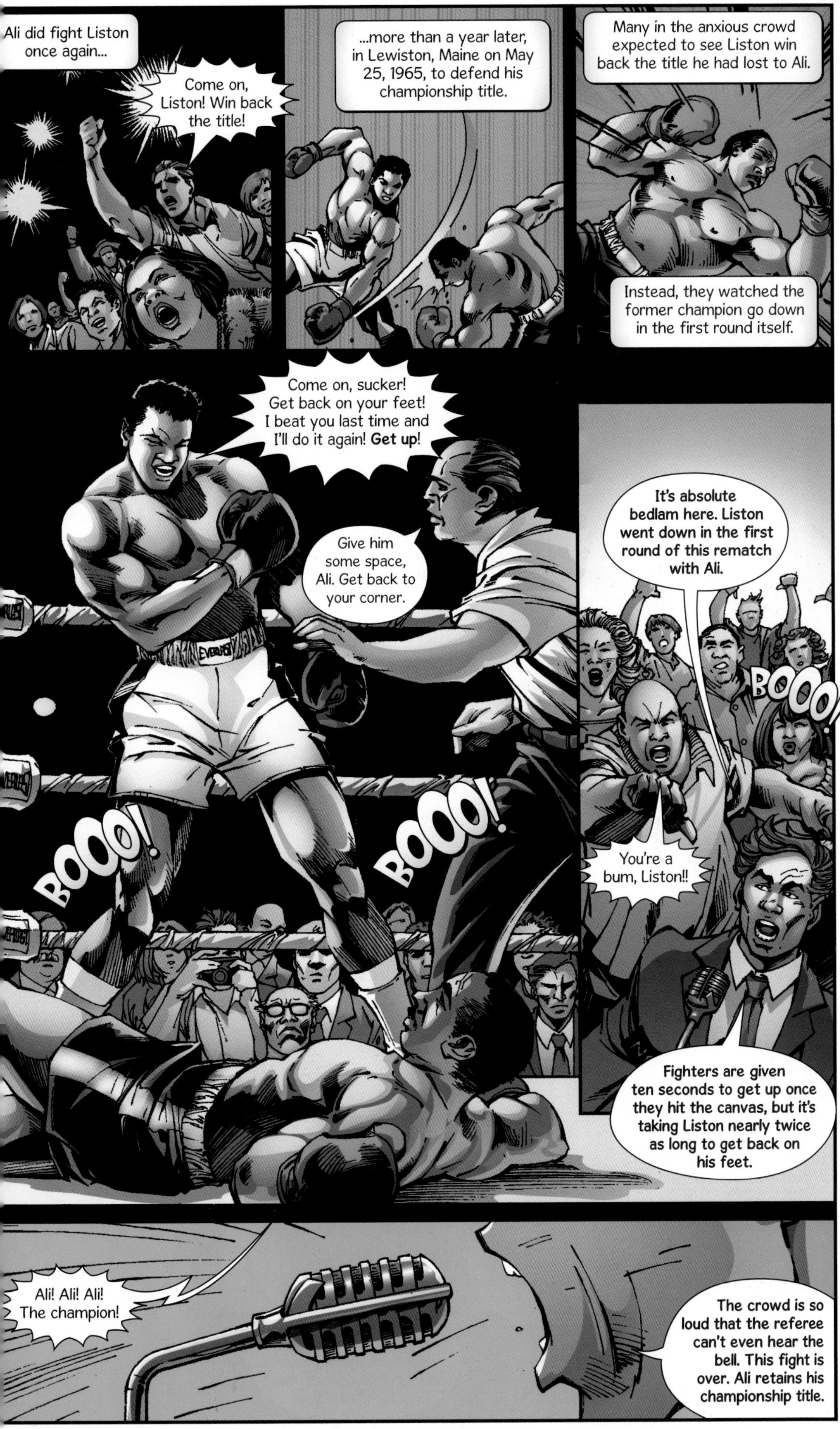

Ali did fight Liston once again...
Come on, Liston! Win back the title!
...more than a year later, in Lewiston, Maine on May 25, 1965, to defend his championship title.
Many in the anxious crowd expected to see Liston win back the title he had lost to Ali.
Instead, they watched the former champion go down in the first round itself.
Come on, sucker! Get back on your feet! I beat you last time and I'll do it again! **Get up**!
Give him some space, Ali. Get back to your corner.
BOOO!
BOOO!
It's absolute bedlam here. Liston went down in the first round of this rematch with Ali.
BOOO!
You're a bum, Liston!!
Fighters are given ten seconds to get up once they hit the canvas, but it's taking Liston nearly twice as long to get back on his feet.
Ali! Ali! Ali! The champion!
The crowd is so loud that the referee can't even hear the bell. This fight is over. Ali retains his championship title.

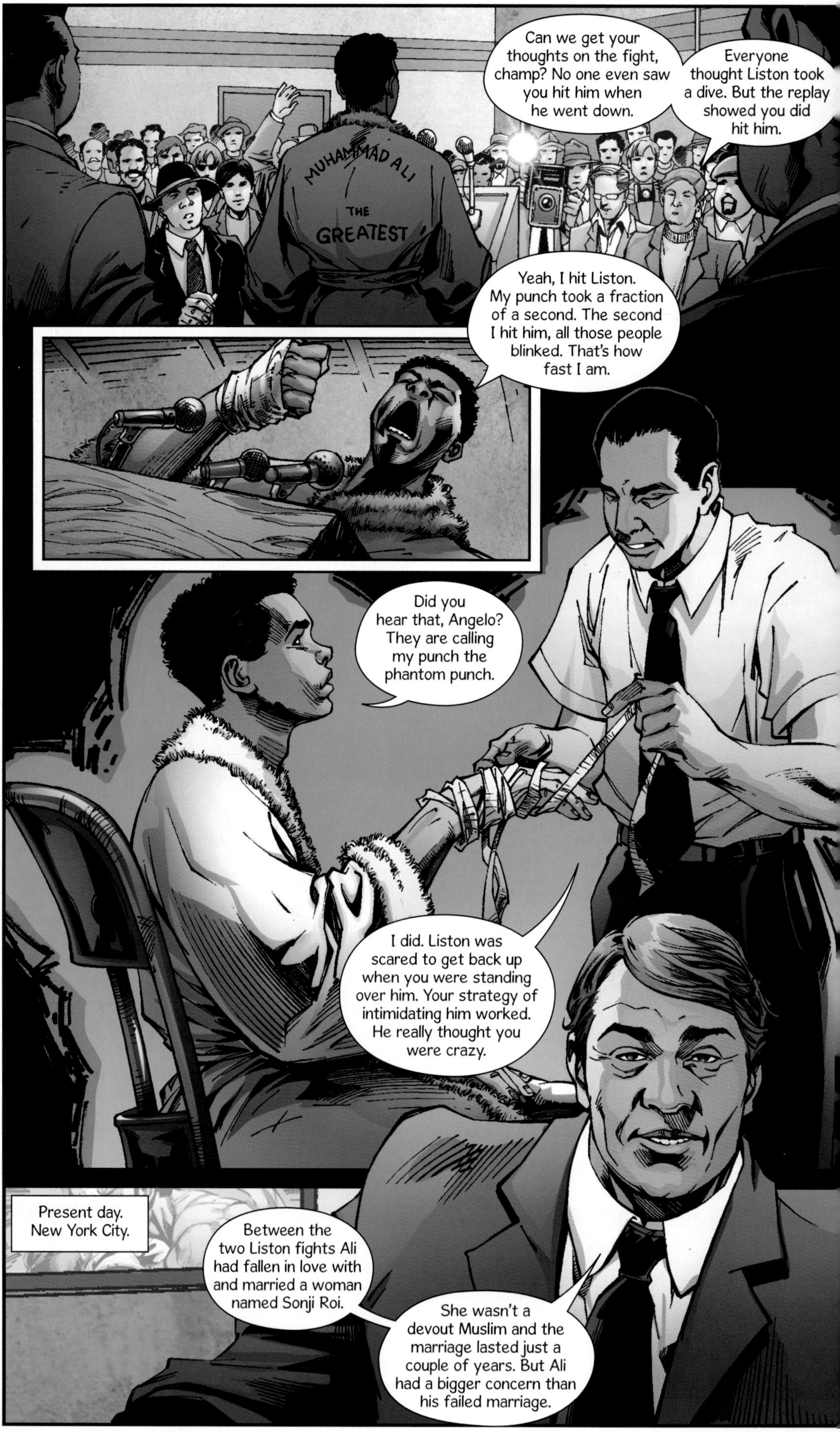
MUHAMMAD ALI THE GREATEST
Can we get your thoughts on the fight, champ? No one even saw you hit him when he went down.
Everyone thought Liston took a dive. But the replay showed you did hit him.
Yeah, I hit Liston. My punch took a fraction of a second. The second I hit him, all those people blinked. That's how fast I am.
Did you hear that, Angelo? They are calling my punch the phantom punch.
I did. Liston was scared to get back up when you were standing over him. Your strategy of intimidating him worked. He really thought you were crazy.
Present day. New York City.
Between the two Liston fights Ali had fallen in love with and married a woman named Sonji Roi.
She wasn't a devout Muslim and the marriage lasted just a couple of years. But Ali had a bigger concern than his failed marriage.

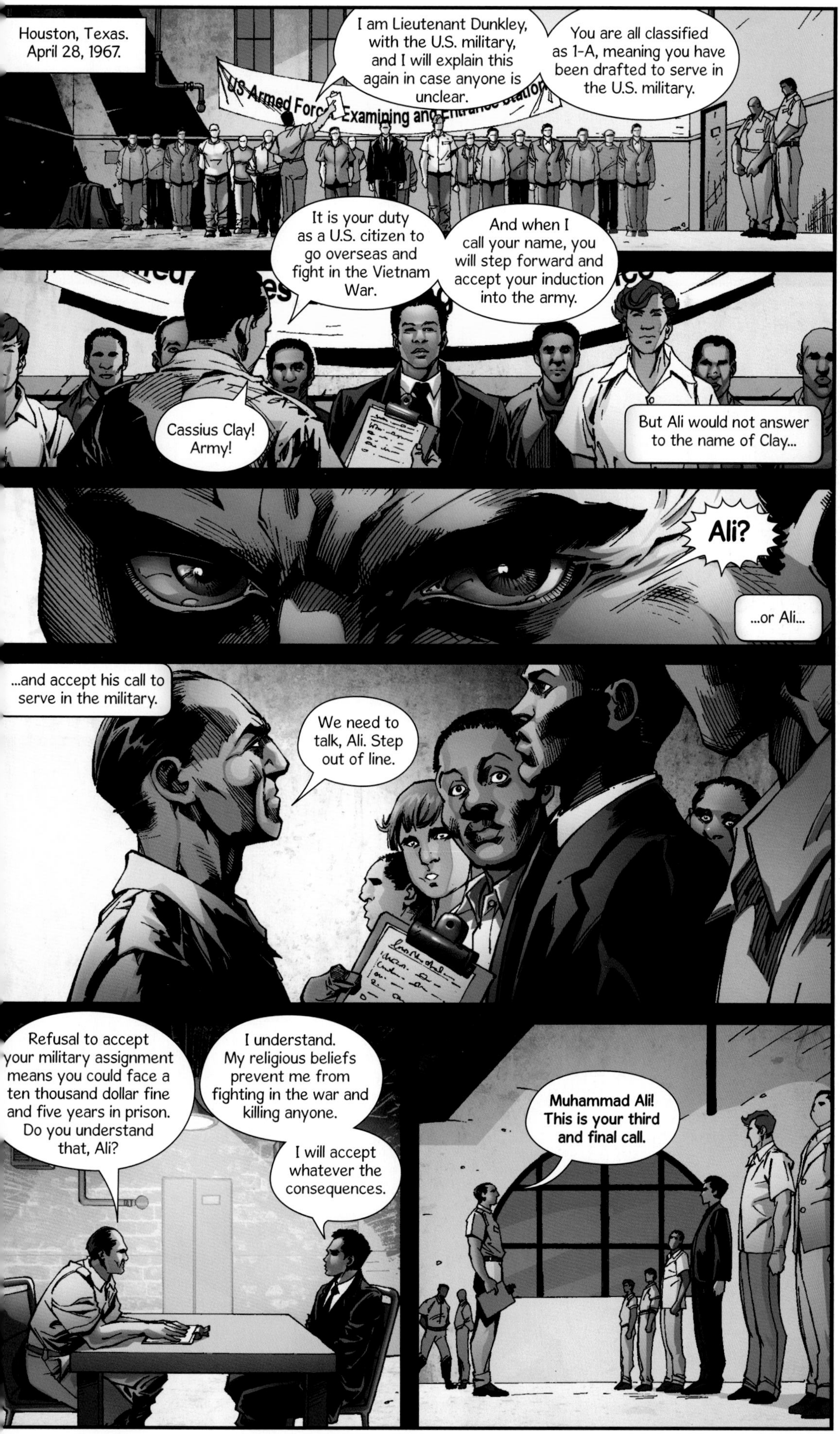
Houston, Texas. April 28, 1967.
I am Lieutenant Dunkley, with the U.S. military, and I will explain this again in case anyone is unclear.
You are all classified as 1-A, meaning you have been drafted to serve in the U.S. military.
US Armed Forces Examining and Entrance Station
It is your duty as a U.S. citizen to go overseas and fight in the Vietnam War.
And when I call your name, you will step forward and accept your induction into the army.
Cassius Clay! Army!
But Ali would not answer to the name of Clay...
Ali?
...or Ali...
...and accept his call to serve in the military.
We need to talk, Ali. Step out of line.
Refusal to accept your military assignment means you could face a ten thousand dollar fine and five years in prison. Do you understand that, Ali?
I understand. My religious beliefs prevent me from fighting in the war and killing anyone.
I will accept whatever the consequences.
Muhammad Ali! This is your third and final call.

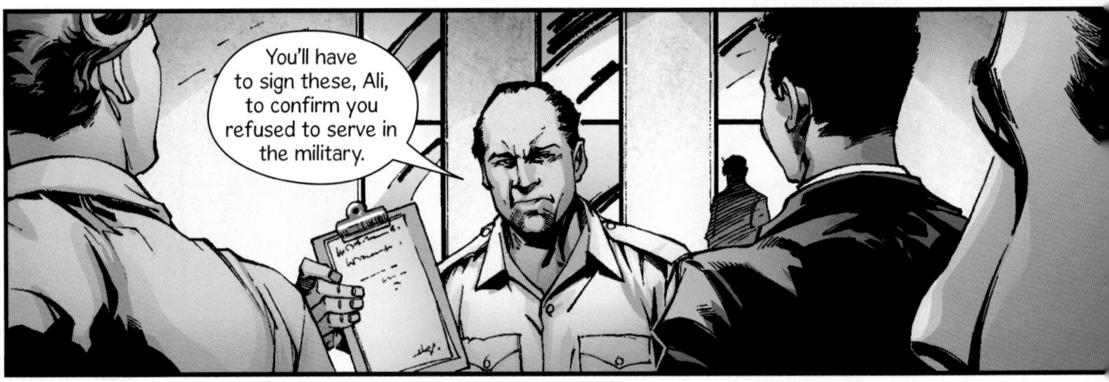
You'll have to sign these, Ali, to confirm you refused to serve in the military.

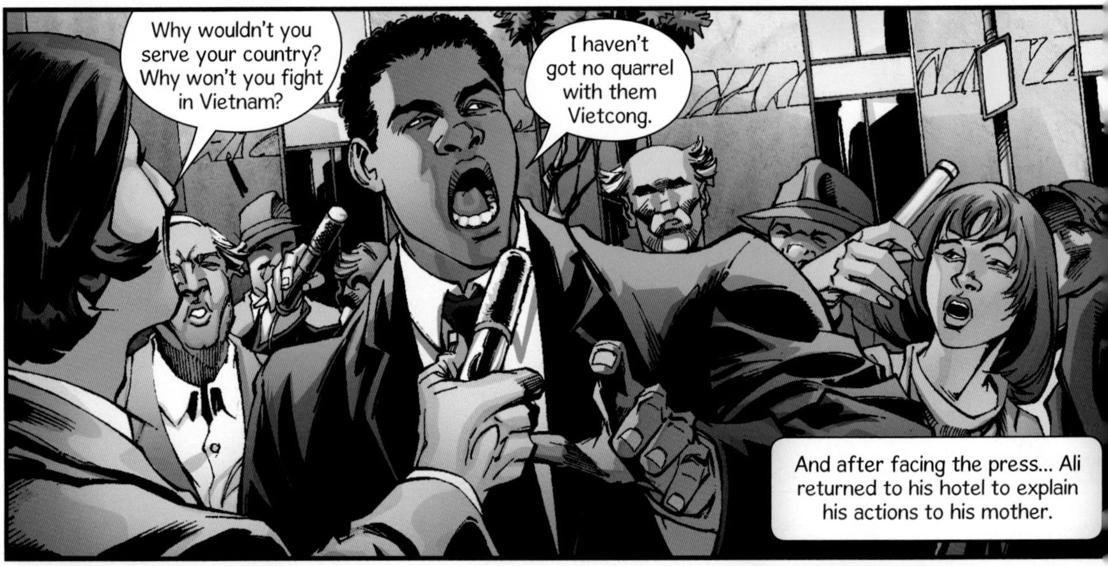
Why wouldn't you serve your country? Why won't you fight in Vietnam?
I haven't got no quarrel with them Vietcong.
And after facing the press... Ali returned to his hotel to explain his actions to his mother.

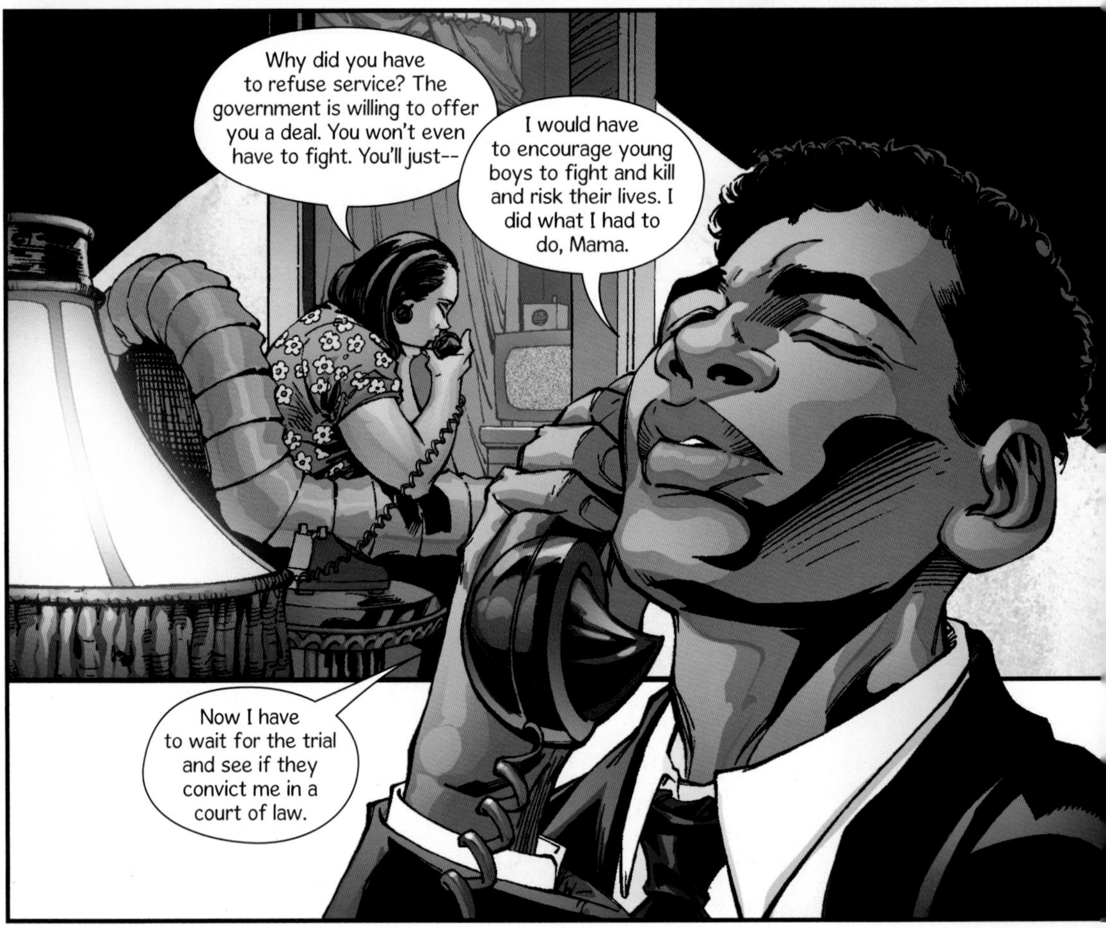
Why did you have to refuse service? The government is willing to offer you a deal. You won't even have to fight. You'll just--
I would have to encourage young boys to fight and kill and risk their lives. I did what I had to do, Mama.
Now I have to wait for the trial and see if they convict me in a court of law.

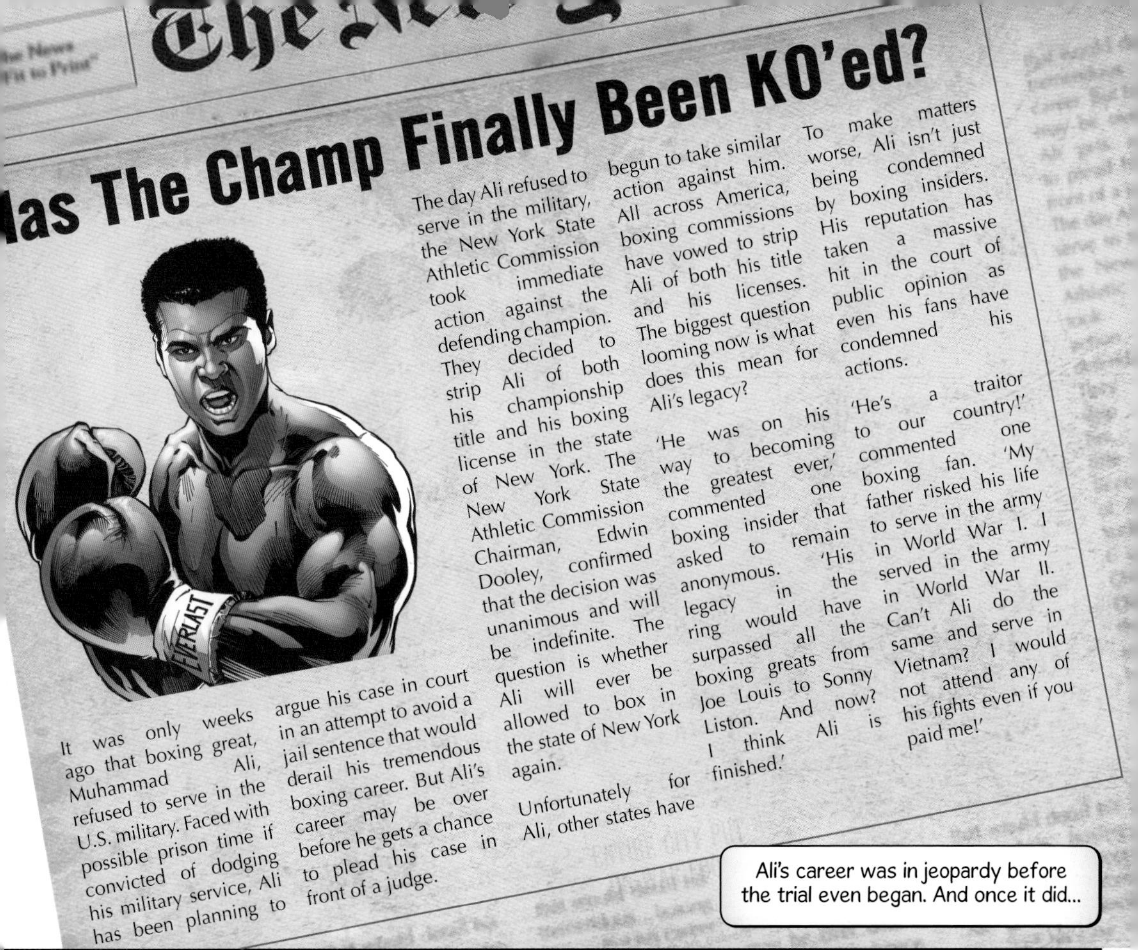

Has The Champ Finally Been KO'ed?

It was only weeks ago that boxing great, Muhammad Ali, refused to serve in the U.S. military. Faced with possible prison time if convicted of dodging his military service, Ali has been planning to argue his case in court in an attempt to avoid a jail sentence that would derail his tremendous boxing career. But Ali's career may be over before he gets a chance to plead his case in front of a judge.

The day Ali refused to serve in the military, the New York State Athletic Commission took immediate action against the defending champion. They decided to strip Ali of both his championship title and his boxing license in the state of New York. The New York State Athletic Commission Chairman, Edwin Dooley, confirmed that the decision was unanimous and will be indefinite. The question is whether Ali will ever be allowed to box in the state of New York again.

Unfortunately for Ali, other states have begun to take similar action against him. All across America, boxing commissions have vowed to strip Ali of both his title and his licenses. The biggest question looming now is what does this mean for Ali's legacy?

'He was on his way to becoming the greatest ever,' commented one boxing insider that asked to remain anonymous. 'His legacy in the ring would have surpassed all the boxing greats from Joe Louis to Sonny Liston. And now? I think Ali is finished.'

To make matters worse, Ali isn't just being condemned by boxing insiders. His reputation has taken a massive hit in the court of public opinion as even his fans have condemned his actions.

'He's a traitor to our country!' commented one boxing fan. 'My father risked his life to serve in the army in World War I. I served in the army in World War II. Can't Ali do the same and serve in Vietnam? I would not attend any of his fights even if you paid me!'

EVERLAST
Ali's career was in jeopardy before the trial even began. And once it did...

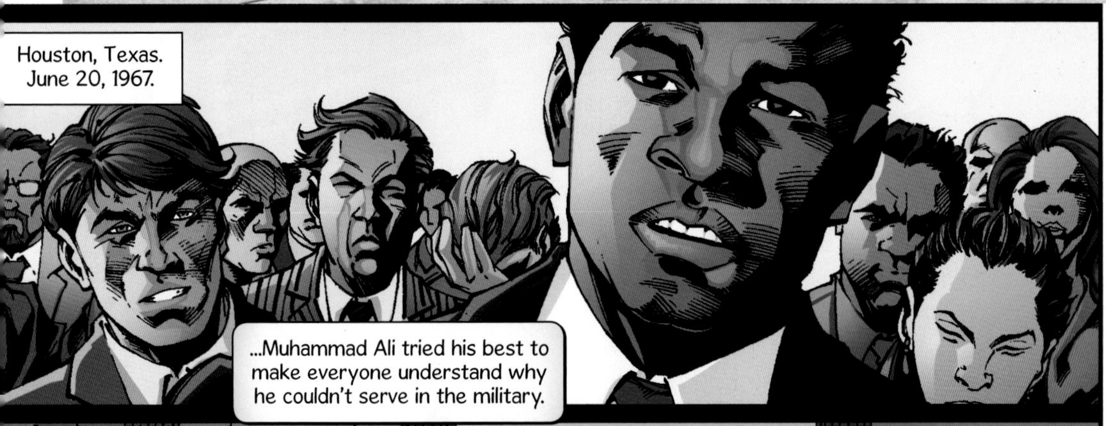
Houston, Texas. June 20, 1967.
...Muhammad Ali tried his best to make everyone understand why he couldn't serve in the military.

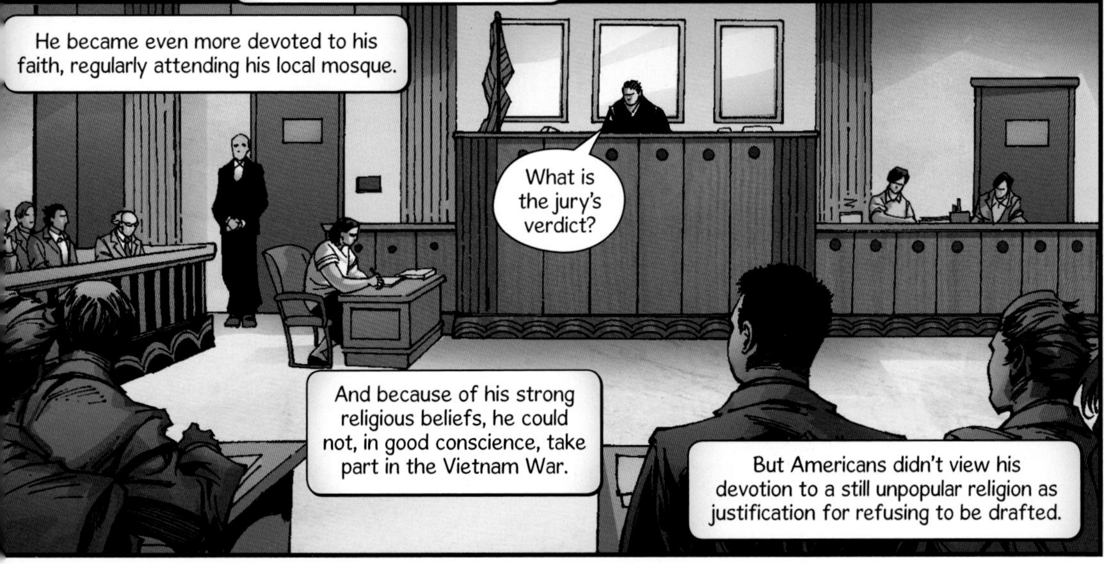
He became even more devoted to his faith, regularly attending his local mosque.
What is the jury's verdict?
And because of his strong religious beliefs, he could not, in good conscience, take part in the Vietnam War.
But Americans didn't view his devotion to a still unpopular religion as justification for refusing to be drafted.

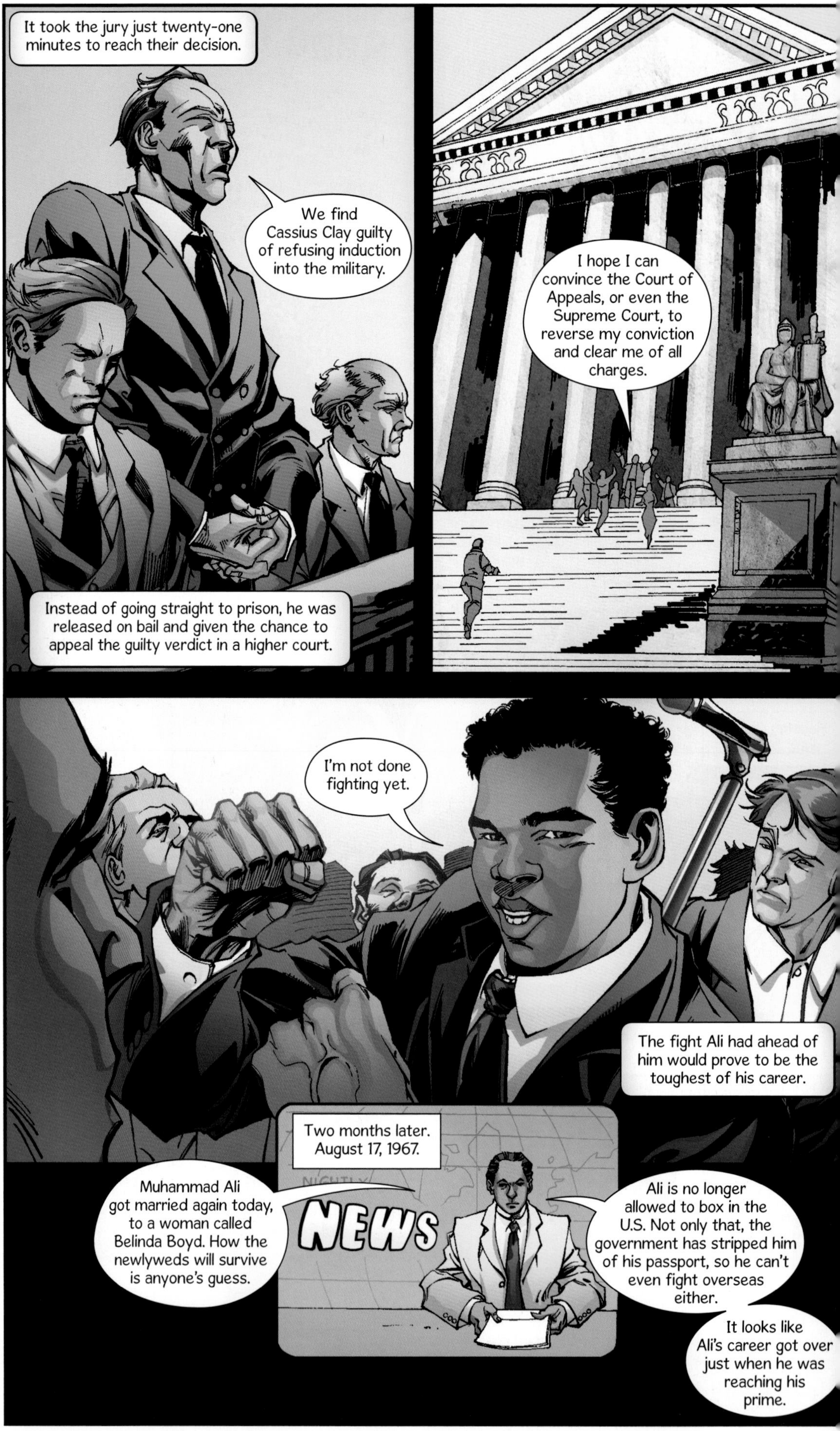
It took the jury just twenty-one minutes to reach their decision.
We find Cassius Clay guilty of refusing induction into the military.
Instead of going straight to prison, he was released on bail and given the chance to appeal the guilty verdict in a higher court.
I hope I can convince the Court of Appeals, or even the Supreme Court, to reverse my conviction and clear me of all charges.
I'm not done fighting yet.
The fight Ali had ahead of him would prove to be the toughest of his career.
Two months later. August 17, 1967.
NEWS
Muhammad Ali got married again today, to a woman called Belinda Boyd. How the newlyweds will survive is anyone's guess.
Ali is no longer allowed to box in the U.S. Not only that, the government has stripped him of his passport, so he can't even fight overseas either.
It looks like Ali's career got over just when he was reaching his prime.

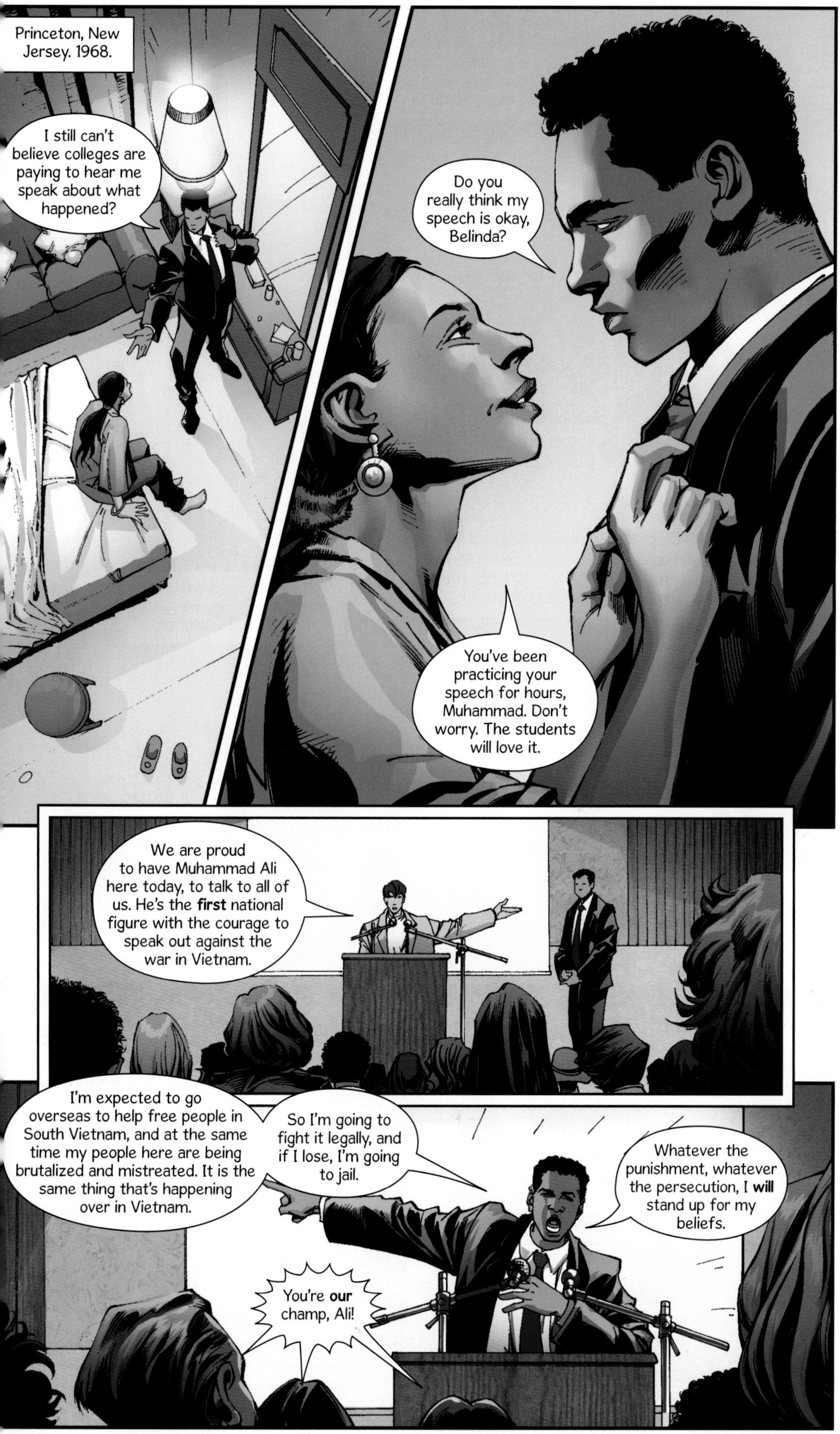
Princeton, New Jersey. 1968.
I still can't believe colleges are paying to hear me speak about what happened?
Do you really think my speech is okay, Belinda?
You've been practicing your speech for hours, Muhammad. Don't worry. The students will love it.
We are proud to have Muhammad Ali here today, to talk to all of us. He's the **first** national figure with the courage to speak out against the war in Vietnam.
I'm expected to go overseas to help free people in South Vietnam, and at the same time my people here are being brutalized and mistreated. It is the same thing that's happening over in Vietnam.
So I'm going to fight it legally, and if I lose, I'm going to jail.
Whatever the punishment, whatever the persecution, I **will** stand up for my beliefs.
You're **our** champ, Ali!

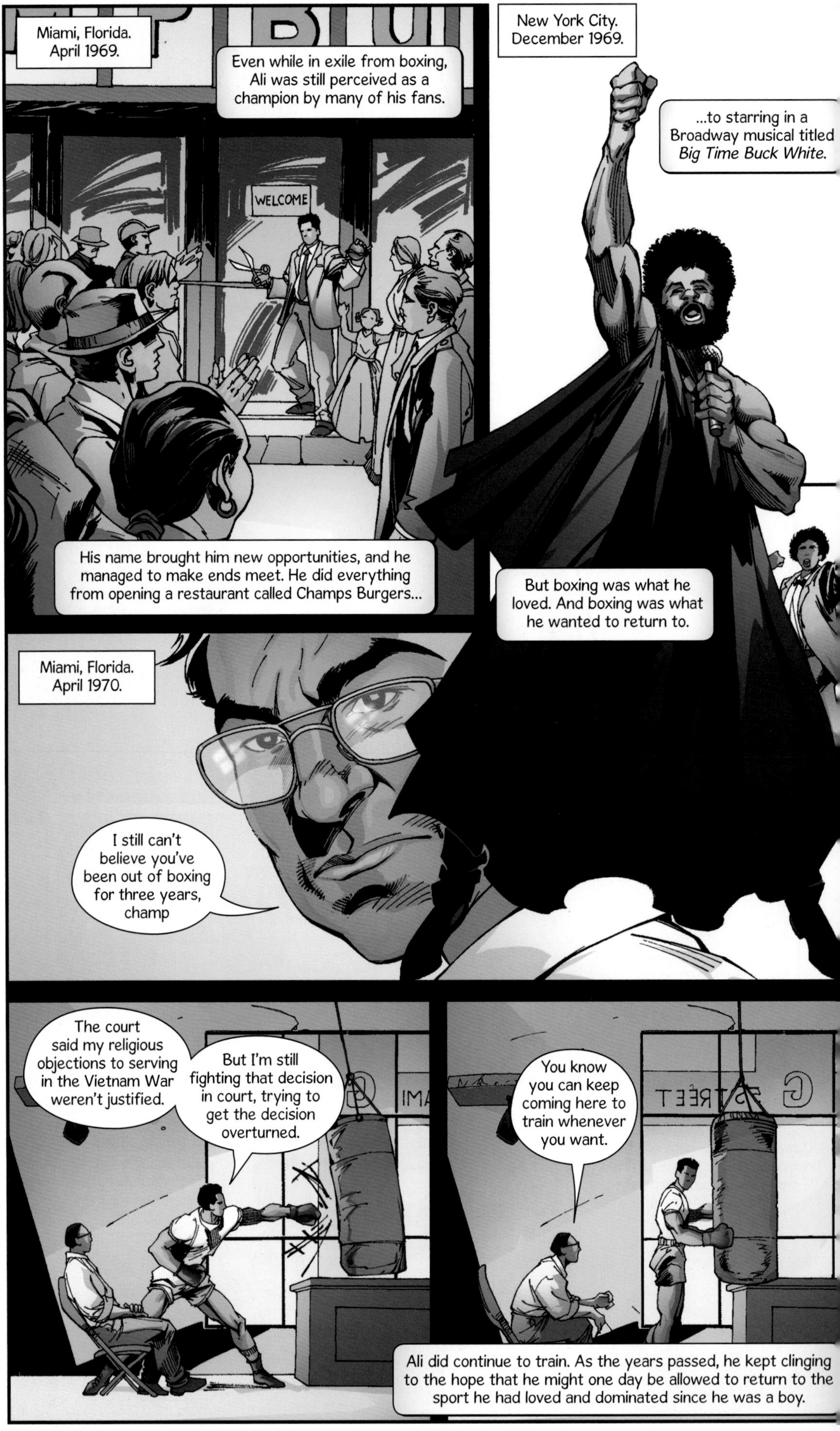
Miami, Florida. April 1969.
Even while in exile from boxing, Ali was still perceived as a champion by many of his fans.
WELCOME
His name brought him new opportunities, and he managed to make ends meet. He did everything from opening a restaurant called Champs Burgers...
New York City. December 1969.
...to starring in a Broadway musical titled *Big Time Buck White*.
But boxing was what he loved. And boxing was what he wanted to return to.
Miami, Florida. April 1970.
I still can't believe you've been out of boxing for three years, champ
The court said my religious objections to serving in the Vietnam War weren't justified.
But I'm still fighting that decision in court, trying to get the decision overturned.
You know you can keep coming here to train whenever you want.
Ali did continue to train. As the years passed, he kept clinging to the hope that he might one day be allowed to return to the sport he had loved and dominated since he was a boy.

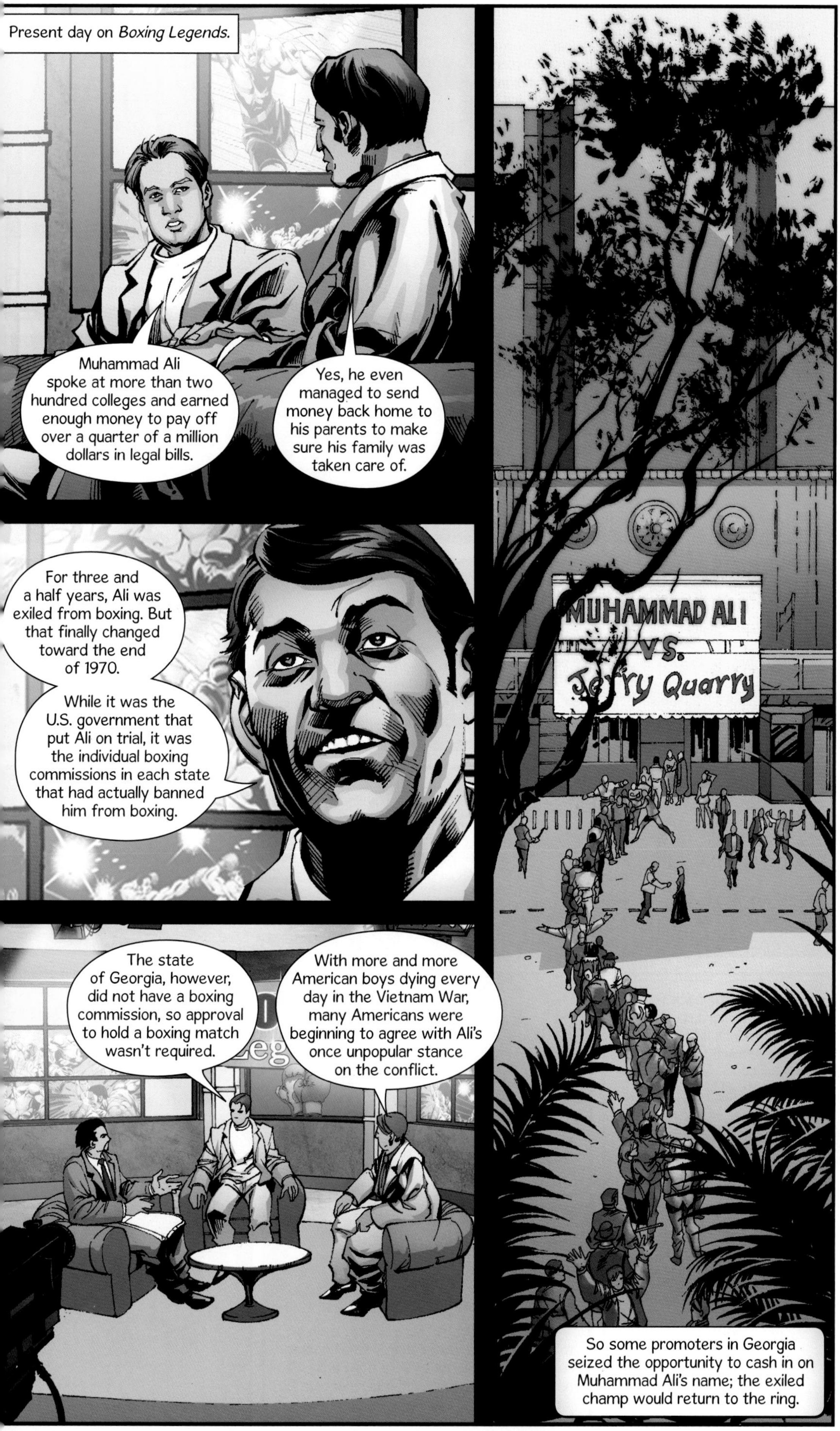
Present day on *Boxing Legends.*
Muhammad Ali spoke at more than two hundred colleges and earned enough money to pay off over a quarter of a million dollars in legal bills.
Yes, he even managed to send money back home to his parents to make sure his family was taken care of.
For three and a half years, Ali was exiled from boxing. But that finally changed toward the end of 1970.
While it was the U.S. government that put Ali on trial, it was the individual boxing commissions in each state that had actually banned him from boxing.
The state of Georgia, however, did not have a boxing commission, so approval to hold a boxing match wasn't required.
With more and more American boys dying every day in the Vietnam War, many Americans were beginning to agree with Ali's once unpopular stance on the conflict.
MUHAMMAD ALI
VS.
Jerry Quarry
So some promoters in Georgia seized the opportunity to cash in on Muhammad Ali's name; the exiled champ would return to the ring.

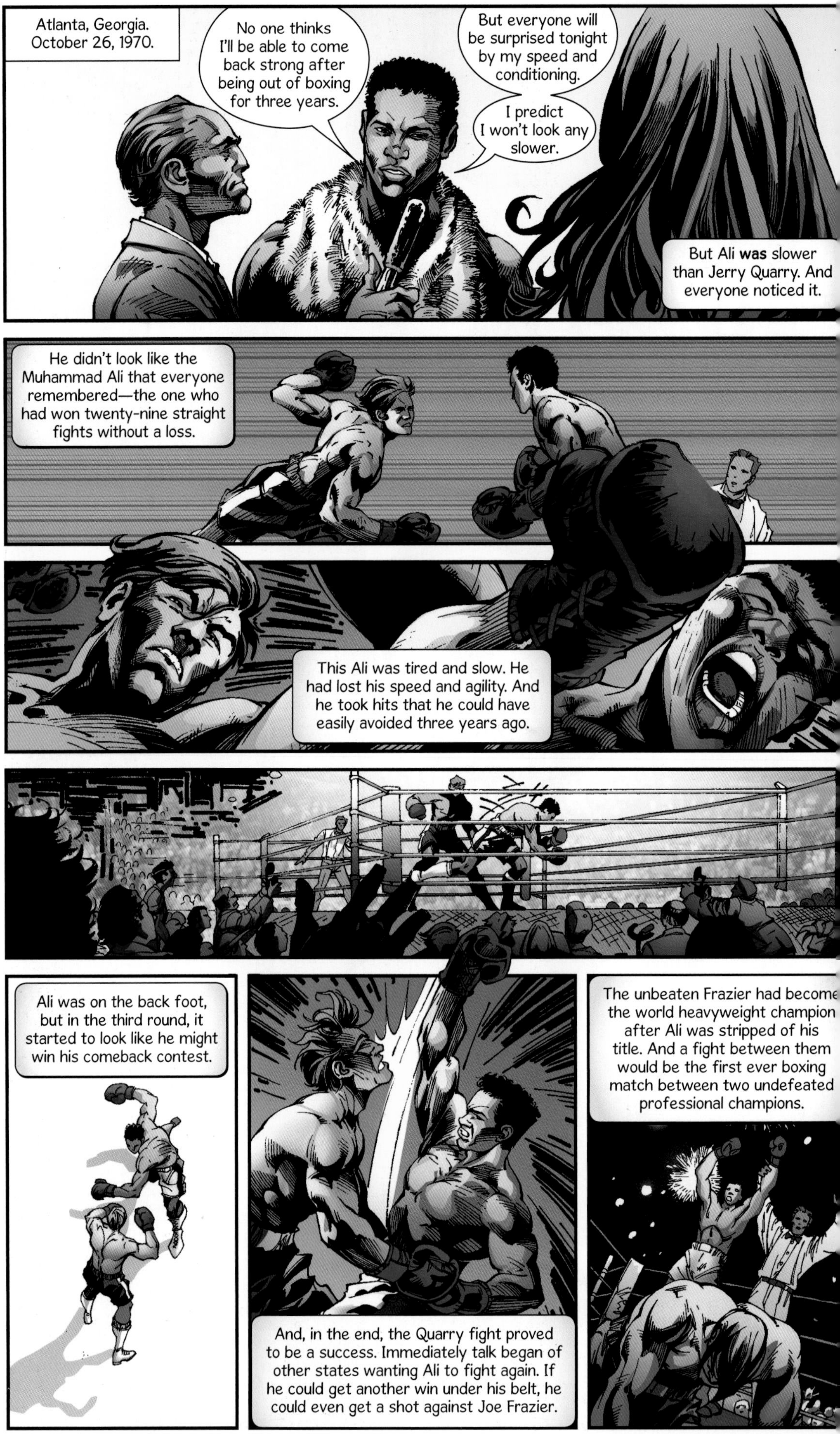

Atlanta, Georgia. October 26, 1970.
No one thinks I'll be able to come back strong after being out of boxing for three years.
But everyone will be surprised tonight by my speed and conditioning.
I predict I won't look any slower.
But Ali **was** slower than Jerry Quarry. And everyone noticed it.
He didn't look like the Muhammad Ali that everyone remembered—the one who had won twenty-nine straight fights without a loss.
This Ali was tired and slow. He had lost his speed and agility. And he took hits that he could have easily avoided three years ago.
Ali was on the back foot, but in the third round, it started to look like he might win his comeback contest.
And, in the end, the Quarry fight proved to be a success. Immediately talk began of other states wanting Ali to fight again. If he could get another win under his belt, he could even get a shot against Joe Frazier.
The unbeaten Frazier had become the world heavyweight champion after Ali was stripped of his title. And a fight between them would be the first ever boxing match between two undefeated professional champions.

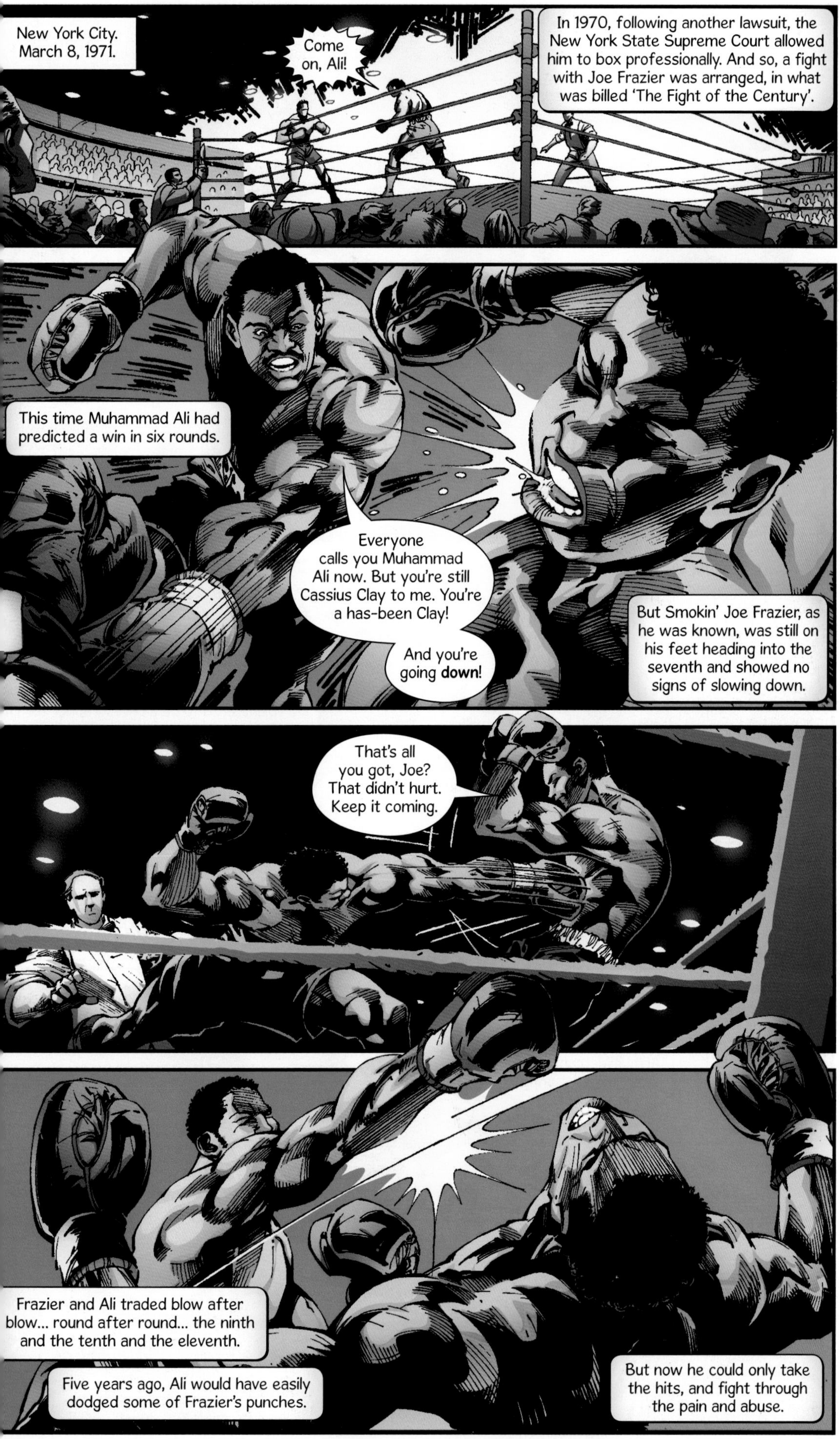
New York City. March 8, 1971.
Come on, Ali!
In 1970, following another lawsuit, the New York State Supreme Court allowed him to box professionally. And so, a fight with Joe Frazier was arranged, in what was billed 'The Fight of the Century'.
This time Muhammad Ali had predicted a win in six rounds.
Everyone calls you Muhammad Ali now. But you're still Cassius Clay to me. You're a has-been Clay!
And you're going **down**!
But Smokin' Joe Frazier, as he was known, was still on his feet heading into the seventh and showed no signs of slowing down.
That's all you got, Joe? That didn't hurt. Keep it coming.
Frazier and Ali traded blow after blow... round after round... the ninth and the tenth and the eleventh.
Five years ago, Ali would have easily dodged some of Frazier's punches.
But now he could only take the hits, and fight through the pain and abuse.

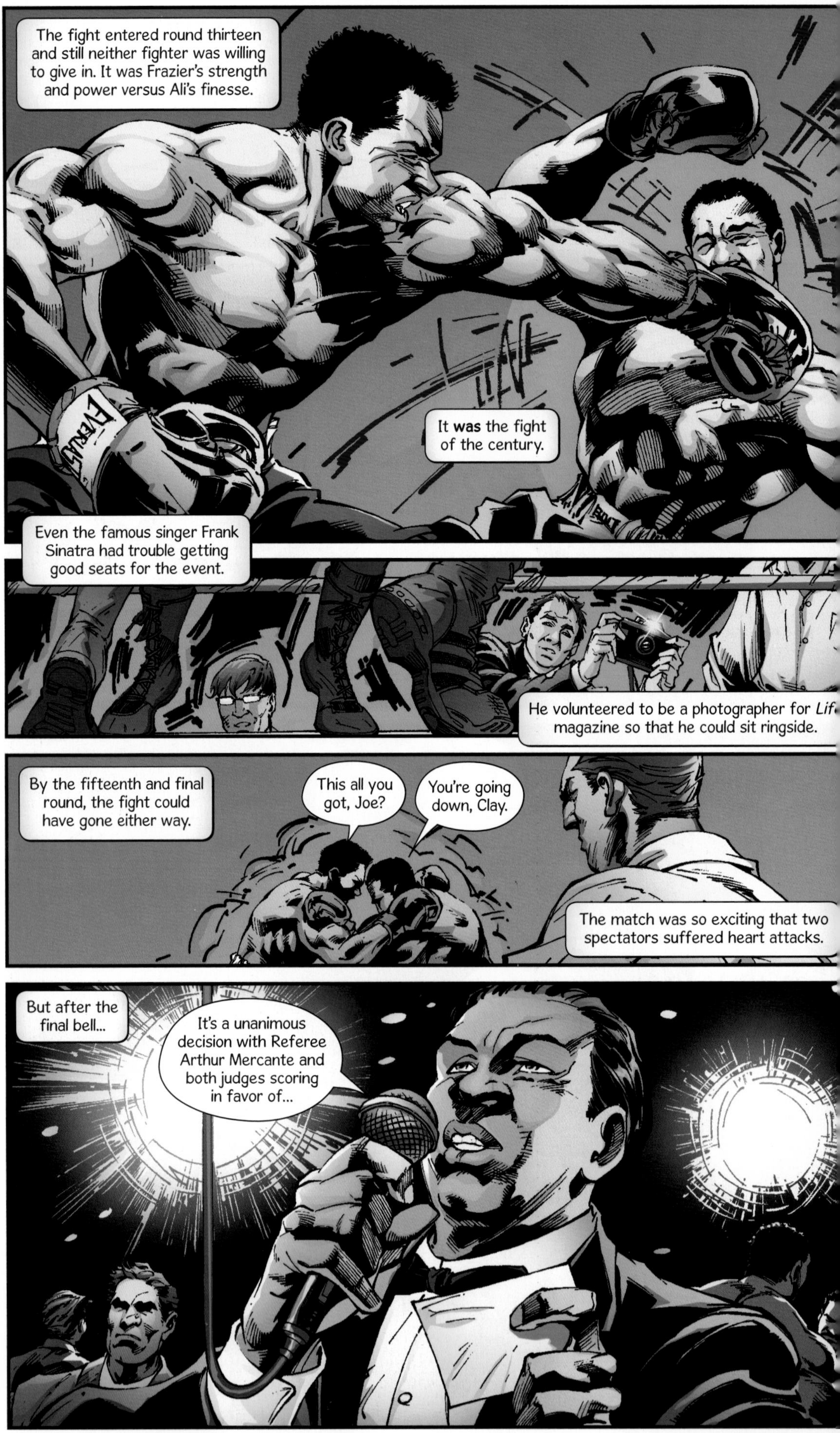
The fight entered round thirteen and still neither fighter was willing to give in. It was Frazier's strength and power versus Ali's finesse.
EVERLAST
It **was** the fight of the century.
Even the famous singer Frank Sinatra had trouble getting good seats for the event.
He volunteered to be a photographer for *Lif*
magazine so that he could sit ringside.
By the fifteenth and final round, the fight could have gone either way.
This all you got, Joe?
You're going down, Clay.
The match was so exciting that two spectators suffered heart attacks.
But after the final bell...
It's a unanimous decision with Referee Arthur Mercante and both judges scoring in favor of...

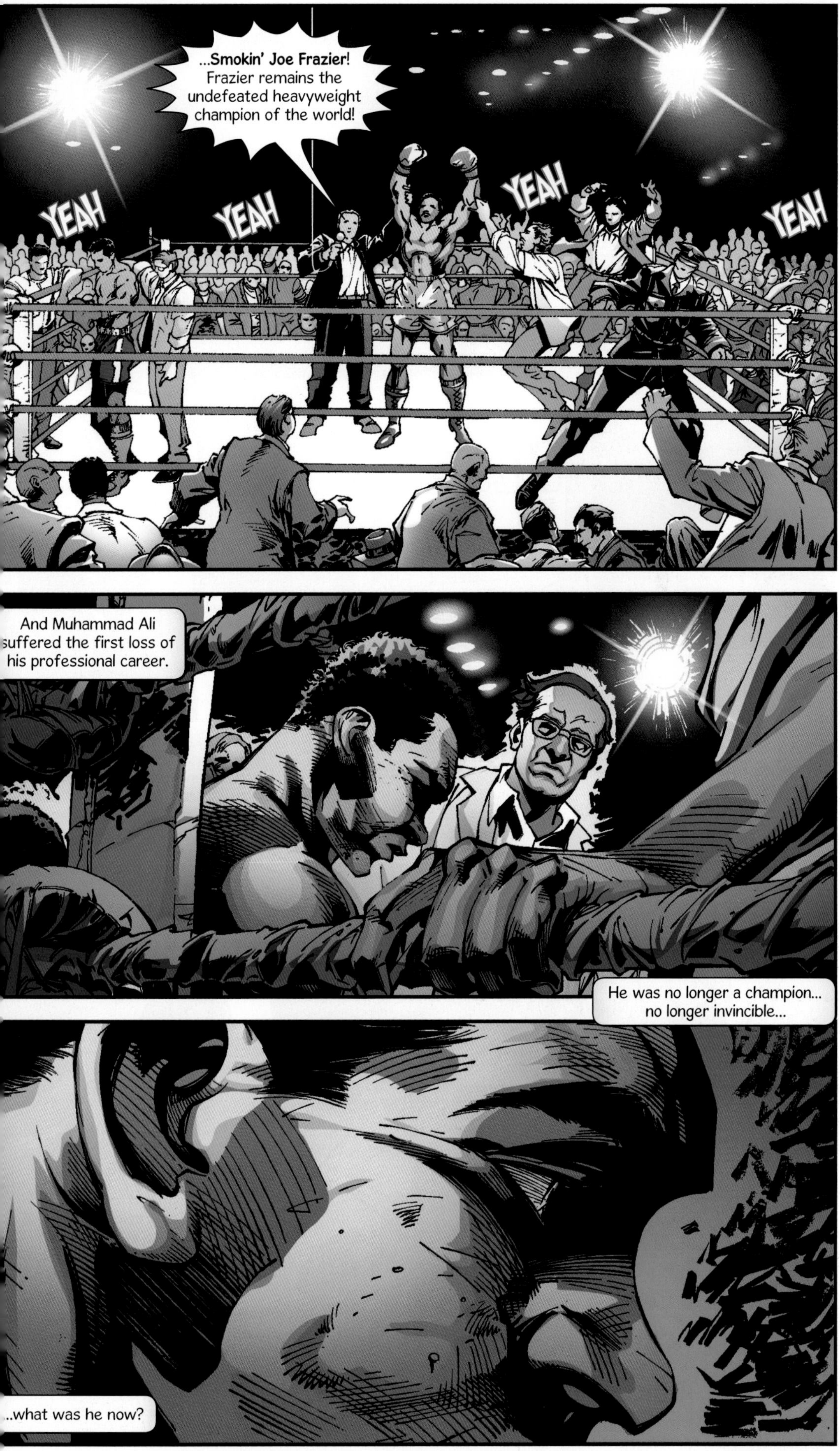
...Smokin' Joe Frazier!
Frazier remains the undefeated heavyweight champion of the world!
YEAH
YEAH
YEAH
YEAH
And Muhammad Ali suffered the first loss of his professional career.
He was no longer a champion... no longer invincible...
..what was he now?

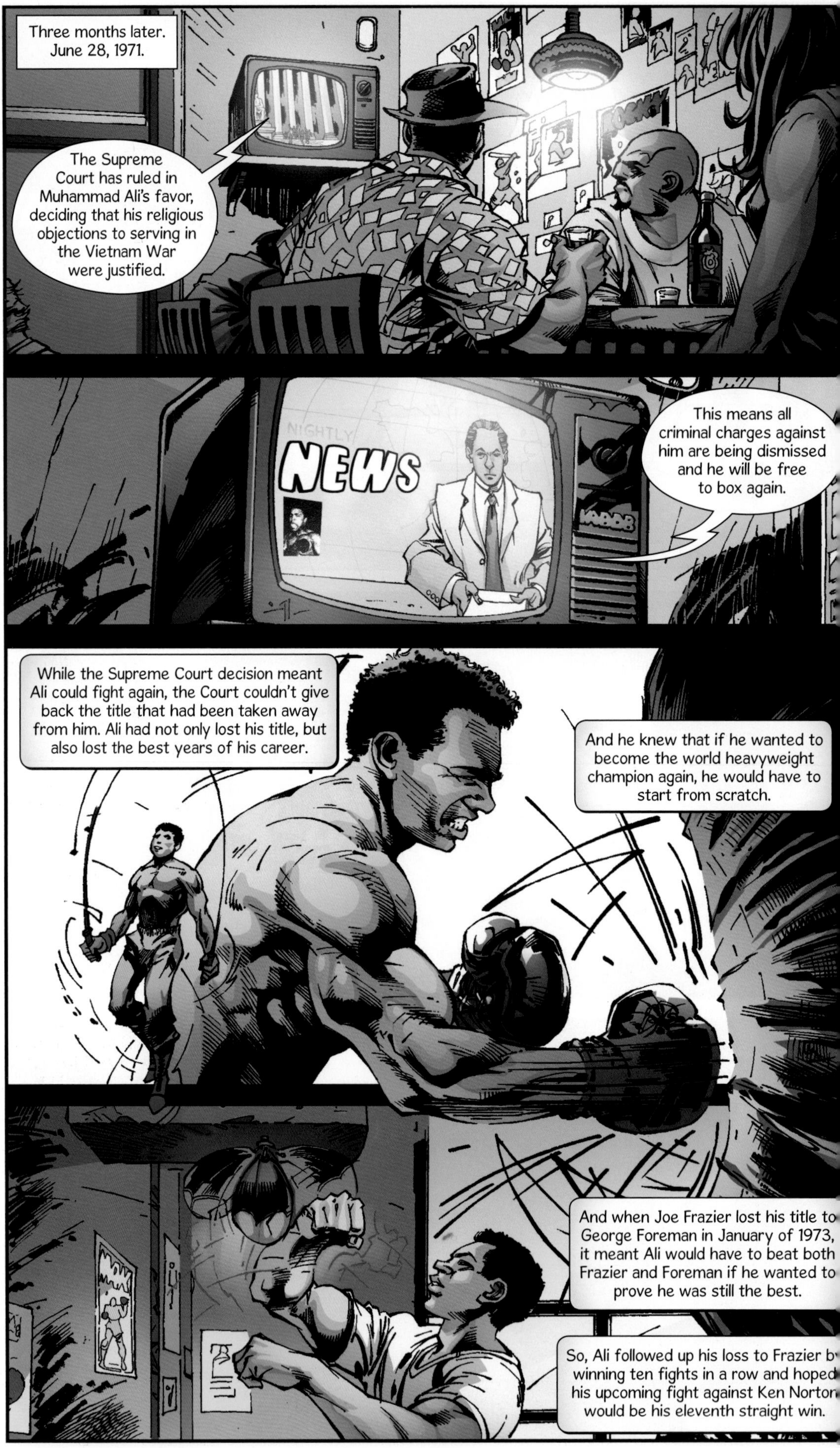
Three months later. June 28, 1971.
The Supreme Court has ruled in Muhammad Ali's favor, deciding that his religious objections to serving in the Vietnam War were justified.
NIGHTLY
NEWS
This means all criminal charges against him are being dismissed and he will be free to box again.
While the Supreme Court decision meant Ali could fight again, the Court couldn't give back the title that had been taken away from him. Ali had not only lost his title, but also lost the best years of his career.
And he knew that if he wanted to become the world heavyweight champion again, he would have to start from scratch.
And when Joe Frazier lost his title to George Foreman in January of 1973, it meant Ali would have to beat both Frazier and Foreman if he wanted to prove he was still the best.
So, Ali followed up his loss to Frazier by winning ten fights in a row and hoped his upcoming fight against Ken Norton would be his eleventh straight win.

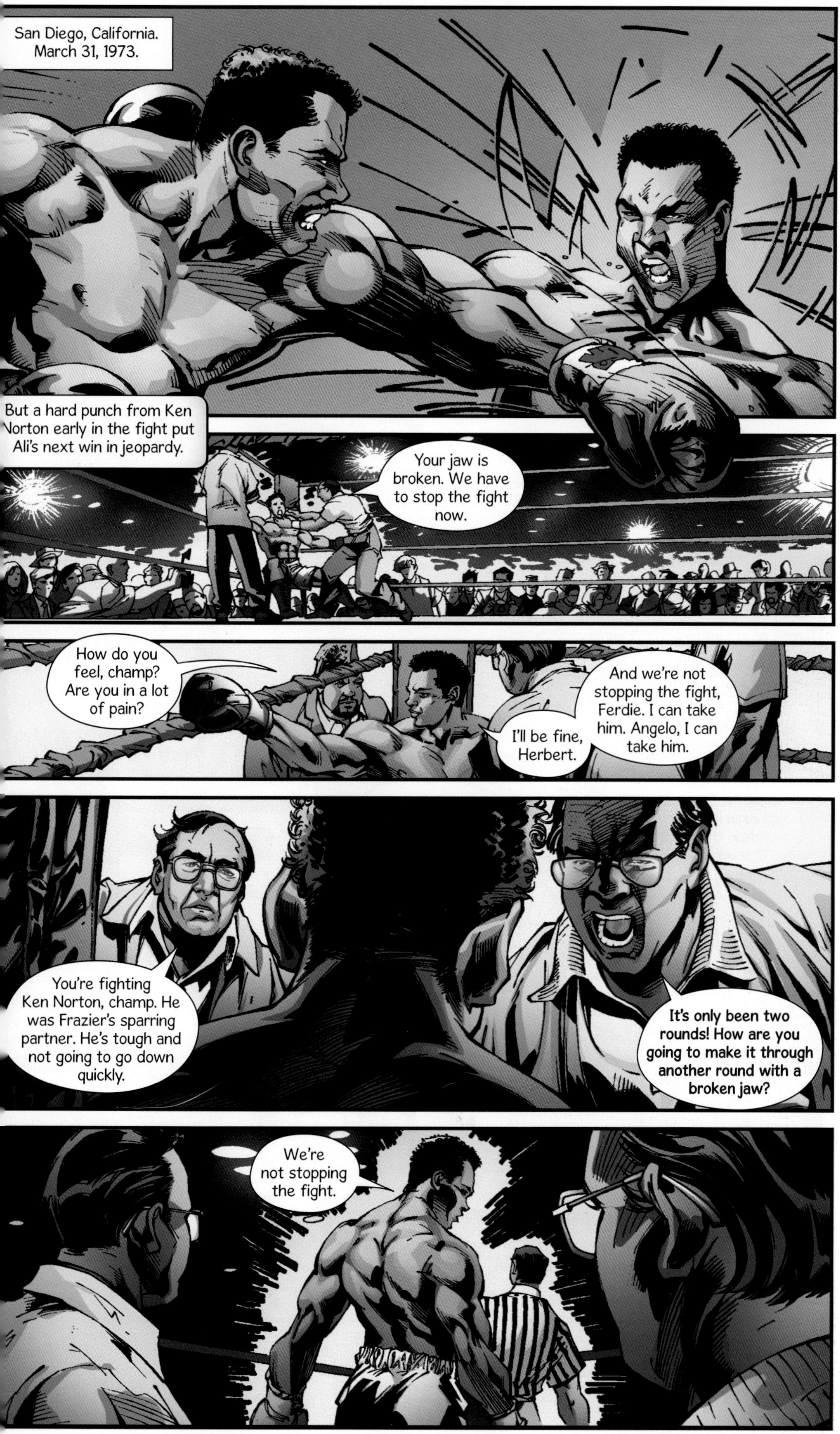
San Diego, California.
March 31, 1973.
But a hard punch from Ken Norton early in the fight put Ali's next win in jeopardy.
Your jaw is broken. We have to stop the fight now.
How do you feel, champ? Are you in a lot of pain?
I'll be fine, Herbert.
And we're not stopping the fight, Ferdie. I can take him. Angelo, I can take him.
You're fighting Ken Norton, champ. He was Frazier's sparring partner. He's tough and not going to go down quickly.
It's only been two rounds! How are you going to make it through another round with a broken jaw?
We're not stopping the fight.

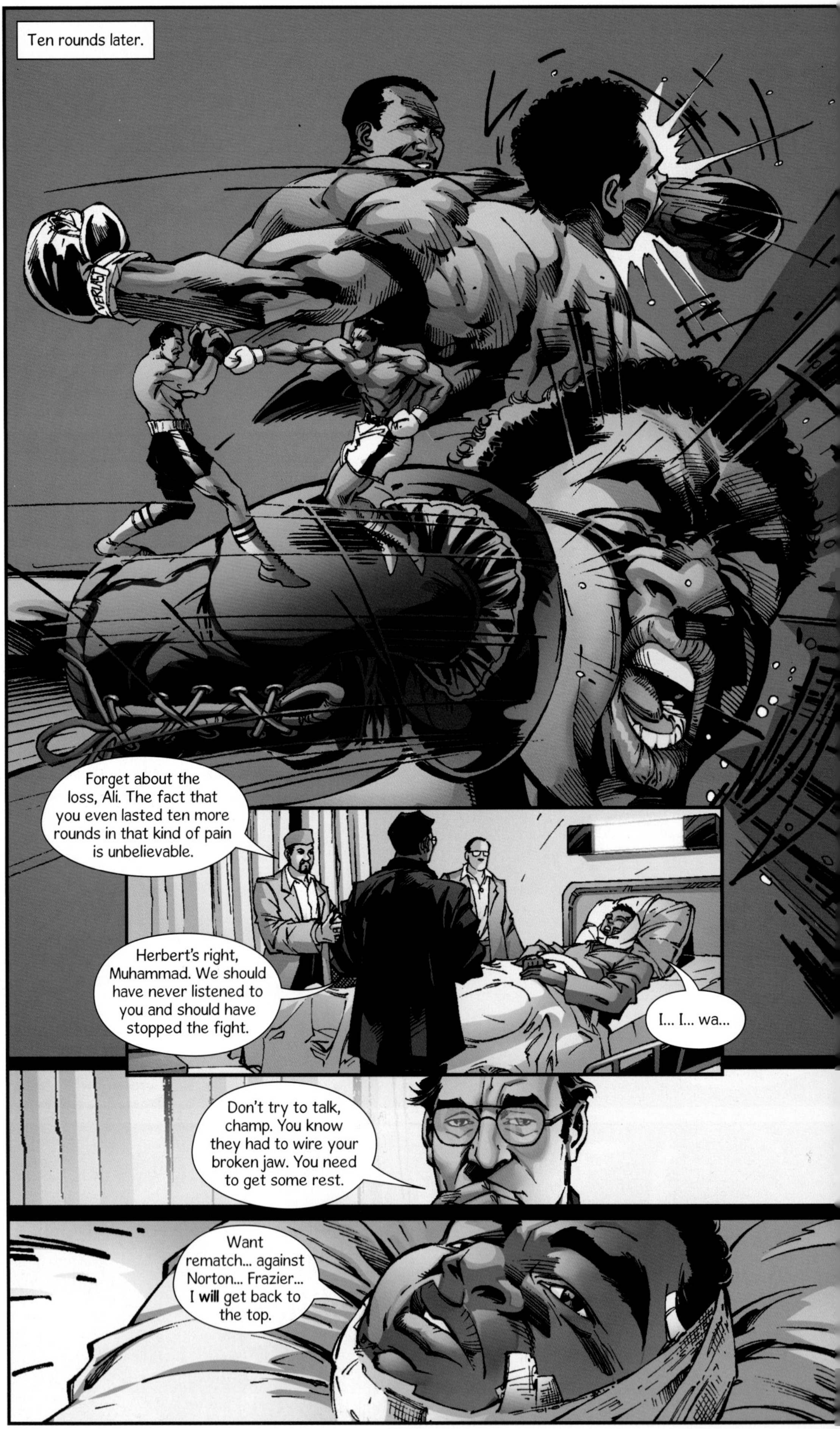
Ten rounds later.
Forget about the loss, Ali. The fact that you even lasted ten more rounds in that kind of pain is unbelievable.
Herbert's right, Muhammad. We should have never listened to you and should have stopped the fight.
I... I... wa...
Don't try to talk, champ. You know they had to wire your broken jaw. You need to get some rest.
Want rematch... against Norton... Frazier... I **will** get back to the top.

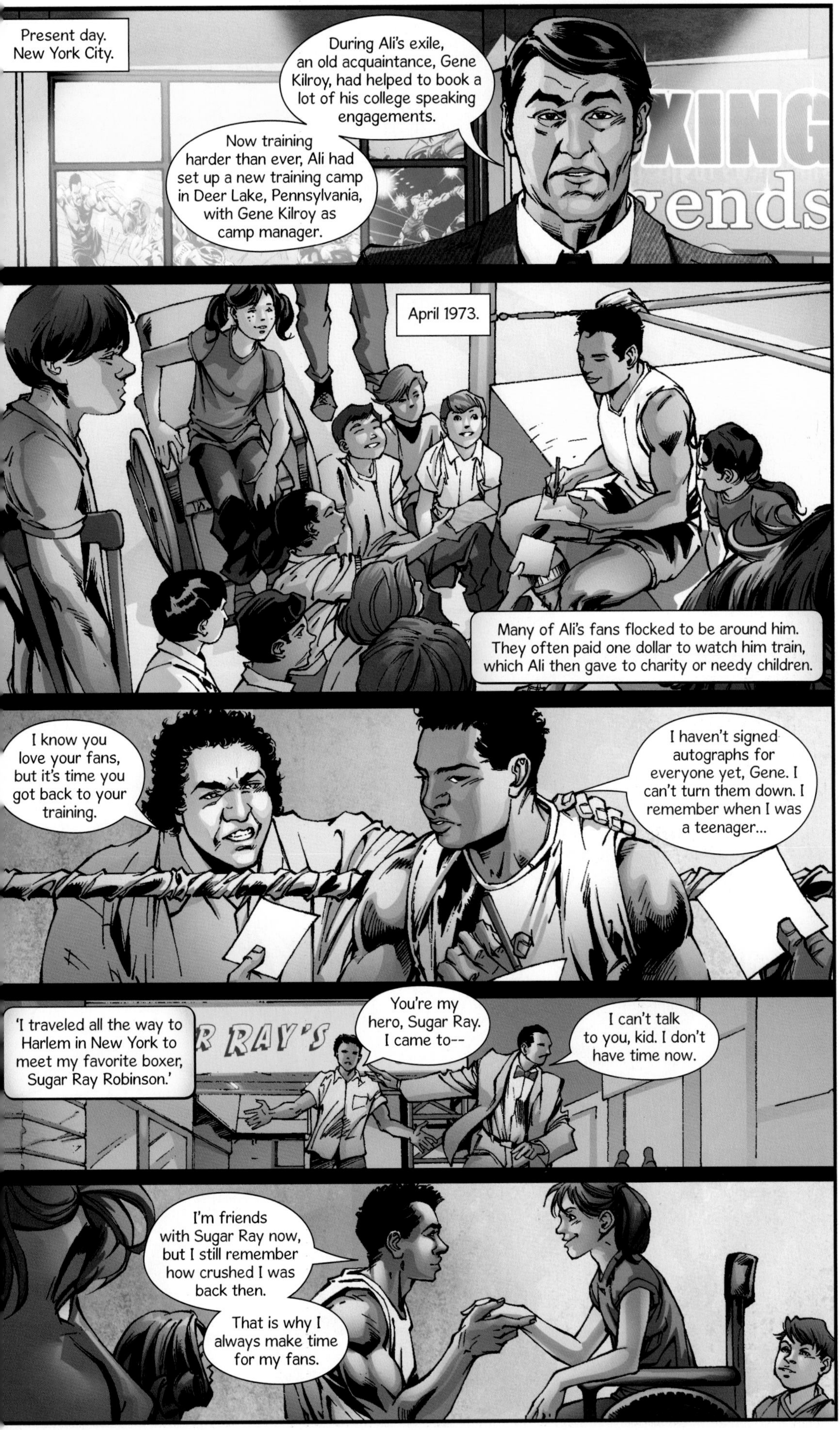

Present day. New York City.
During Ali's exile, an old acquaintance, Gene Kilroy, had helped to book a lot of his college speaking engagements.
Now training harder than ever, Ali had set up a new training camp in Deer Lake, Pennsylvania, with Gene Kilroy as camp manager.
April 1973.
Many of Ali's fans flocked to be around him. They often paid one dollar to watch him train, which Ali then gave to charity or needy children.
I know you love your fans, but it's time you got back to your training.
I haven't signed autographs for everyone yet, Gene. I can't turn them down. I remember when I was a teenager...
'I traveled all the way to Harlem in New York to meet my favorite boxer, Sugar Ray Robinson.'
You're my hero, Sugar Ray. I came to--
I can't talk to you, kid. I don't have time now.
I'm friends with Sugar Ray now, but I still remember how crushed I was back then.
That is why I always make time for my fans.

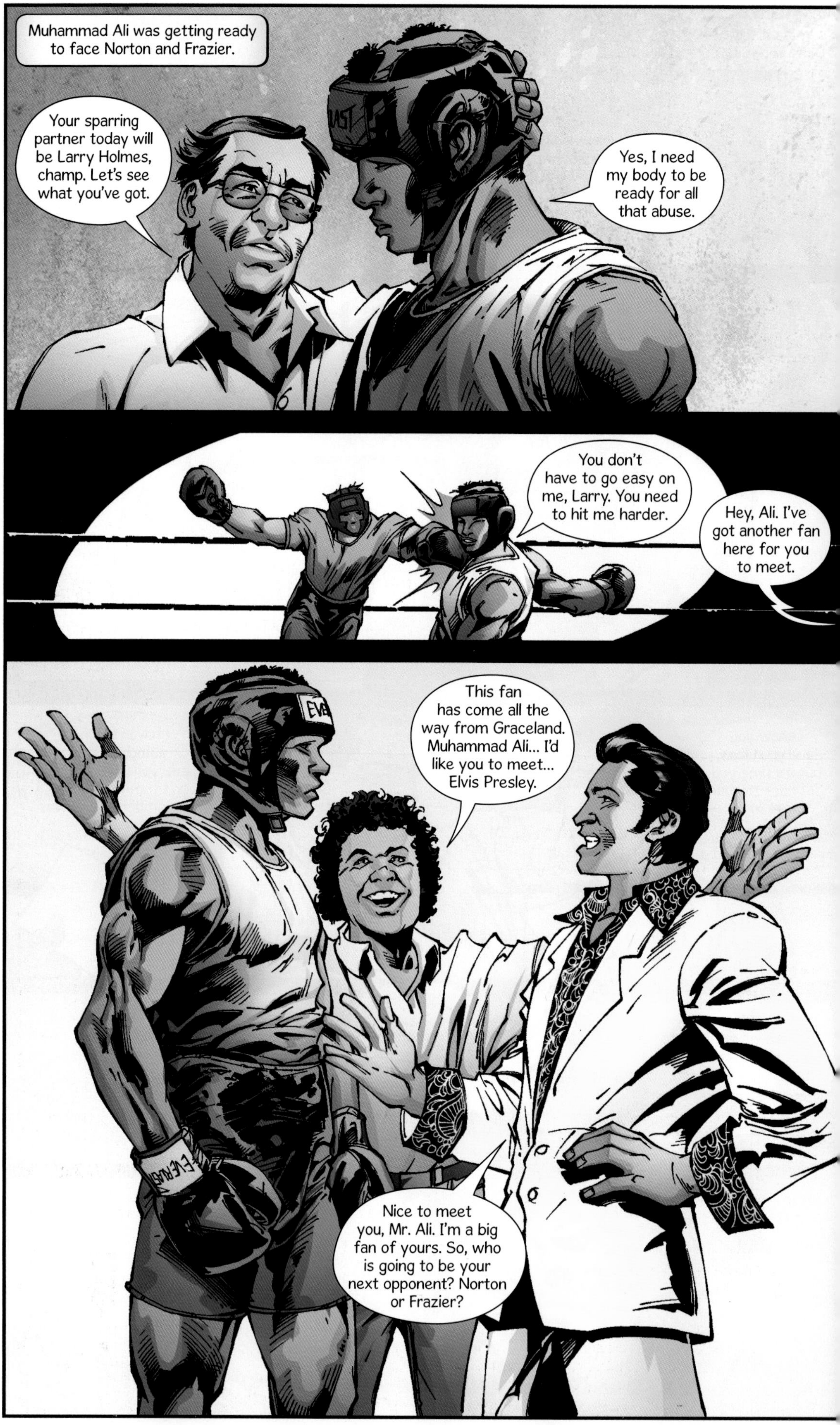
Muhammad Ali was getting ready to face Norton and Frazier.
Your sparring partner today will be Larry Holmes, champ. Let's see what you've got.
Yes, I need my body to be ready for all that abuse.
You don't have to go easy on me, Larry. You need to hit me harder.
Hey, Ali. I've got another fan here for you to meet.
This fan has come all the way from Graceland. Muhammad Ali... I'd like you to meet... Elvis Presley.
Nice to meet you, Mr. Ali. I'm a big fan of yours. So, who is going to be your next opponent? Norton or Frazier?

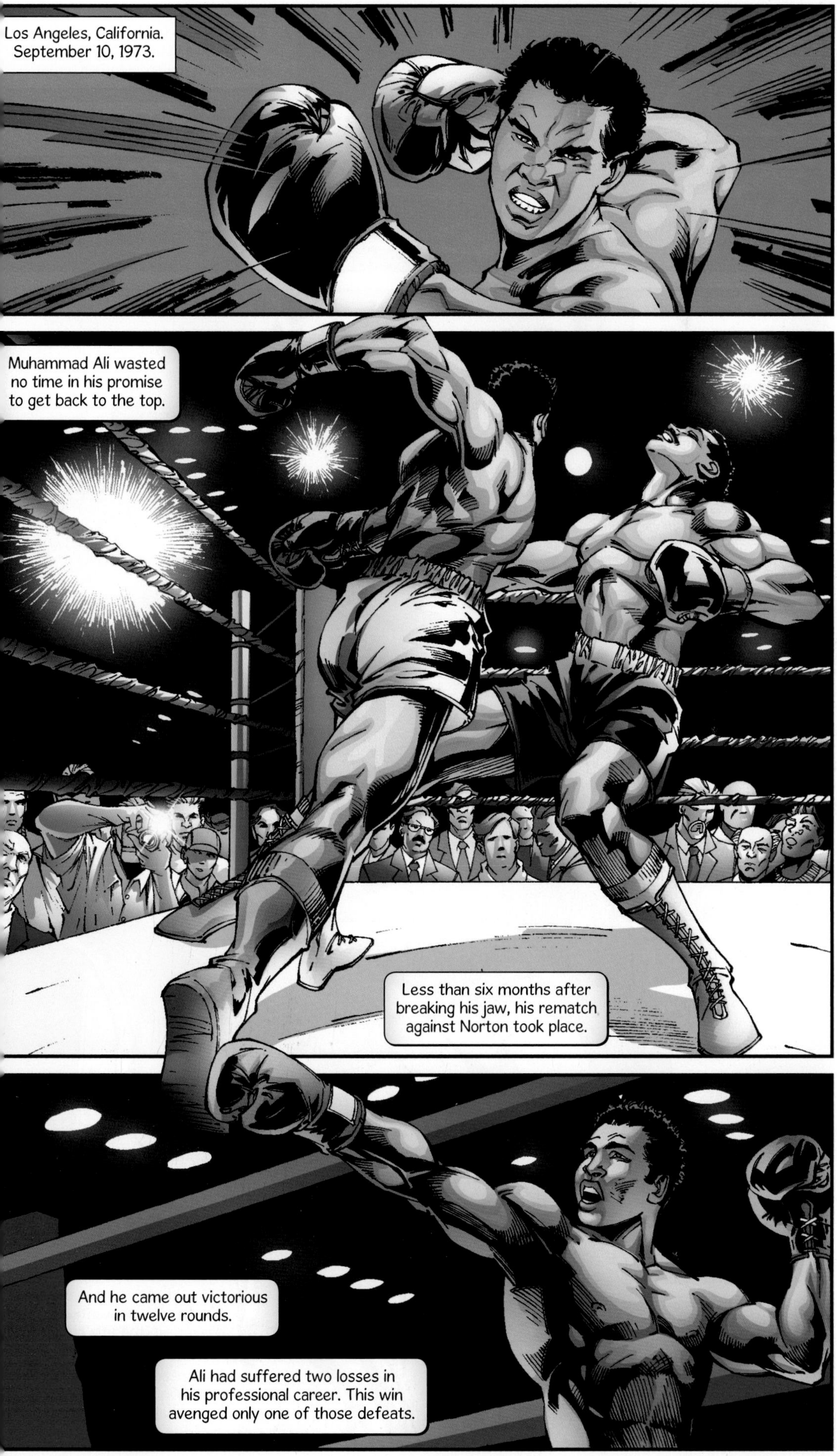

Los Angeles, California.
September 10, 1973.
Muhammad Ali wasted no time in his promise to get back to the top.
Less than six months after breaking his jaw, his rematch against Norton took place.
And he came out victorious in twelve rounds.
Ali had suffered two losses in his professional career. This win avenged only one of those defeats.

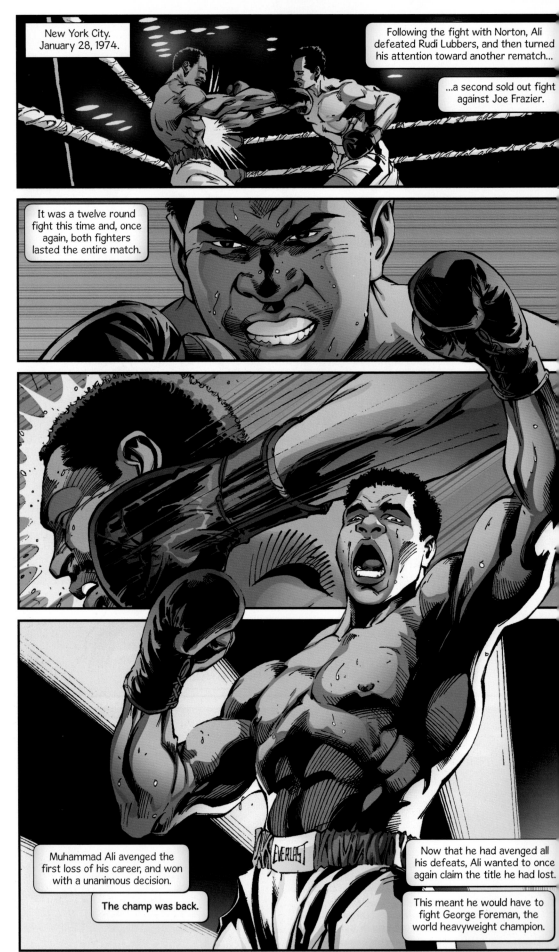

New York City.
January 28, 1974.

Following the fight with Norton, Ali defeated Rudi Lubbers, and then turned his attention toward another rematch...

...a second sold out fight against Joe Frazier.

It was a twelve round fight this time and, once again, both fighters lasted the entire match.

Muhammad Ali avenged the first loss of his career, and won with a unanimous decision.

The champ was back.

Now that he had avenged all his defeats, Ali wanted to once again claim the title he had lost.

This meant he would have to fight George Foreman, the world heavyweight champion.

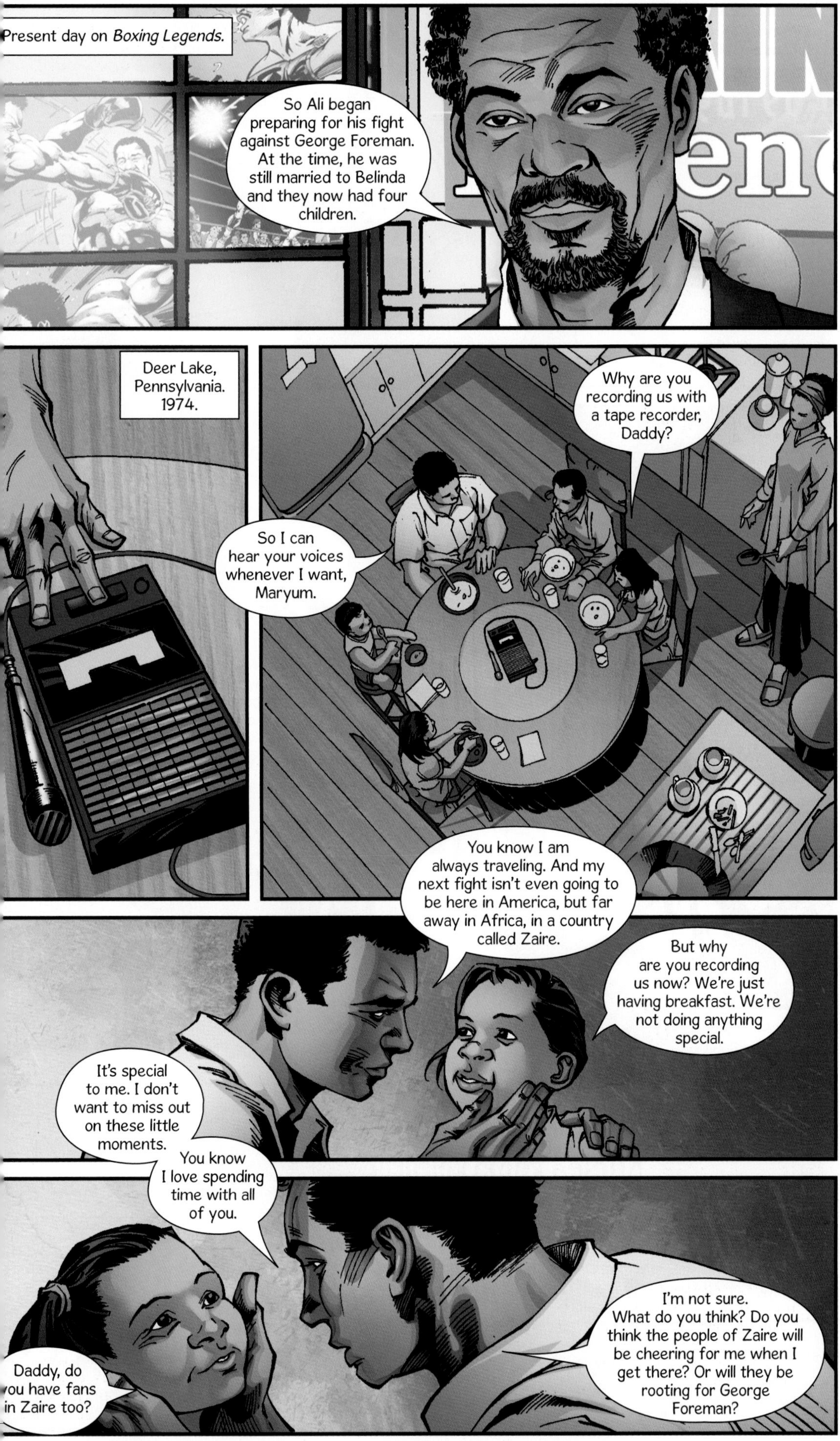

Present day on *Boxing Legends.*
So Ali began preparing for his fight against George Foreman. At the time, he was still married to Belinda and they now had four children.
Deer Lake, Pennsylvania. 1974.
Why are you recording us with a tape recorder, Daddy?
So I can hear your voices whenever I want, Maryum.
You know I am always traveling. And my next fight isn't even going to be here in America, but far away in Africa, in a country called Zaire.
But why are you recording us now? We're just having breakfast. We're not doing anything special.
It's special to me. I don't want to miss out on these little moments.
You know I love spending time with all of you.
Daddy, do you have fans in Zaire too?
I'm not sure. What do you think? Do you think the people of Zaire will be cheering for me when I get there? Or will they be rooting for George Foreman?

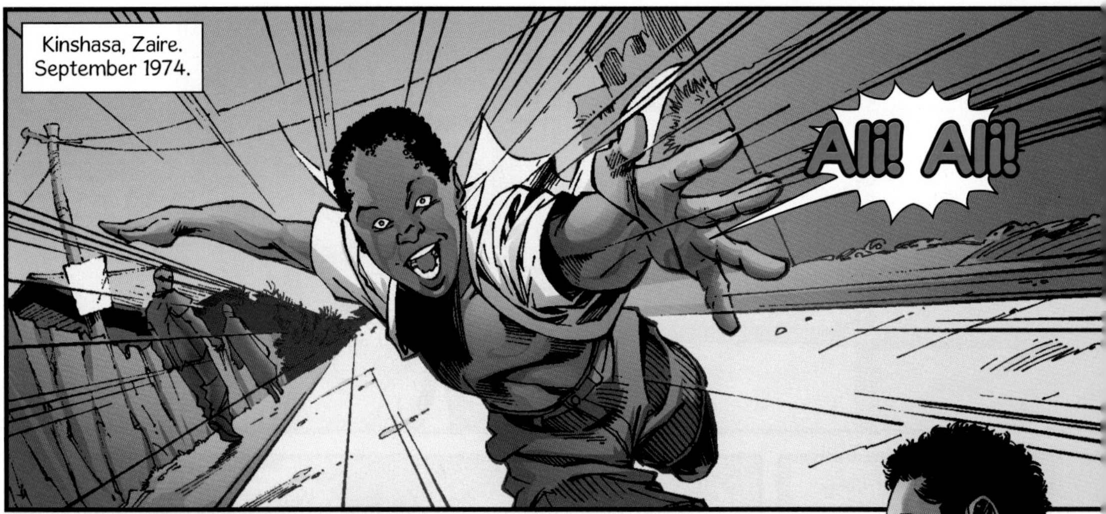
Kinshasa, Zaire.
September 1974.
Ali! Ali!

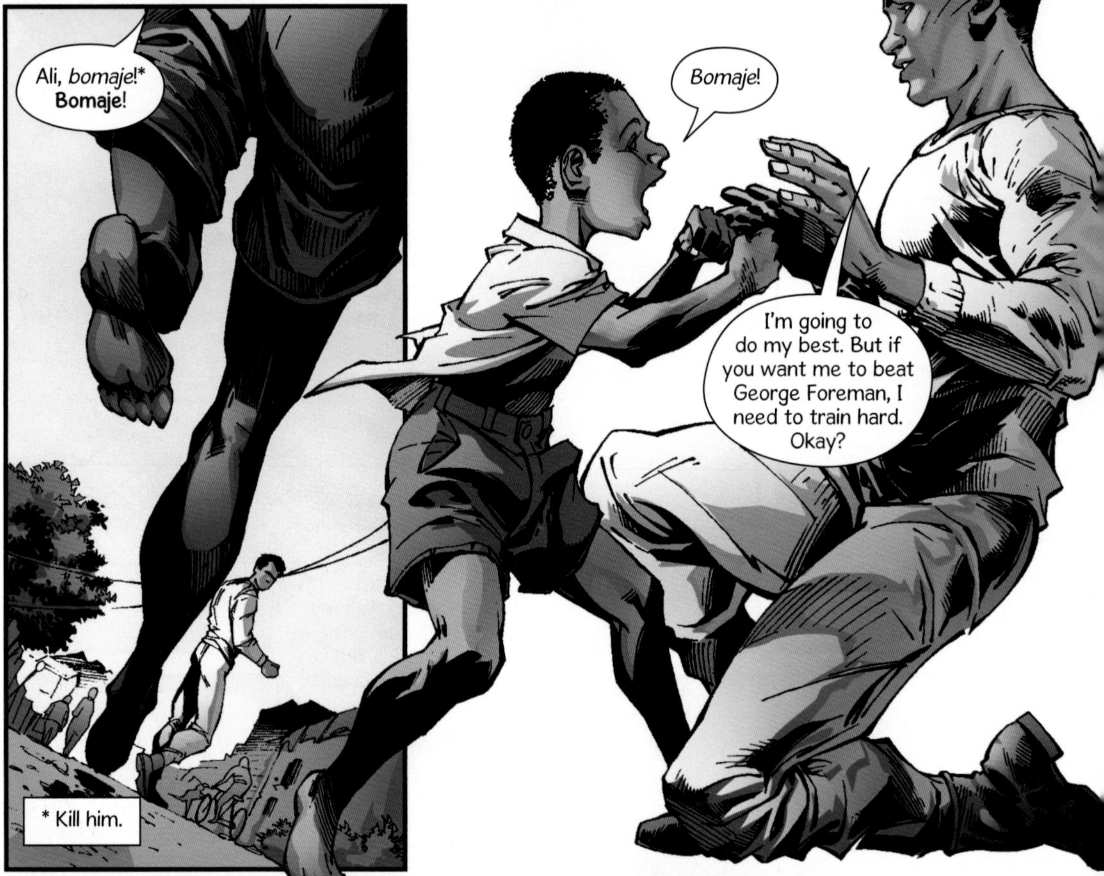
Ali, *bomaje*!*
Bomaje!
Bomaje!
I'm going to do my best. But if you want me to beat George Foreman, I need to train hard. Okay?
* Kill him.

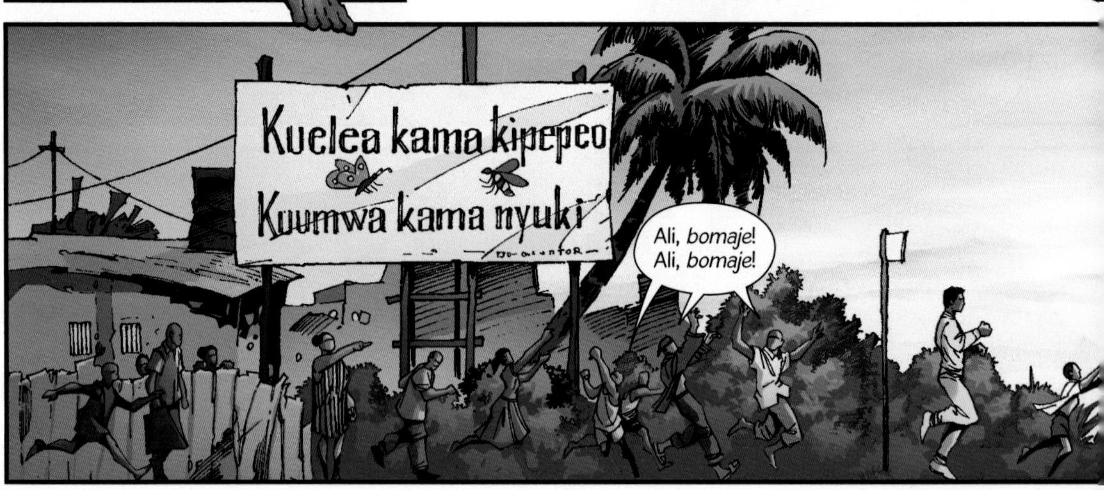
Kuelea kama kipepeo
Kuumwa kama nyuki
Ali, *bomaje*!
Ali, *bomaje*!

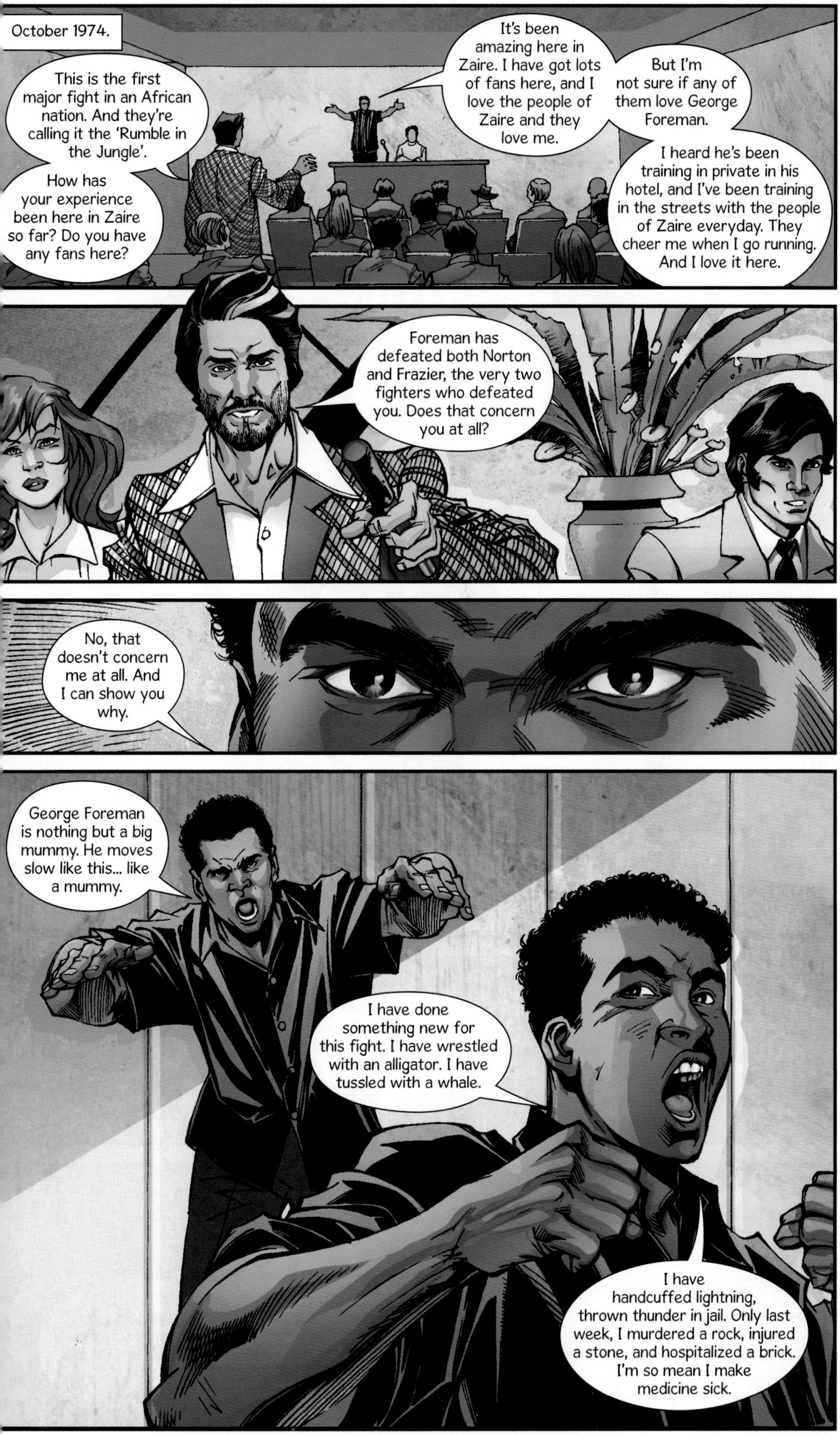
October 1974.
This is the first major fight in an African nation. And they're calling it the 'Rumble in the Jungle'.
How has your experience been here in Zaire so far? Do you have any fans here?
It's been amazing here in Zaire. I have got lots of fans here, and I love the people of Zaire and they love me.
But I'm not sure if any of them love George Foreman.
I heard he's been training in private in his hotel, and I've been training in the streets with the people of Zaire everyday. They cheer me when I go running. And I love it here.
Foreman has defeated both Norton and Frazier, the very two fighters who defeated you. Does that concern you at all?
No, that doesn't concern me at all. And I can show you why.
George Foreman is nothing but a big mummy. He moves slow like this... like a mummy.
I have done something new for this fight. I have wrestled with an alligator. I have tussled with a whale.
I have handcuffed lightning, thrown thunder in jail. Only last week, I murdered a rock, injured a stone, and hospitalized a brick. I'm so mean I make medicine sick.

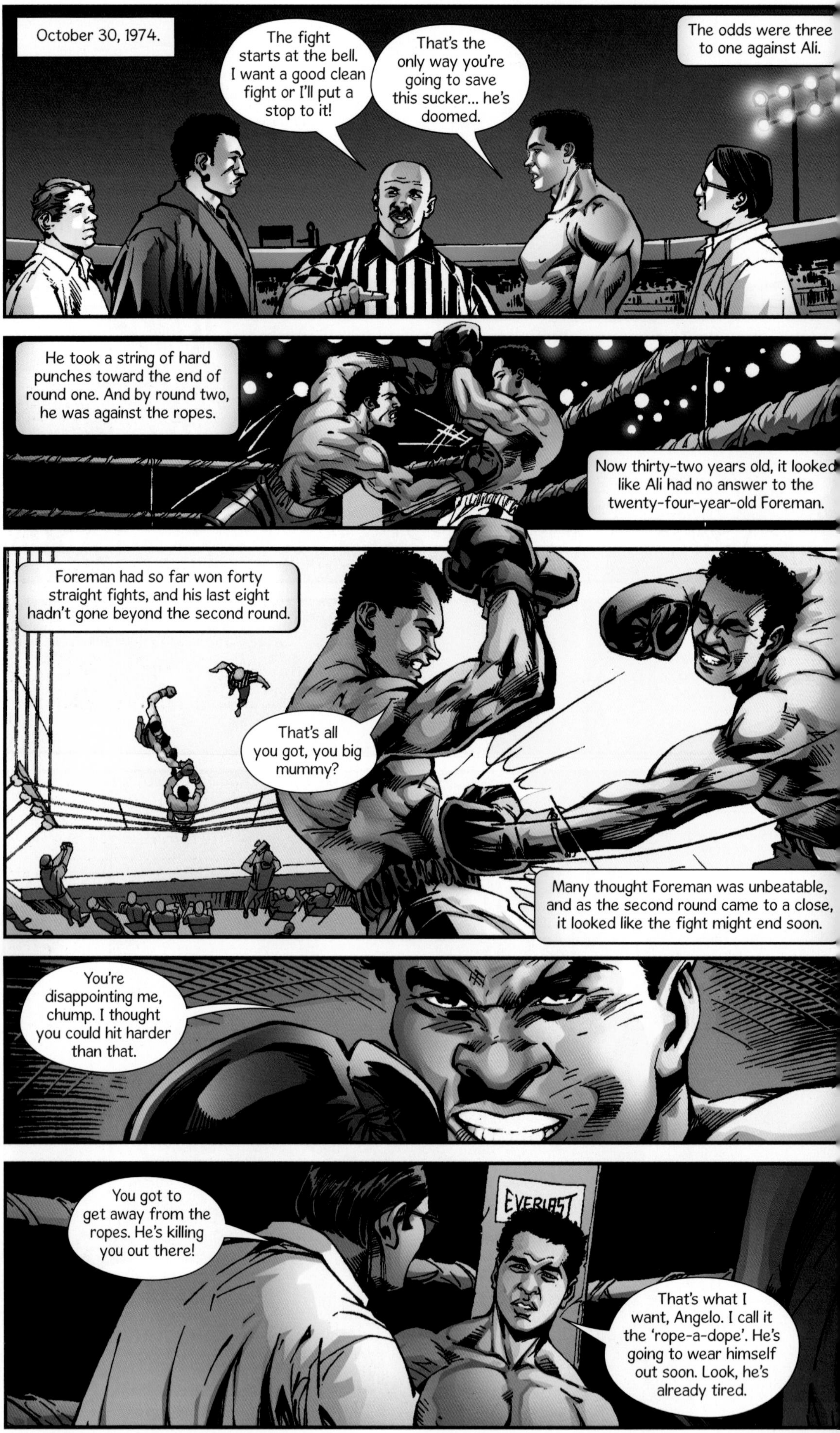

October 30, 1974.
The fight starts at the bell. I want a good clean fight or I'll put a stop to it!
That's the only way you're going to save this sucker... he's doomed.
The odds were three to one against Ali.
He took a string of hard punches toward the end of round one. And by round two, he was against the ropes.
Now thirty-two years old, it looked like Ali had no answer to the twenty-four-year-old Foreman.
Foreman had so far won forty straight fights, and his last eight hadn't gone beyond the second round.
That's all you got, you big mummy?
Many thought Foreman was unbeatable, and as the second round came to a close, it looked like the fight might end soon.
You're disappointing me, chump. I thought you could hit harder than that.
You got to get away from the ropes. He's killing you out there!
EVERLAST
That's what I want, Angelo. I call it the 'rope-a-dope'. He's going to wear himself out soon. Look, he's already tired.

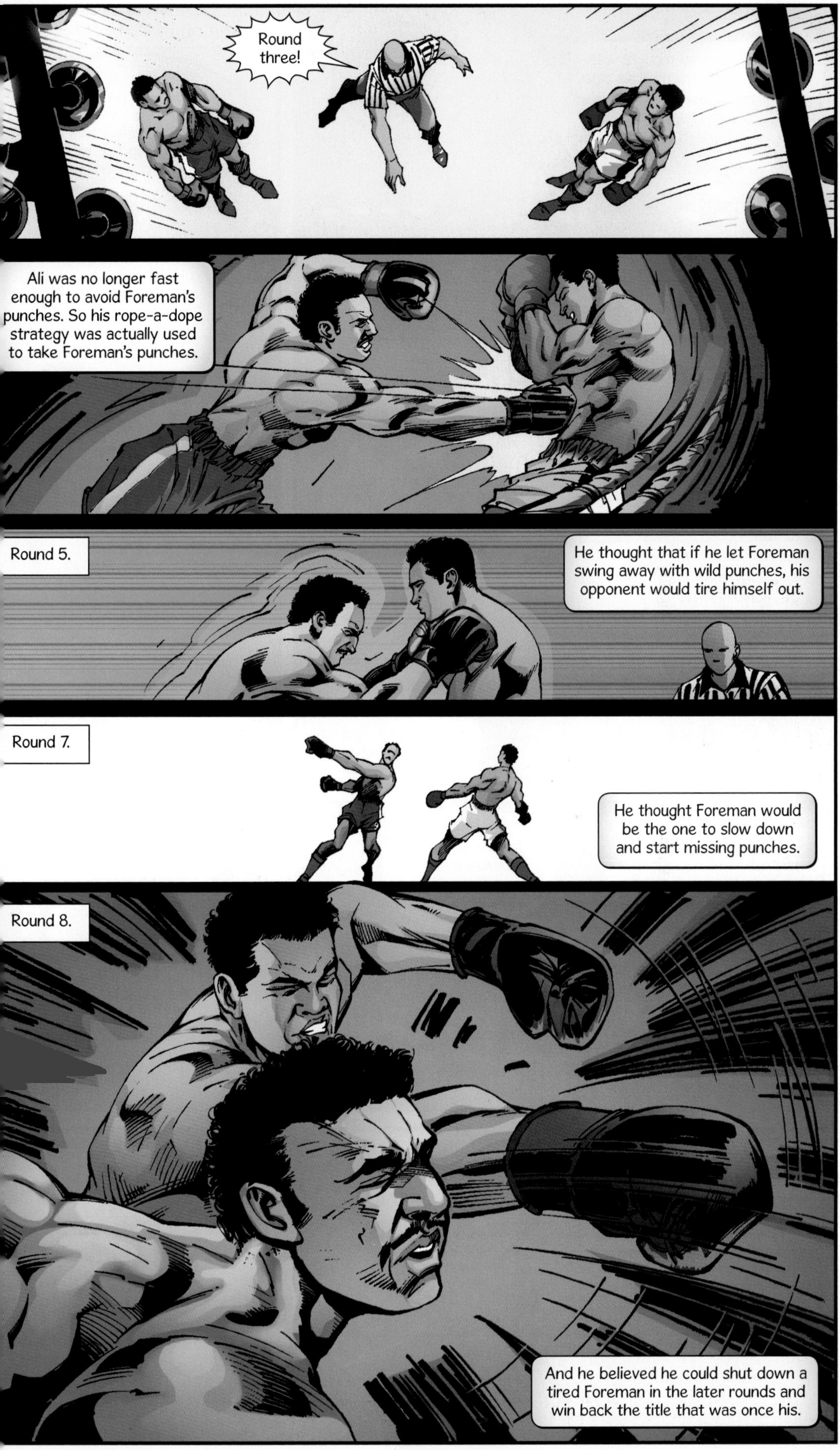
Round three!
Ali was no longer fast enough to avoid Foreman's punches. So his rope-a-dope strategy was actually used to take Foreman's punches.
Round 5.
He thought that if he let Foreman swing away with wild punches, his opponent would tire himself out.
Round 7.
He thought Foreman would be the one to slow down and start missing punches.
Round 8.
And he believed he could shut down a tired Foreman in the later rounds and win back the title that was once his.

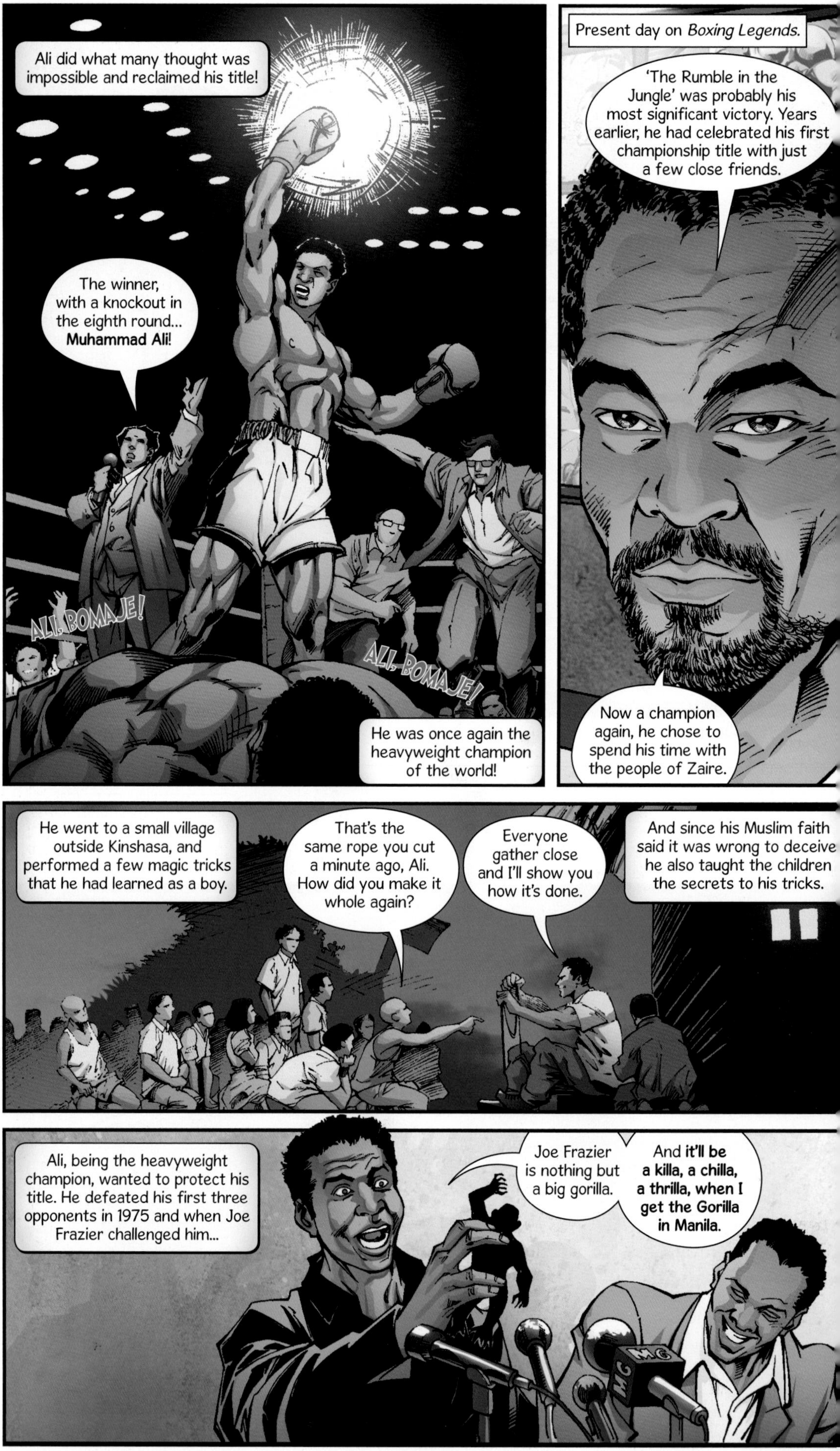

Ali did what many thought was impossible and reclaimed his title!
The winner, with a knockout in the eighth round... **Muhammad Ali!**
ALI, BOMAJE!
ALI, BOMAJE!
He was once again the heavyweight champion of the world!
Present day on *Boxing Legends.*
'The Rumble in the Jungle' was probably his most significant victory. Years earlier, he had celebrated his first championship title with just a few close friends.
Now a champion again, he chose to spend his time with the people of Zaire.
He went to a small village outside Kinshasa, and performed a few magic tricks that he had learned as a boy.
That's the same rope you cut a minute ago, Ali. How did you make it whole again?
Everyone gather close and I'll show you how it's done.
And since his Muslim faith said it was wrong to deceive he also taught the children the secrets to his tricks.
Ali, being the heavyweight champion, wanted to protect his title. He defeated his first three opponents in 1975 and when Joe Frazier challenged him...
Joe Frazier is nothing but a big gorilla.
And **it'll be a killa, a chilla, a thrilla, when I get the Gorilla in Manila.**

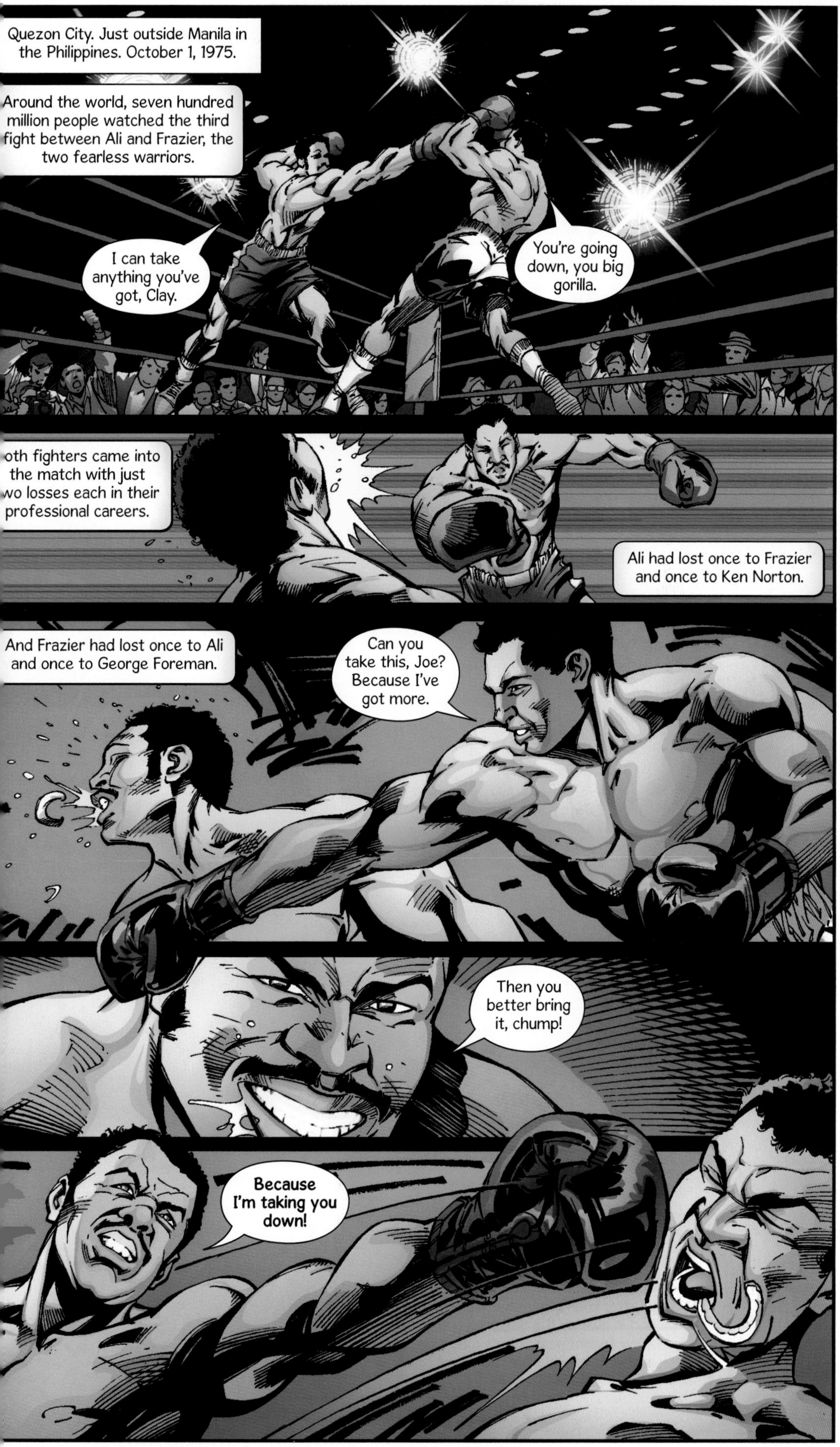

Quezon City. Just outside Manila in the Philippines. October 1, 1975.
Around the world, seven hundred million people watched the third fight between Ali and Frazier, the two fearless warriors.
I can take anything you've got, Clay.
You're going down, you big gorilla.
oth fighters came into the match with just wo losses each in their professional careers.
Ali had lost once to Frazier and once to Ken Norton.
And Frazier had lost once to Ali and once to George Foreman.
Can you take this, Joe? Because I've got more.
Then you better bring it, chump!
Because I'm taking you down!

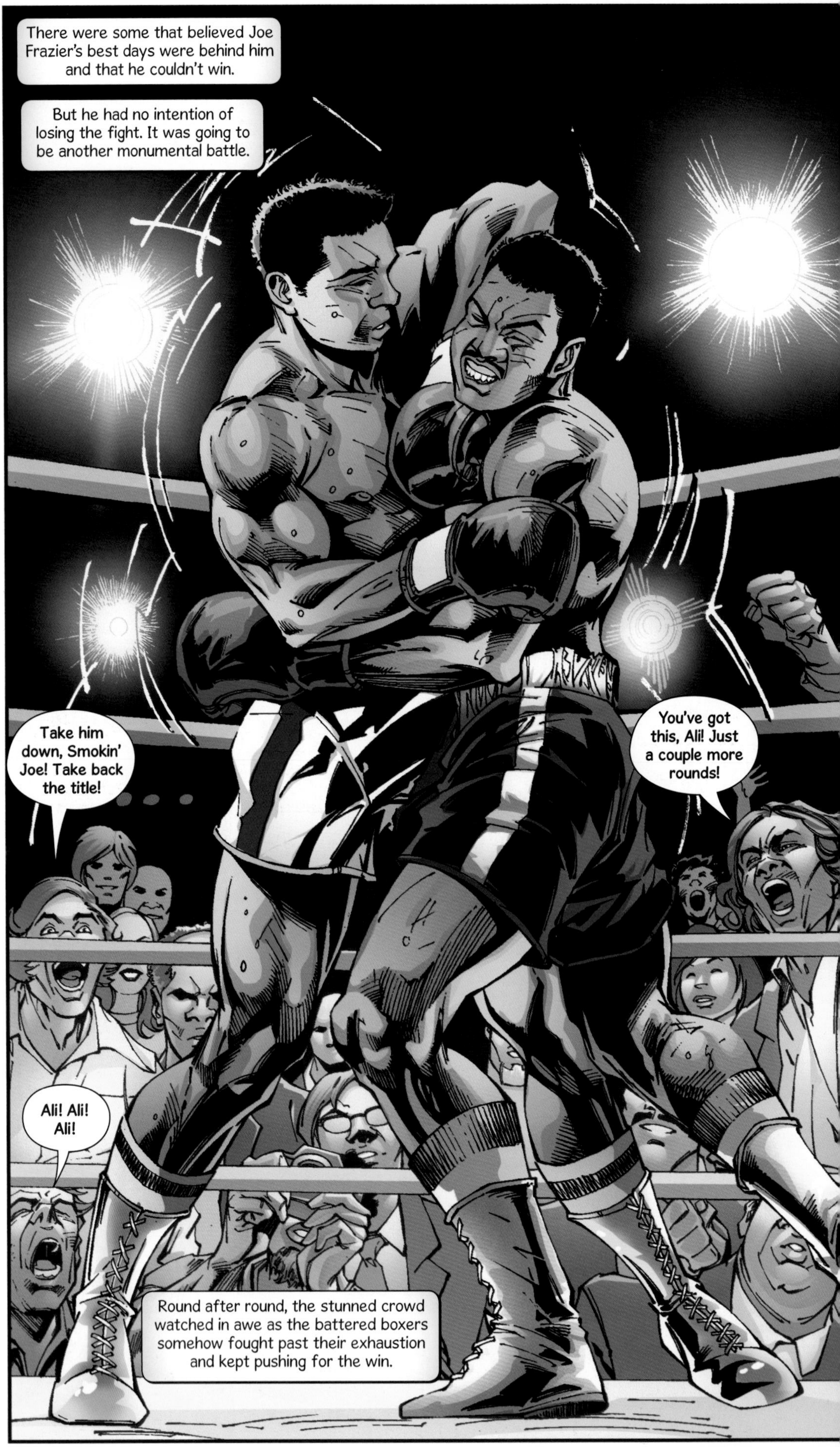
There were some that believed Joe Frazier's best days were behind him and that he couldn't win.
But he had no intention of losing the fight. It was going to be another monumental battle.
Take him down, Smokin' Joe! Take back the title!
You've got this, Ali! Just a couple more rounds!
Ali! Ali! Ali!
Round after round, the stunned crowd watched in awe as the battered boxers somehow fought past their exhaustion and kept pushing for the win.

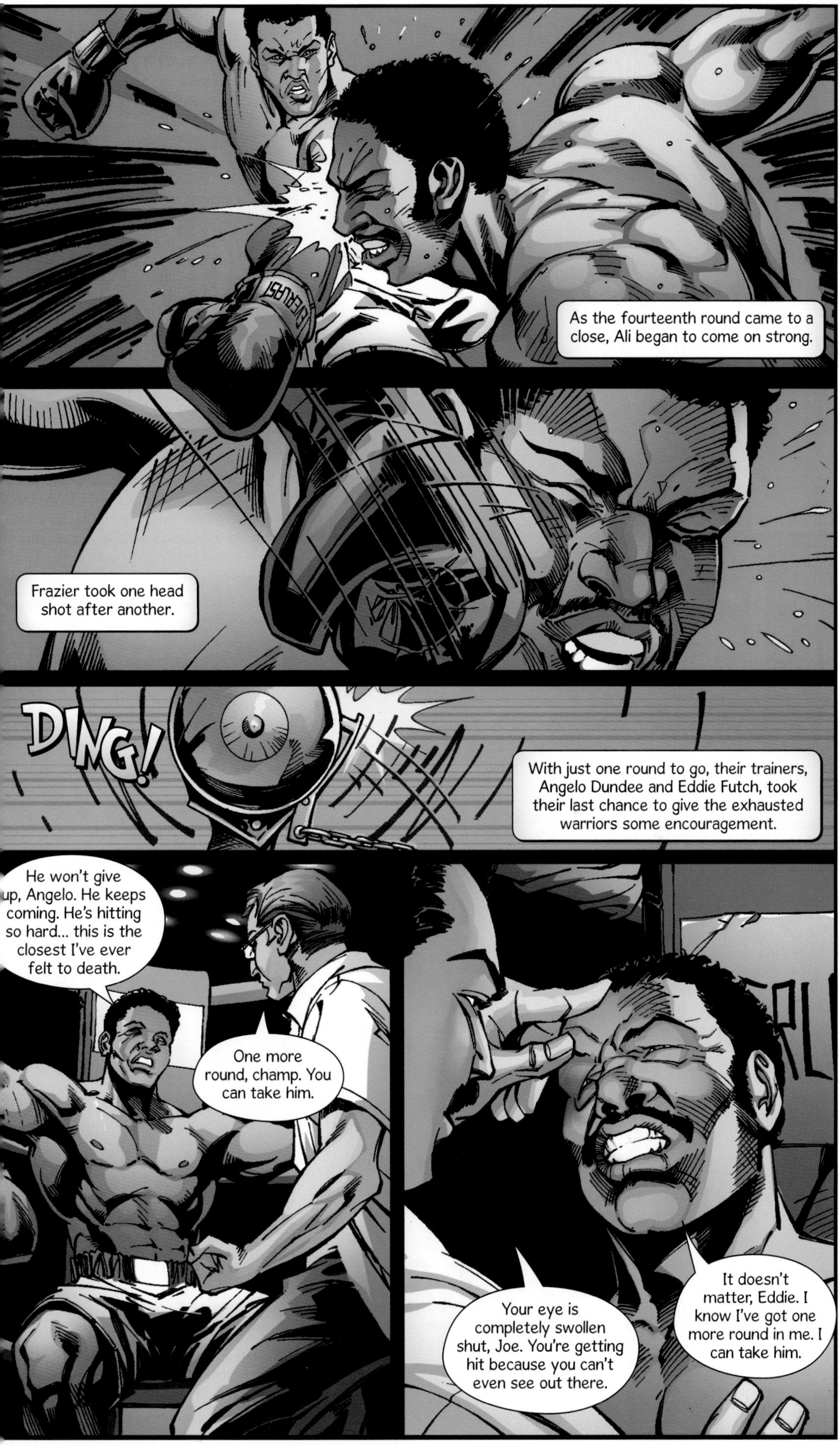
As the fourteenth round came to a close, Ali began to come on strong.
Frazier took one head shot after another.
DING!
With just one round to go, their trainers, Angelo Dundee and Eddie Futch, took their last chance to give the exhausted warriors some encouragement.
He won't give up, Angelo. He keeps coming. He's hitting so hard... this is the closest I've ever felt to death.
One more round, champ. You can take him.
Your eye is completely swollen shut, Joe. You're getting hit because you can't even see out there.
It doesn't matter, Eddie. I know I've got one more round in me. I can take him.

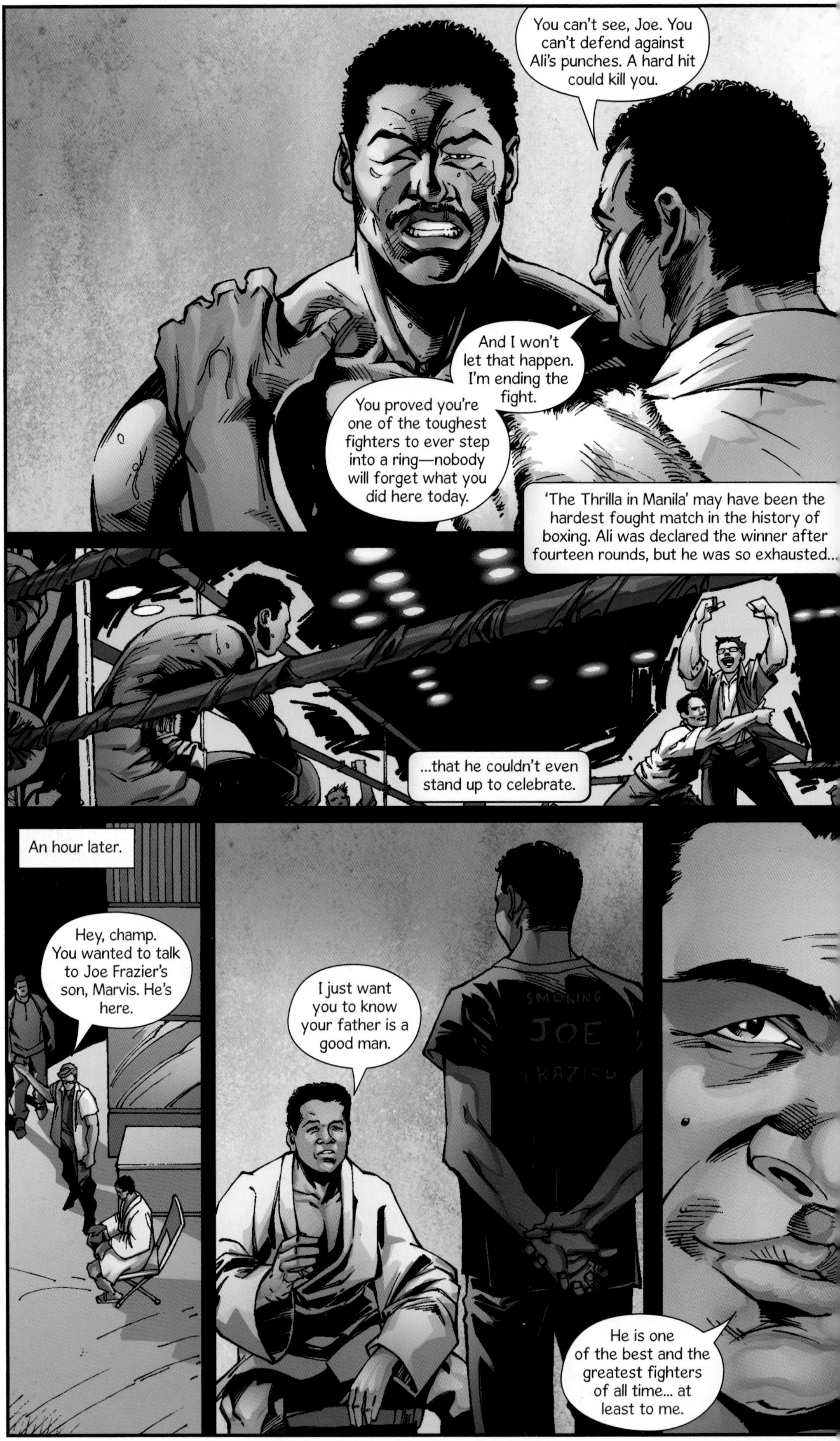
You can't see, Joe. You can't defend against Ali's punches. A hard hit could kill you.
And I won't let that happen. I'm ending the fight.
You proved you're one of the toughest fighters to ever step into a ring—nobody will forget what you did here today.
'The Thrilla in Manila' may have been the hardest fought match in the history of boxing. Ali was declared the winner after fourteen rounds, but he was so exhausted...
...that he couldn't even stand up to celebrate.
An hour later.
Hey, champ. You wanted to talk to Joe Frazier's son, Marvis. He's here.
I just want you to know your father is a good man.
He is one of the best and the greatest fighters of all time... at least to me.

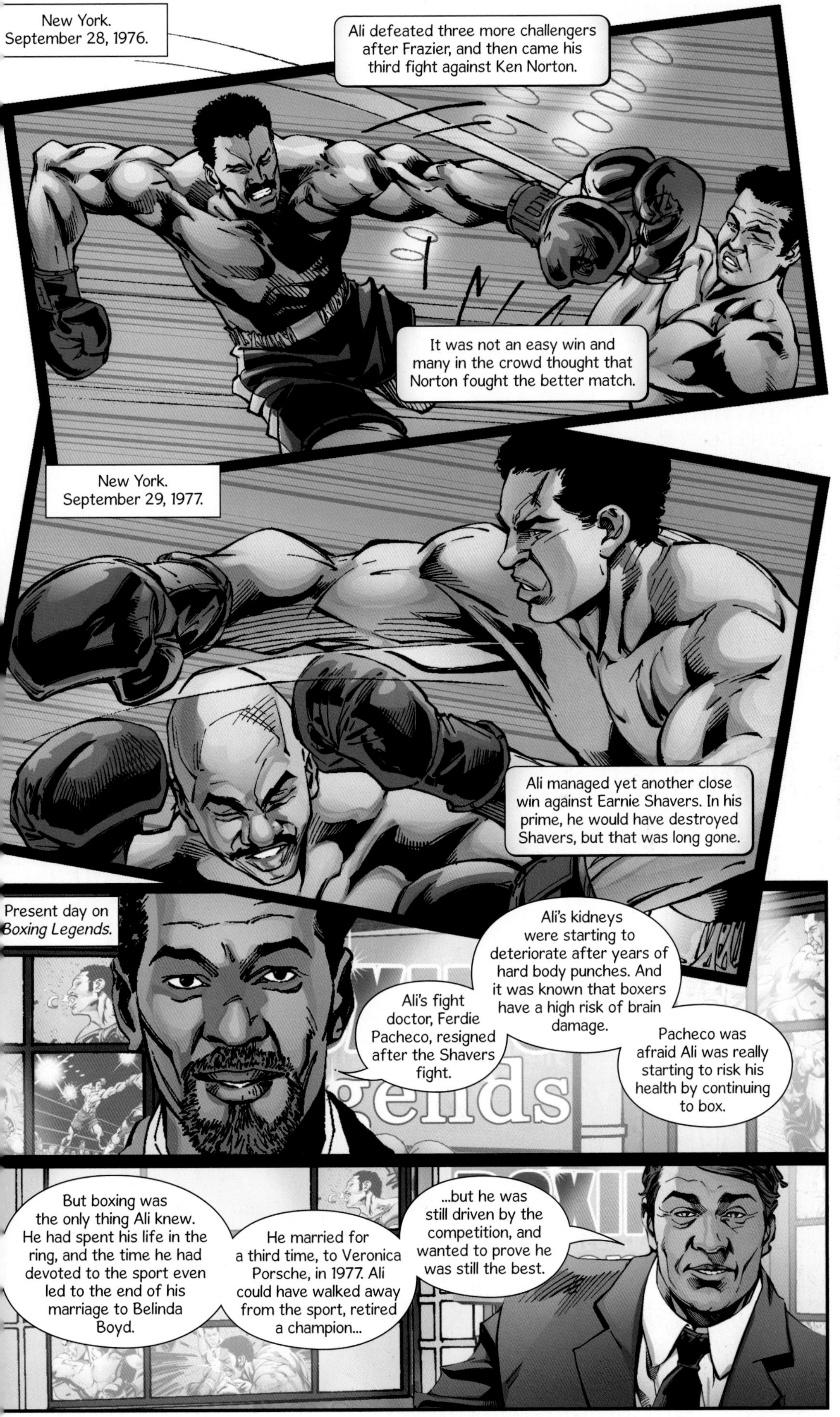

New York. September 28, 1976.
Ali defeated three more challengers after Frazier, and then came his third fight against Ken Norton.
It was not an easy win and many in the crowd thought that Norton fought the better match.
New York. September 29, 1977.
Ali managed yet another close win against Earnie Shavers. In his prime, he would have destroyed Shavers, but that was long gone.
Present day on *Boxing Legends*.
Ali's fight doctor, Ferdie Pacheco, resigned after the Shavers fight.
Ali's kidneys were starting to deteriorate after years of hard body punches. And it was known that boxers have a high risk of brain damage.
Pacheco was afraid Ali was really starting to risk his health by continuing to box.
But boxing was the only thing Ali knew. He had spent his life in the ring, and the time he had devoted to the sport even led to the end of his marriage to Belinda Boyd.
He married for a third time, to Veronica Porsche, in 1977. Ali could have walked away from the sport, retired a champion...
...but he was still driven by the competition, and wanted to prove he was still the best.

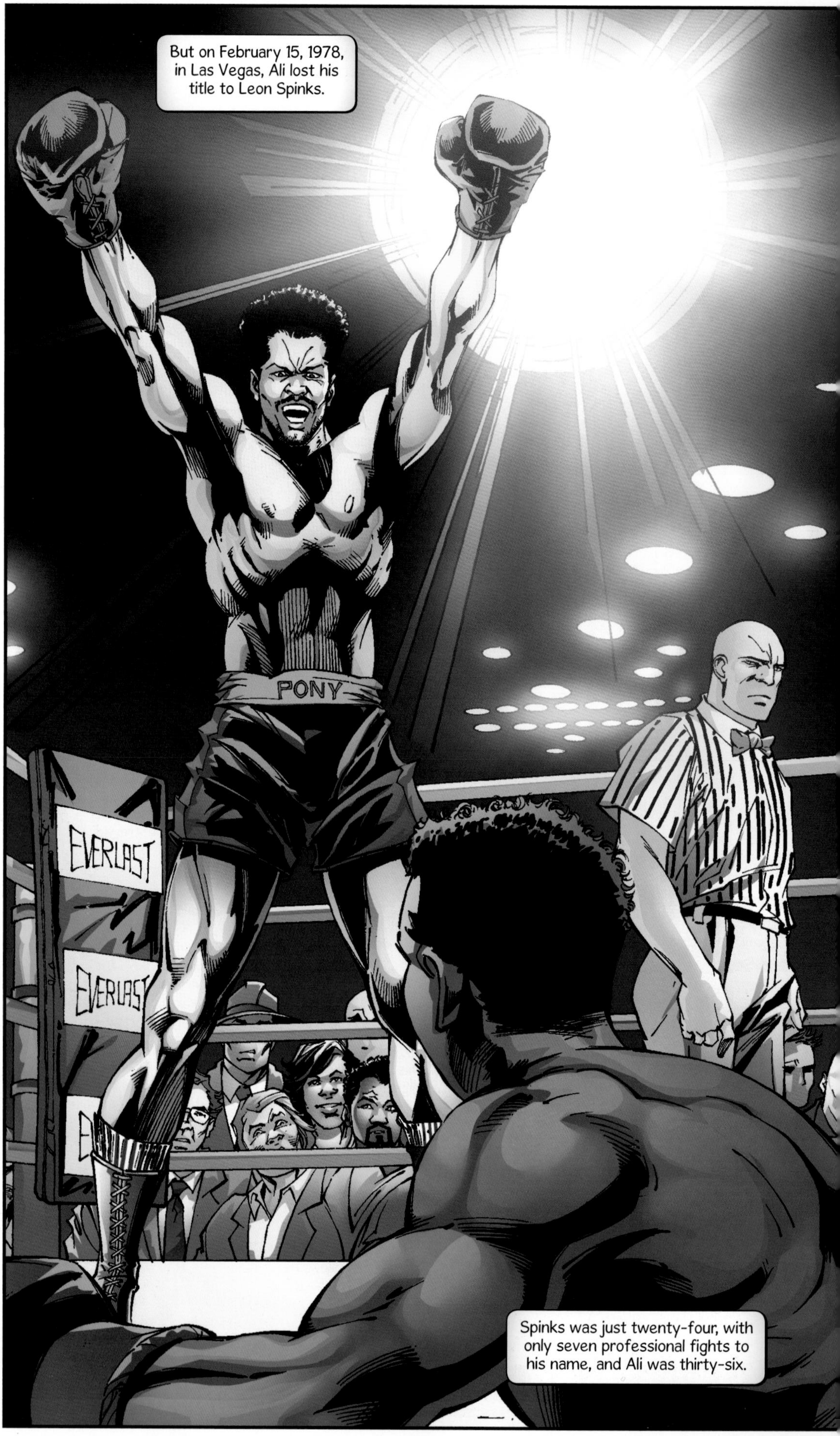
But on February 15, 1978, in Las Vegas, Ali lost his title to Leon Spinks.
PONY
EVERLAST
EVERLAST
Spinks was just twenty-four, with only seven professional fights to his name, and Ali was thirty-six.

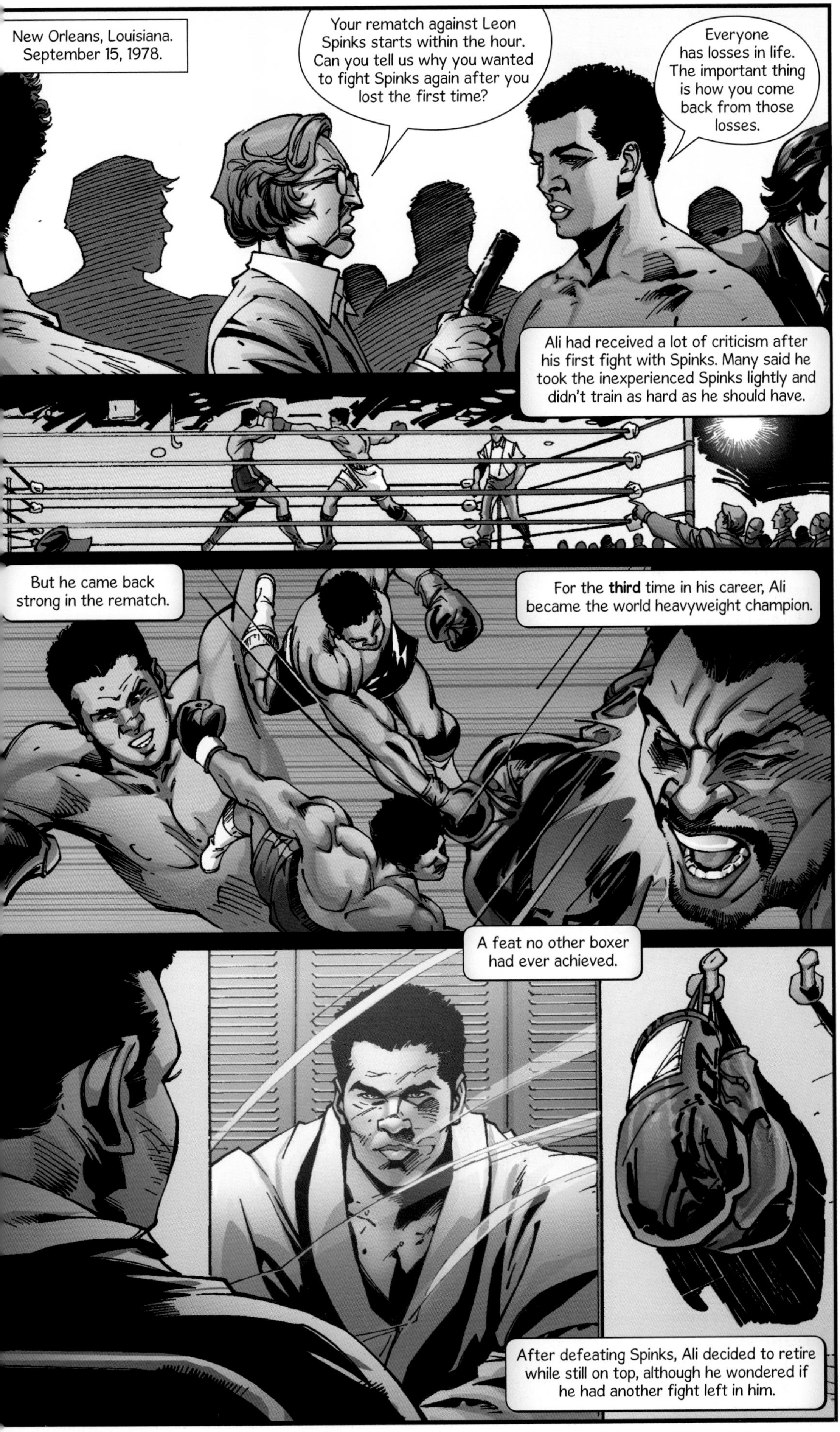

New Orleans, Louisiana. September 15, 1978.
Your rematch against Leon Spinks starts within the hour. Can you tell us why you wanted to fight Spinks again after you lost the first time?
Everyone has losses in life. The important thing is how you come back from those losses.
Ali had received a lot of criticism after his first fight with Spinks. Many said he took the inexperienced Spinks lightly and didn't train as hard as he should have.
But he came back strong in the rematch.
For the **third** time in his career, Ali became the world heavyweight champion.
A feat no other boxer had ever achieved.
After defeating Spinks, Ali decided to retire while still on top, although he wondered if he had another fight left in him.

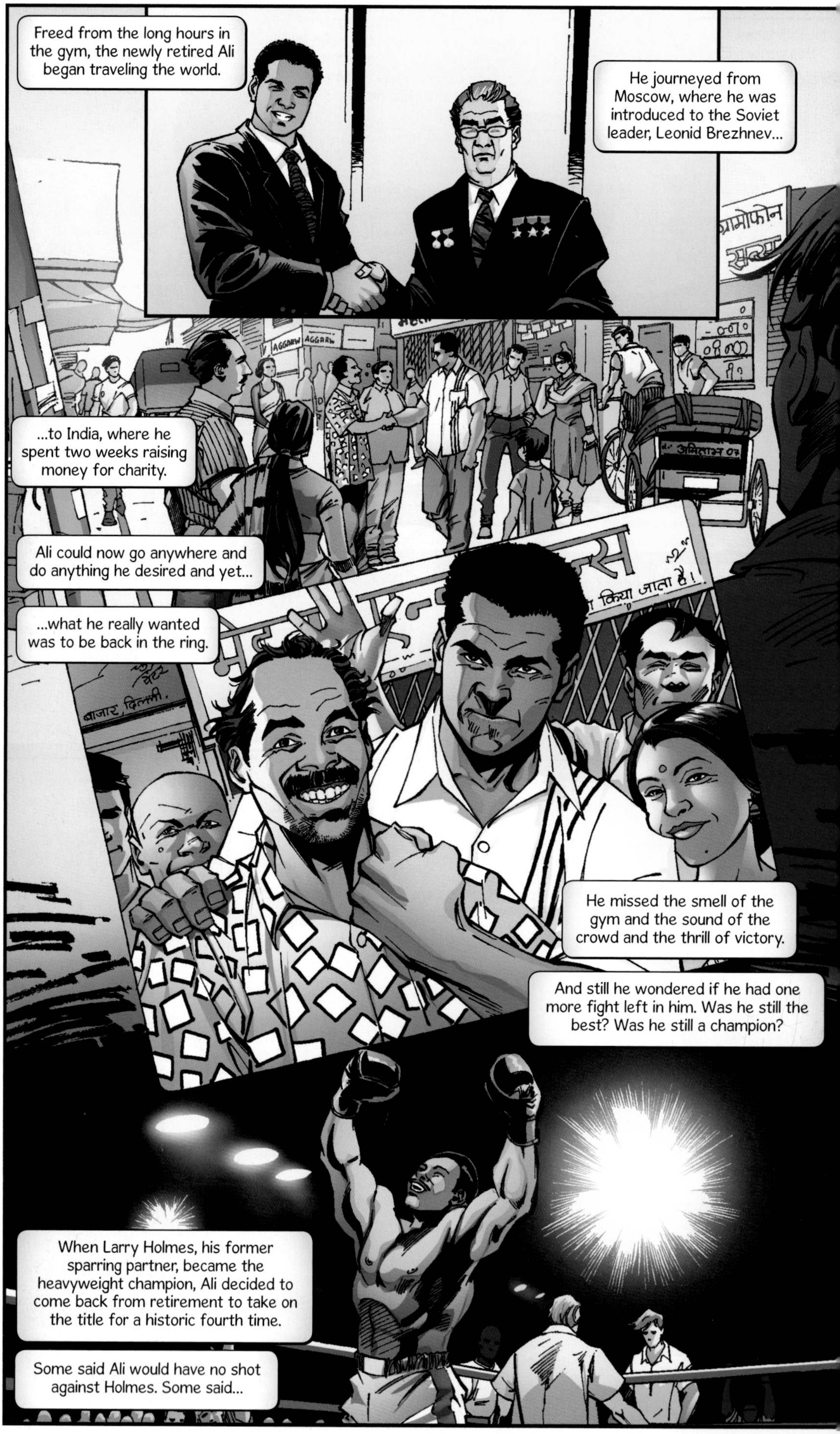

Freed from the long hours in the gym, the newly retired Ali began traveling the world.
He journeyed from Moscow, where he was introduced to the Soviet leader, Leonid Brezhnev...
...to India, where he spent two weeks raising money for charity.
Ali could now go anywhere and do anything he desired and yet...
...what he really wanted was to be back in the ring.
He missed the smell of the gym and the sound of the crowd and the thrill of victory.
And still he wondered if he had one more fight left in him. Was he still the best? Was he still a champion?
When Larry Holmes, his former sparring partner, became the heavyweight champion, Ali decided to come back from retirement to take on the title for a historic fourth time.
Some said Ali would have no shot against Holmes. Some said...

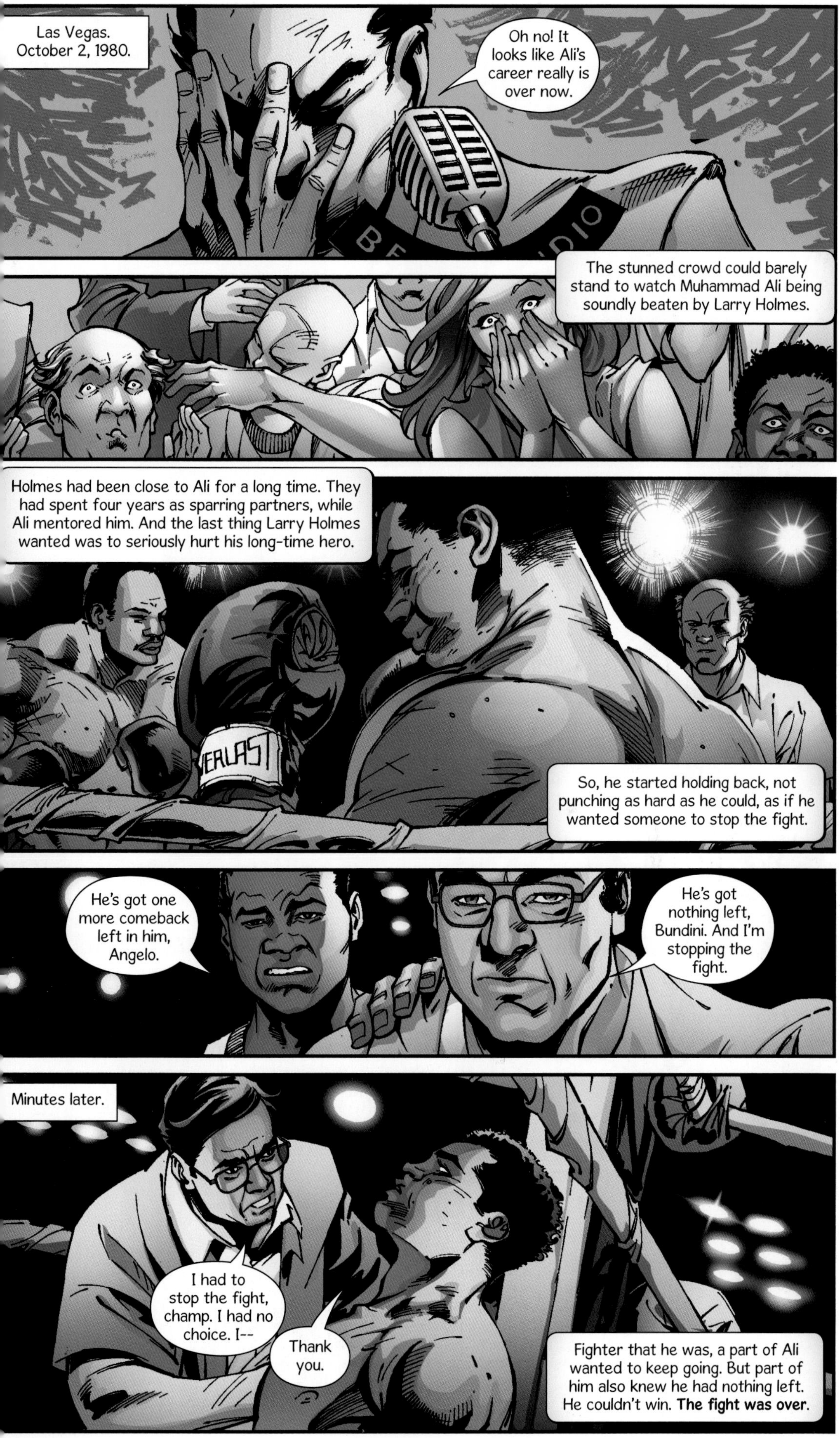
Las Vegas. October 2, 1980.
Oh no! It looks like Ali's career really is over now.
The stunned crowd could barely stand to watch Muhammad Ali being soundly beaten by Larry Holmes.
Holmes had been close to Ali for a long time. They had spent four years as sparring partners, while Ali mentored him. And the last thing Larry Holmes wanted was to seriously hurt his long-time hero.
So, he started holding back, not punching as hard as he could, as if he wanted someone to stop the fight.
He's got one more comeback left in him, Angelo.
He's got nothing left, Bundini. And I'm stopping the fight.
Minutes later.
I had to stop the fight, champ. I had no choice. I--
Thank you.
Fighter that he was, a part of Ali wanted to keep going. But part of him also knew he had nothing left. He couldn't win. **The fight was over.**

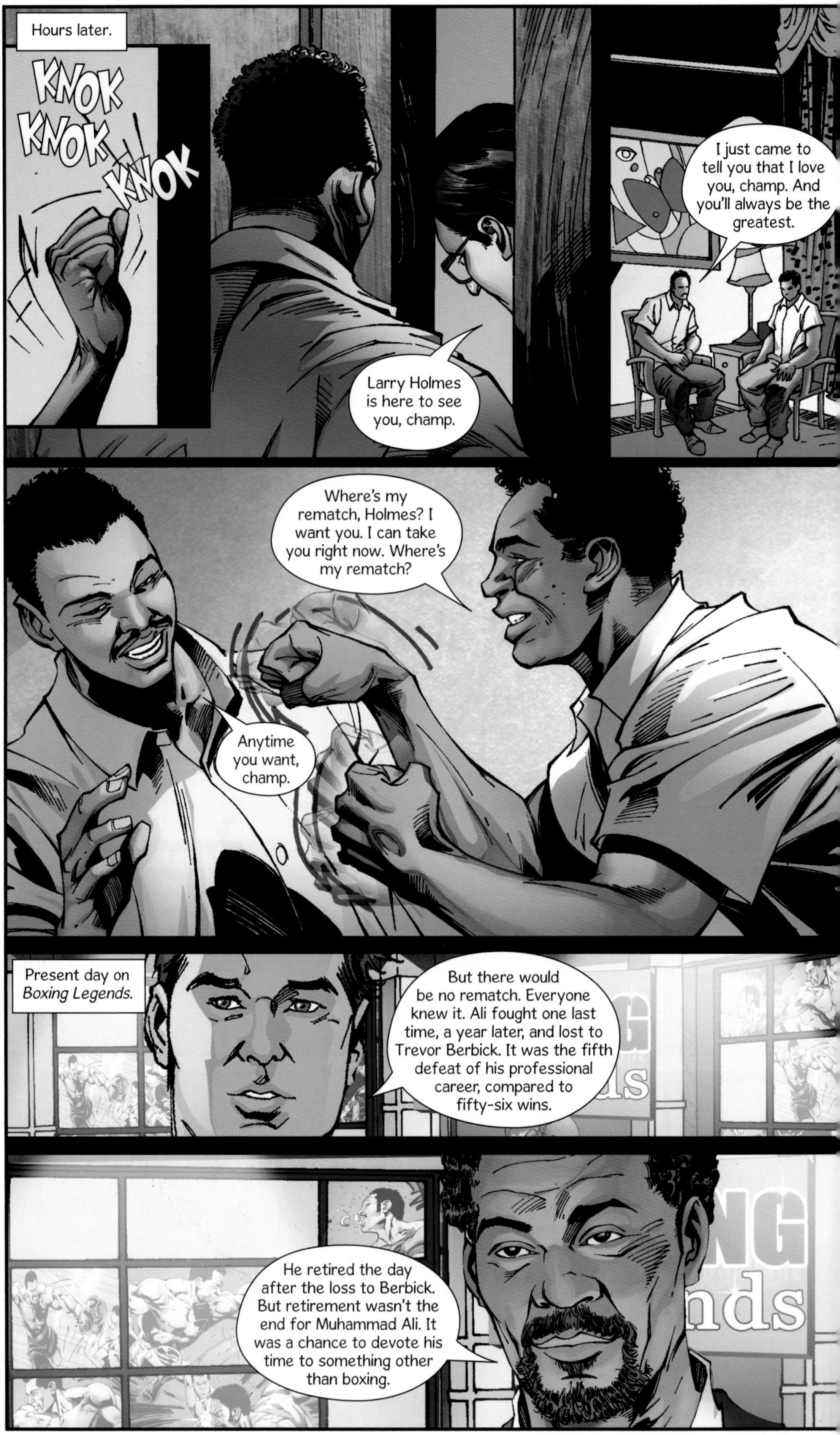
Hours later.
KNOK KNOK KNOK
Larry Holmes is here to see you, champ.
I just came to tell you that I love you, champ. And you'll always be the greatest.
Where's my rematch, Holmes? I want you. I can take you right now. Where's my rematch?
Anytime you want, champ.
Present day on *Boxing Legends.*
But there would be no rematch. Everyone knew it. Ali fought one last time, a year later, and lost to Trevor Berbick. It was the fifth defeat of his professional career, compared to fifty-six wins.
He retired the day after the loss to Berbick. But retirement wasn't the end for Muhammad Ali. It was a chance to devote his time to something other than boxing.

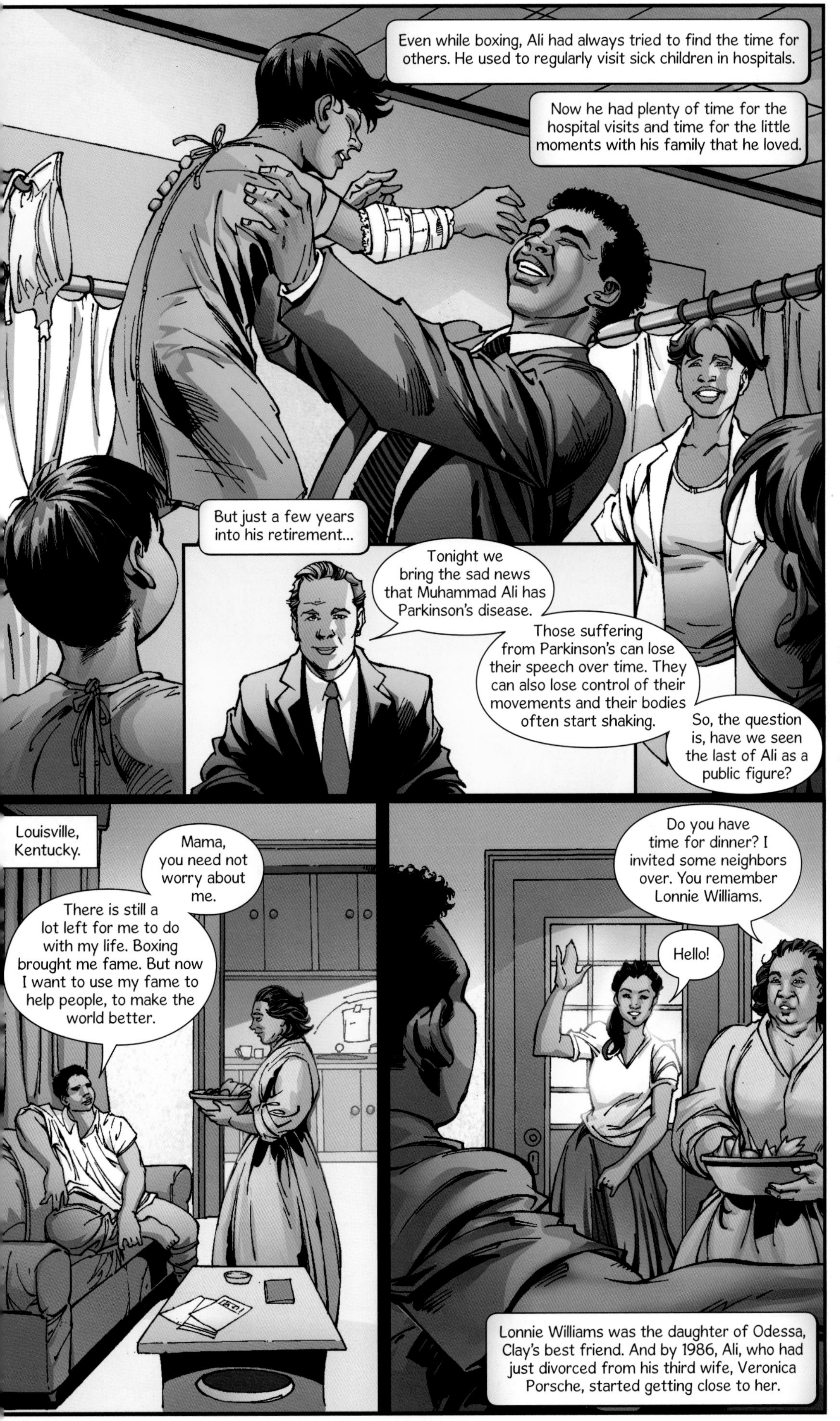

Even while boxing, Ali had always tried to find the time for others. He used to regularly visit sick children in hospitals.
Now he had plenty of time for the hospital visits and time for the little moments with his family that he loved.
But just a few years into his retirement...
Tonight we bring the sad news that Muhammad Ali has Parkinson's disease.
Those suffering from Parkinson's can lose their speech over time. They can also lose control of their movements and their bodies often start shaking.
So, the question is, have we seen the last of Ali as a public figure?
Louisville, Kentucky.
Mama, you need not worry about me.
There is still a lot left for me to do with my life. Boxing brought me fame. But now I want to use my fame to help people, to make the world better.
Do you have time for dinner? I invited some neighbors over. You remember Lonnie Williams.
Hello!
Lonnie Williams was the daughter of Odessa, Clay's best friend. And by 1986, Ali, who had just divorced from his third wife, Veronica Porsche, started getting close to her.

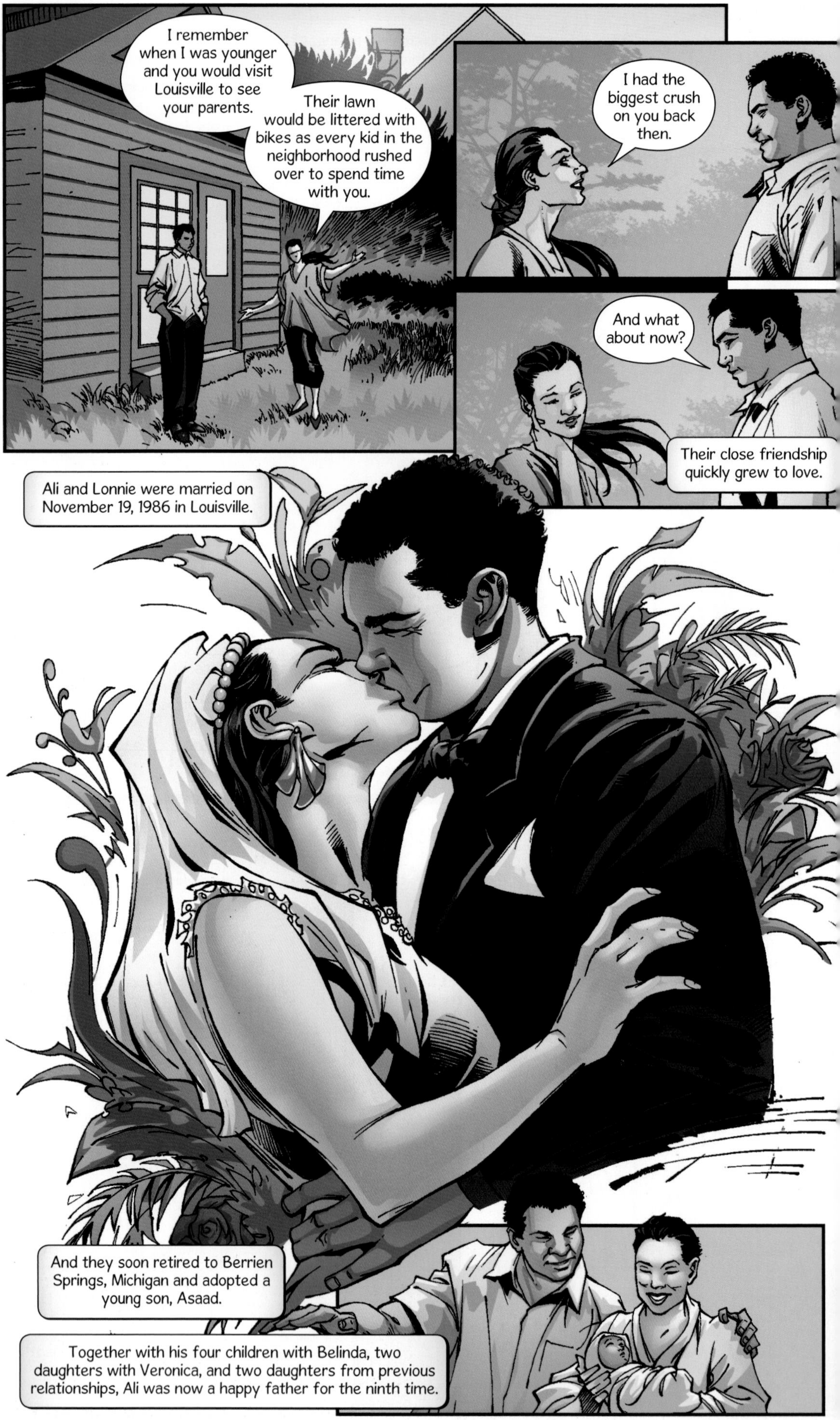
I remember when I was younger and you would visit Louisville to see your parents.
Their lawn would be littered with bikes as every kid in the neighborhood rushed over to spend time with you.
I had the biggest crush on you back then.
And what about now?
Their close friendship quickly grew to love.
Ali and Lonnie were married on November 19, 1986 in Louisville.
And they soon retired to Berrien Springs, Michigan and adopted a young son, Asaad.
Together with his four children with Belinda, two daughters with Veronica, and two daughters from previous relationships, Ali was now a happy father for the ninth time.

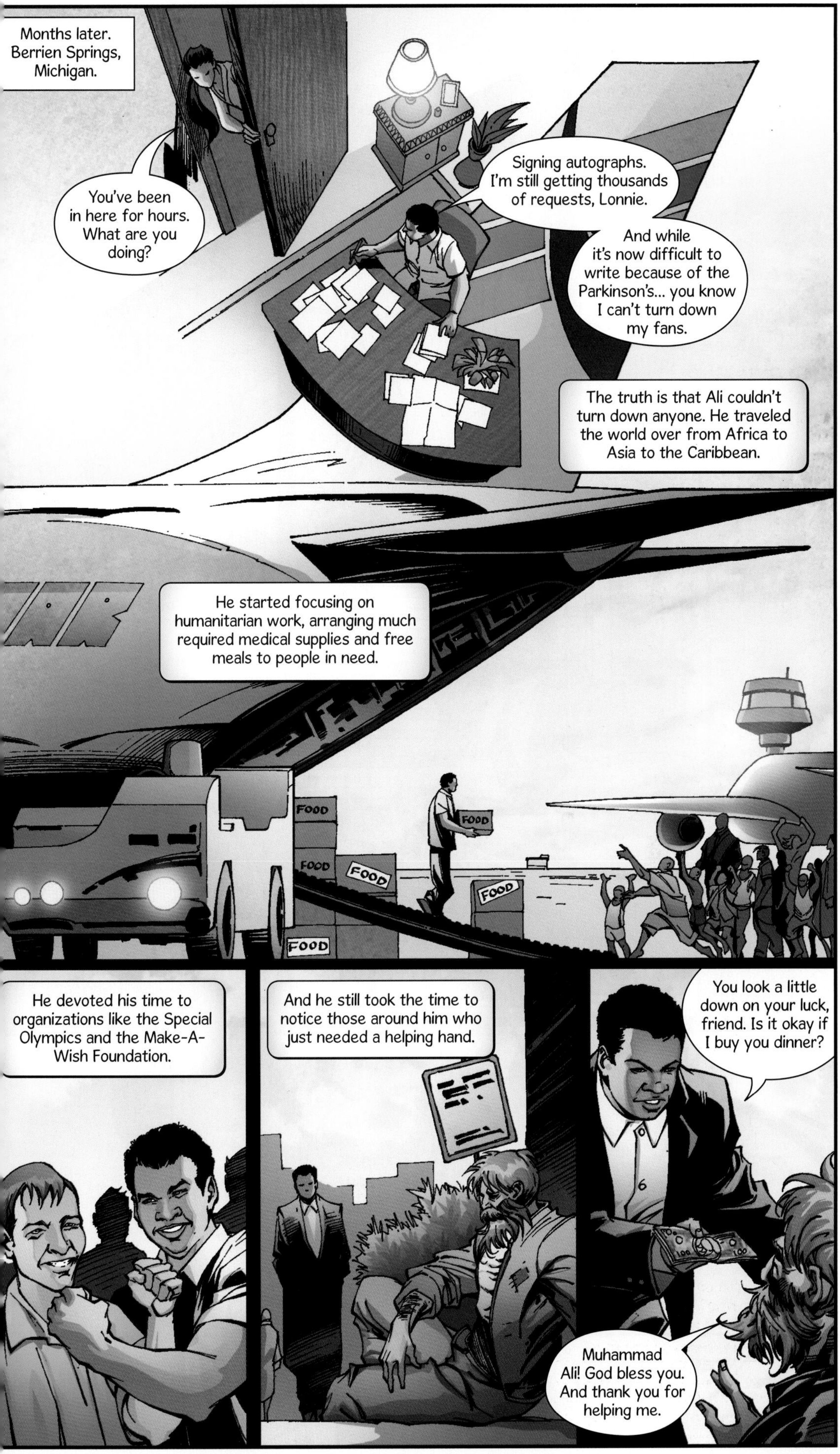

Months later. Berrien Springs, Michigan.
You've been in here for hours. What are you doing?
Signing autographs. I'm still getting thousands of requests, Lonnie.
And while it's now difficult to write because of the Parkinson's... you know I can't turn down my fans.
The truth is that Ali couldn't turn down anyone. He traveled the world over from Africa to Asia to the Caribbean.
He started focusing on humanitarian work, arranging much required medical supplies and free meals to people in need.
FOOD
FOOD
FOOD
FOOD
FOOD
FOOD
He devoted his time to organizations like the Special Olympics and the Make-A-Wish Foundation.
And he still took the time to notice those around him who just needed a helping hand.
You look a little down on your luck, friend. Is it okay if I buy you dinner?
Muhammad Ali! God bless you. And thank you for helping me.

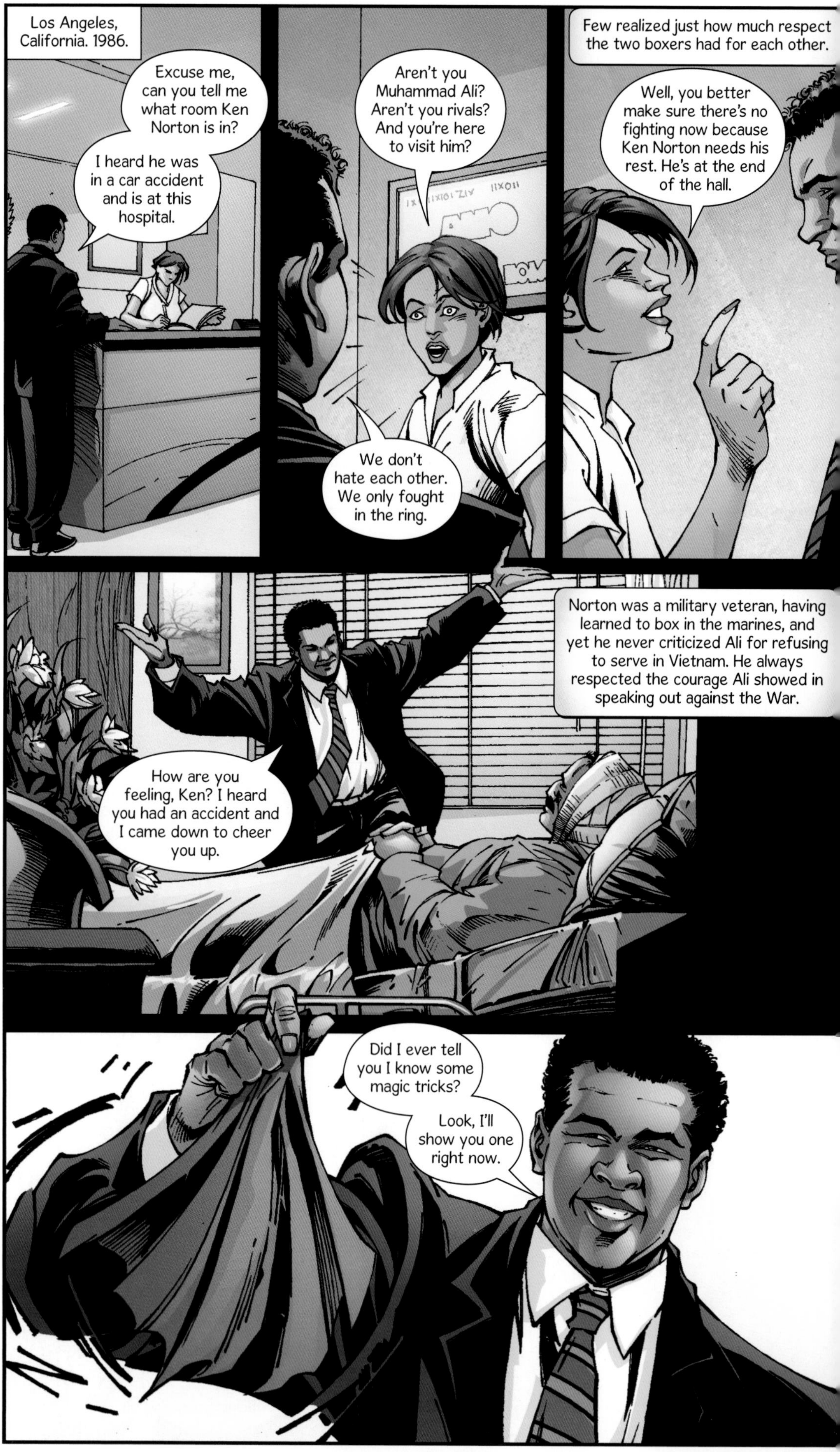
Los Angeles, California. 1986.
Excuse me, can you tell me what room Ken Norton is in?
I heard he was in a car accident and is at this hospital.
Aren't you Muhammad Ali? Aren't you rivals? And you're here to visit him?
We don't hate each other. We only fought in the ring.
Few realized just how much respect the two boxers had for each other.
Well, you better make sure there's no fighting now because Ken Norton needs his rest. He's at the end of the hall.
Norton was a military veteran, having learned to box in the marines, and yet he never criticized Ali for refusing to serve in Vietnam. He always respected the courage Ali showed in speaking out against the War.
How are you feeling, Ken? I heard you had an accident and I came down to cheer you up.
Did I ever tell you I know some magic tricks?
Look, I'll show you one right now.

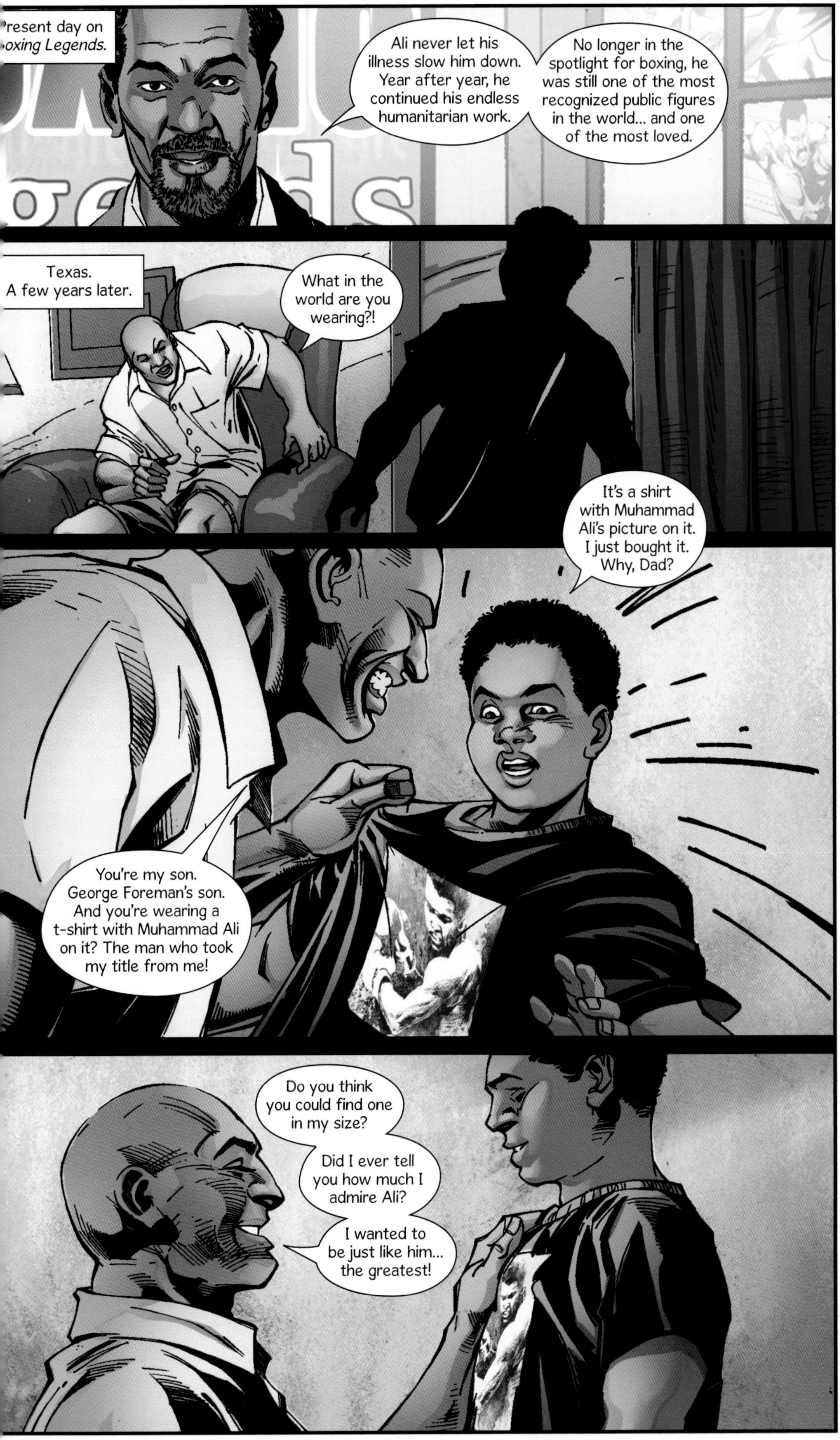
'resent day on
oxing Legends.
Ali never let his illness slow him down. Year after year, he continued his endless humanitarian work.
No longer in the spotlight for boxing, he was still one of the most recognized public figures in the world... and one of the most loved.
Texas.
A few years later.
What in the world are you wearing?!
It's a shirt with Muhammad Ali's picture on it. I just bought it. Why, Dad?
You're my son. George Foreman's son. And you're wearing a t-shirt with Muhammad Ali on it? The man who took my title from me!
Do you think you could find one in my size?
Did I ever tell you how much I admire Ali?
I wanted to be just like him... the greatest!

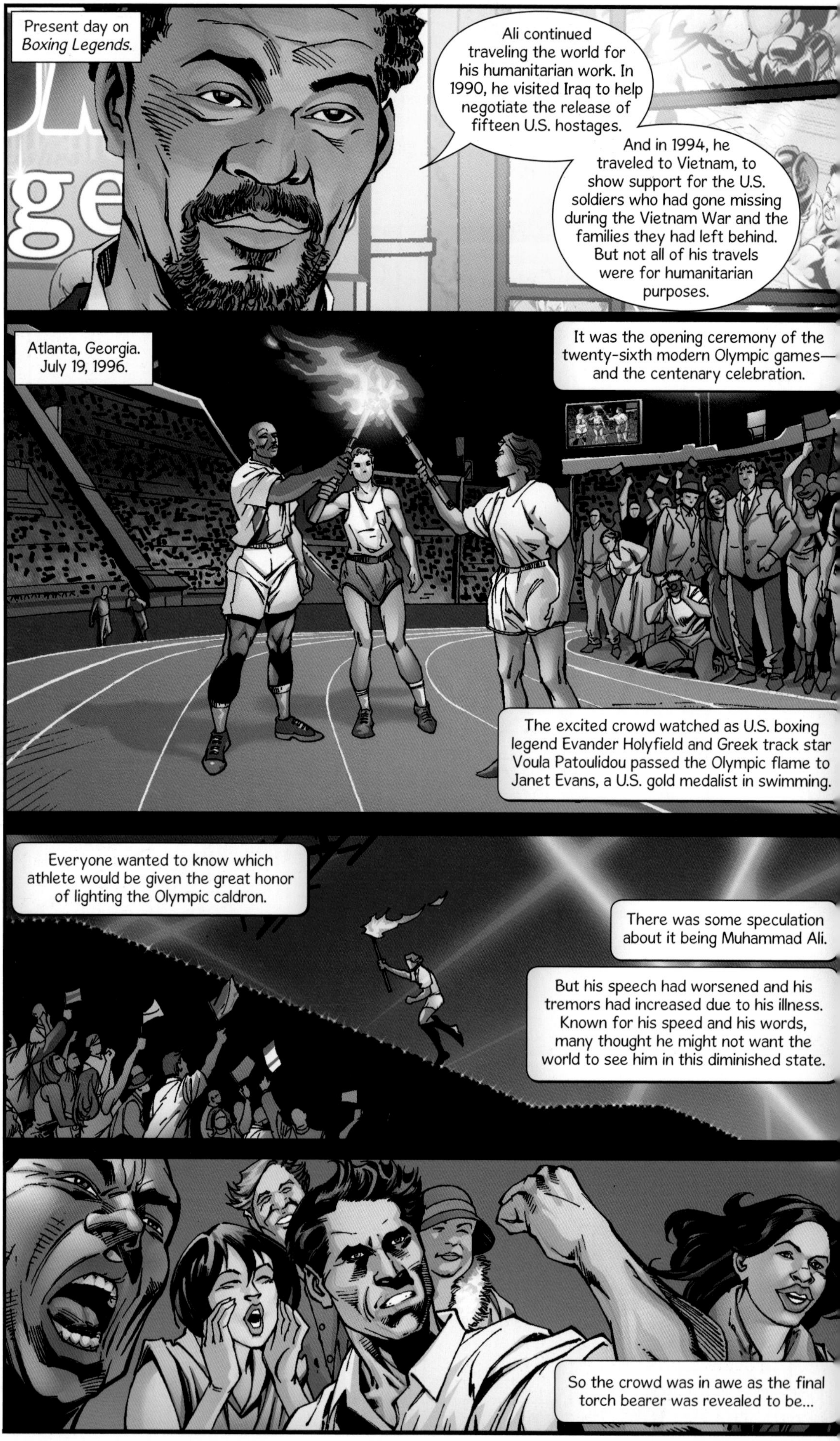
Present day on *Boxing Legends*.
Ali continued traveling the world for his humanitarian work. In 1990, he visited Iraq to help negotiate the release of fifteen U.S. hostages.
And in 1994, he traveled to Vietnam, to show support for the U.S. soldiers who had gone missing during the Vietnam War and the families they had left behind. But not all of his travels were for humanitarian purposes.
Atlanta, Georgia. July 19, 1996.
It was the opening ceremony of the twenty-sixth modern Olympic games—and the centenary celebration.
The excited crowd watched as U.S. boxing legend Evander Holyfield and Greek track star Voula Patoulidou passed the Olympic flame to Janet Evans, a U.S. gold medalist in swimming.
Everyone wanted to know which athlete would be given the great honor of lighting the Olympic caldron.
There was some speculation about it being Muhammad Ali.
But his speech had worsened and his tremors had increased due to his illness. Known for his speed and his words, many thought he might not want the world to see him in this diminished state.
So the crowd was in awe as the final torch bearer was revealed to be...

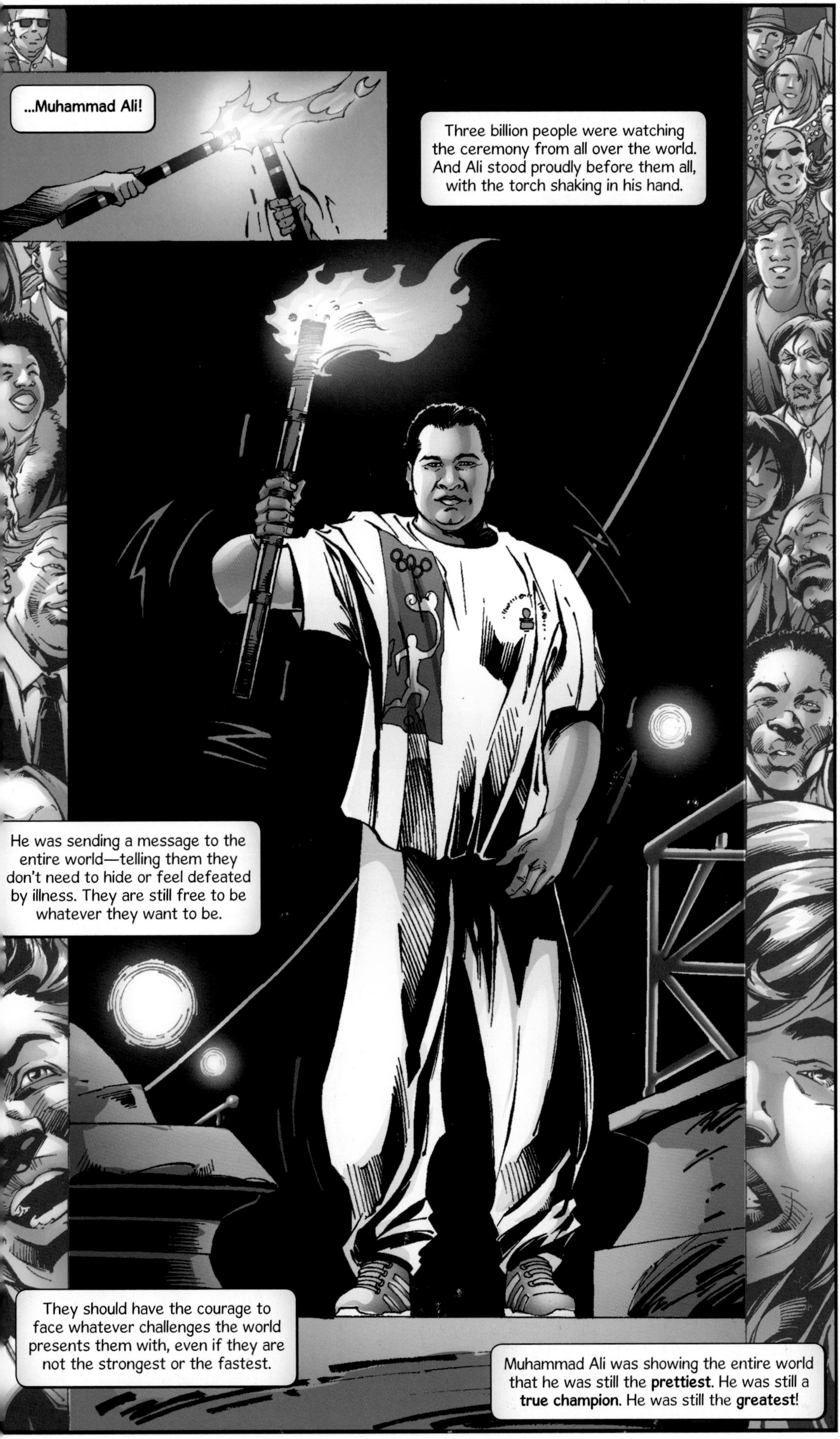

...Muhammad Ali!
Three billion people were watching the ceremony from all over the world. And Ali stood proudly before them all, with the torch shaking in his hand.
He was sending a message to the entire world—telling them they don't need to hide or feel defeated by illness. They are still free to be whatever they want to be.
They should have the courage to face whatever challenges the world presents them with, even if they are not the strongest or the fastest.
Muhammad Ali was showing the entire world that he was still the **prettiest**. He was still a **true champion**. He was still the **greatest**!

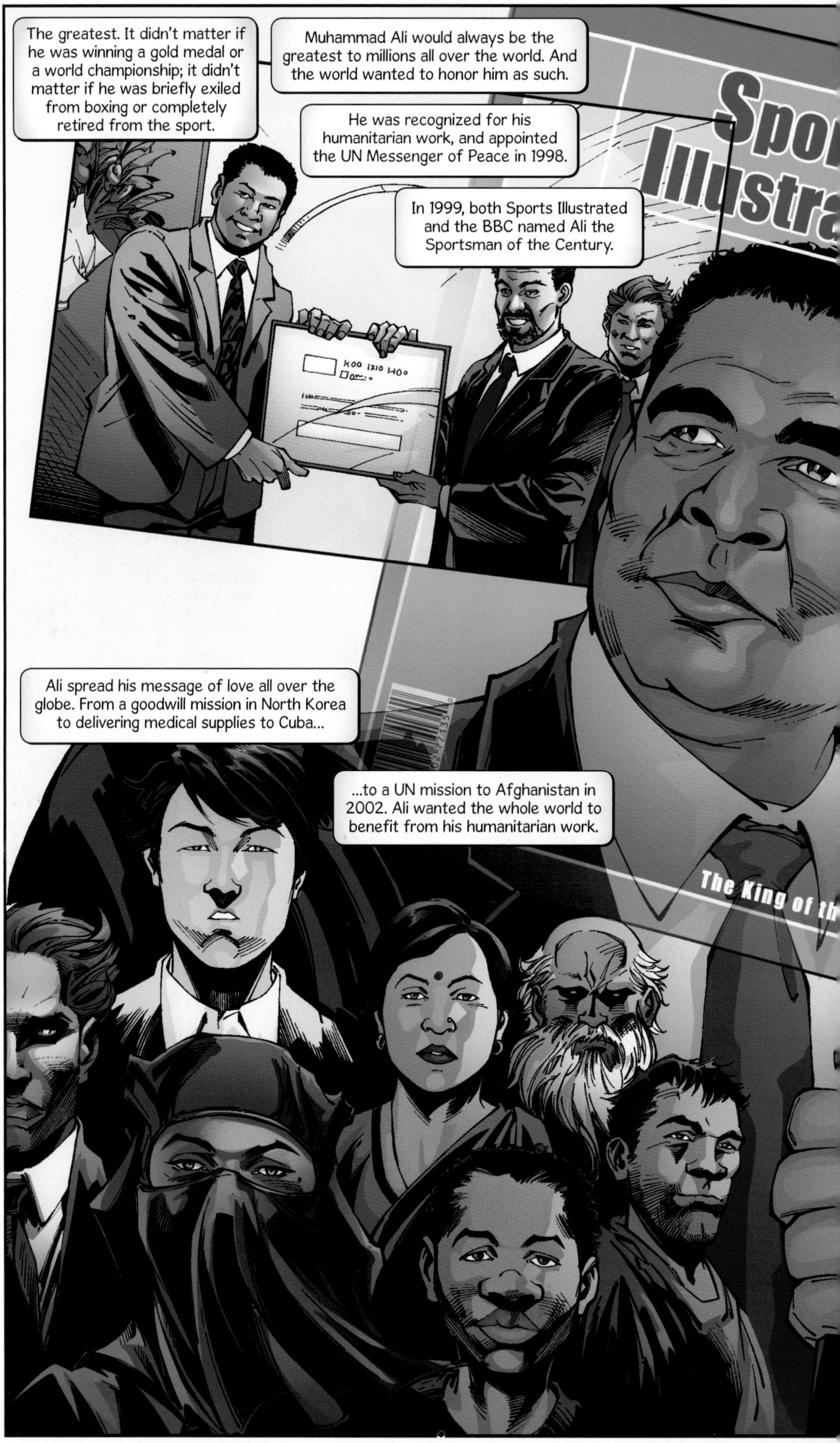
The greatest. It didn't matter if he was winning a gold medal or a world championship; it didn't matter if he was briefly exiled from boxing or completely retired from the sport.
Muhammad Ali would always be the greatest to millions all over the world. And the world wanted to honor him as such.
He was recognized for his humanitarian work, and appointed the UN Messenger of Peace in 1998.
In 1999, both Sports Illustrated and the BBC named Ali the Sportsman of the Century.
Ali spread his message of love all over the globe. From a goodwill mission in North Korea to delivering medical supplies to Cuba...
...to a UN mission to Afghanistan in 2002. Ali wanted the whole world to benefit from his humanitarian work.

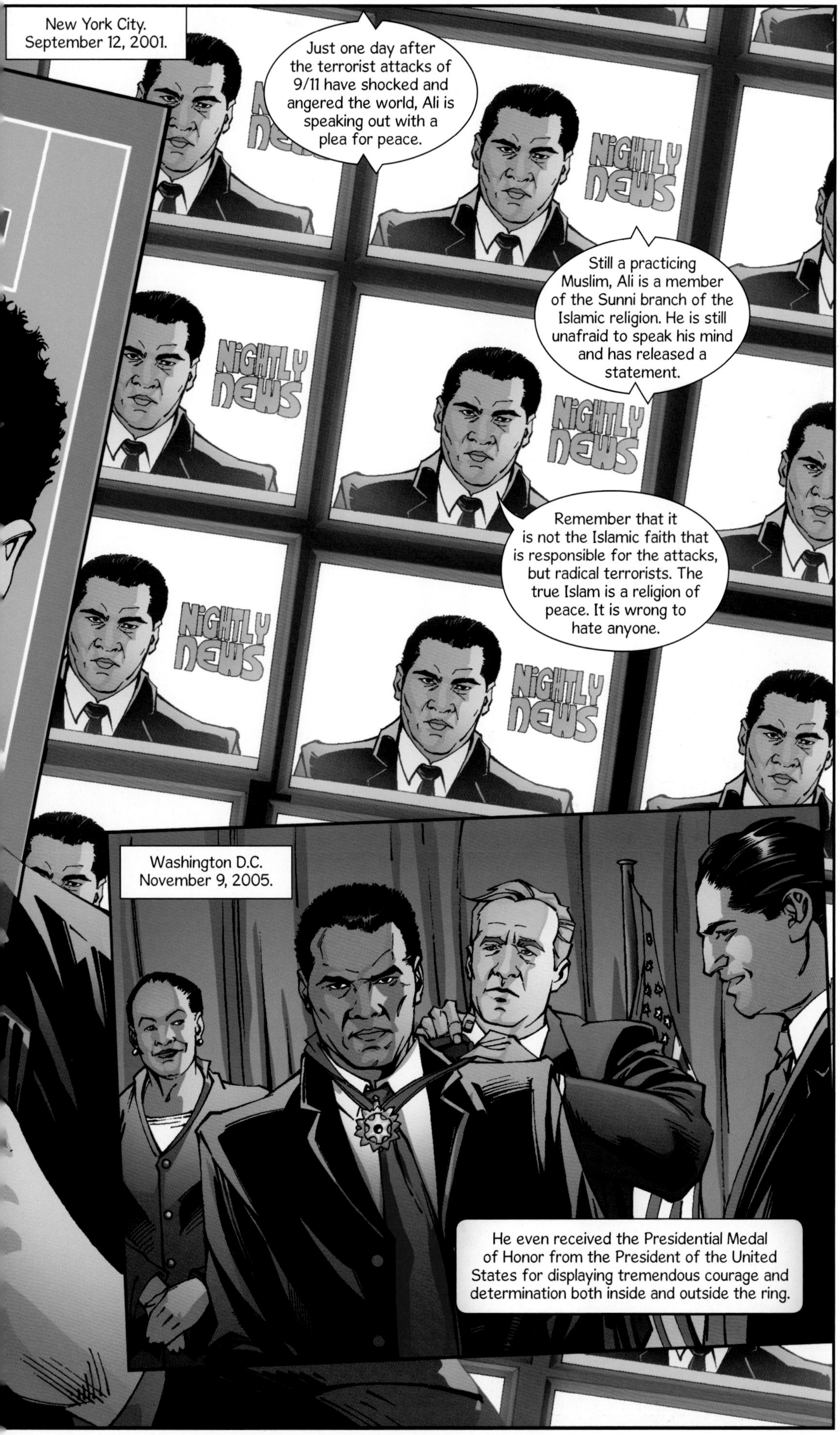
New York City. September 12, 2001.
Just one day after the terrorist attacks of 9/11 have shocked and angered the world, Ali is speaking out with a plea for peace.
NiGHTLY NEWS
Still a practicing Muslim, Ali is a member of the Sunni branch of the Islamic religion. He is still unafraid to speak his mind and has released a statement.
Remember that it is not the Islamic faith that is responsible for the attacks, but radical terrorists. The true Islam is a religion of peace. It is wrong to hate anyone.
Washington D.C. November 9, 2005.
He even received the Presidential Medal of Honor from the President of the United States for displaying tremendous courage and determination both inside and outside the ring.

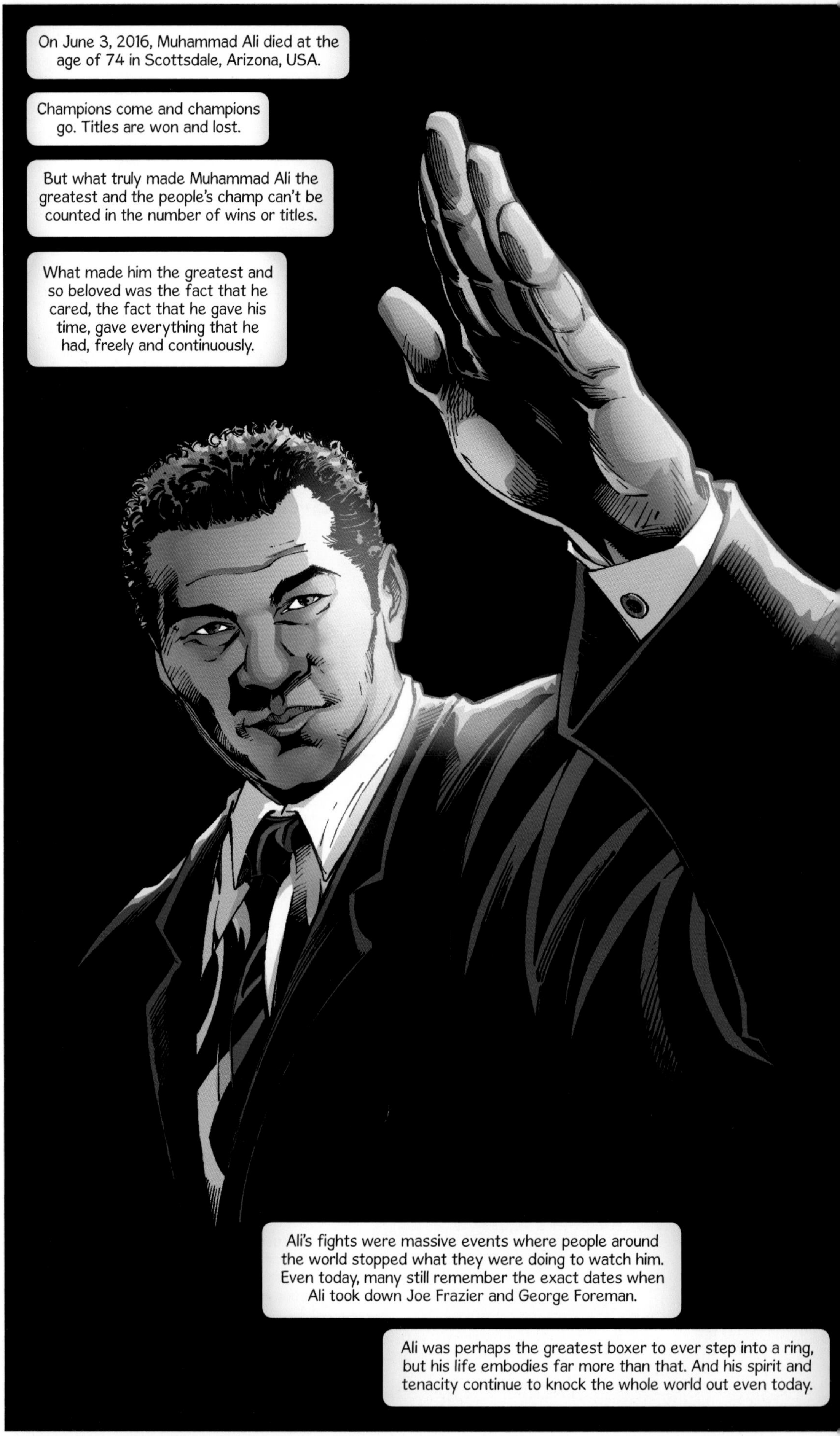
On June 3, 2016, Muhammad Ali died at the age of 74 in Scottsdale, Arizona, USA.
Champions come and champions go. Titles are won and lost.
But what truly made Muhammad Ali the greatest and the people's champ can't be counted in the number of wins or titles.
What made him the greatest and so beloved was the fact that he cared, the fact that he gave his time, gave everything that he had, freely and continuously.
Ali's fights were massive events where people around the world stopped what they were doing to watch him. Even today, many still remember the exact dates when Ali took down Joe Frazier and George Foreman.
Ali was perhaps the greatest boxer to ever step into a ring, but his life embodies far more than that. And his spirit and tenacity continue to knock the whole world out even today.

PRIZE FIGHTERS!

Muhammad Ali was nicknamed 'The Greatest', but in boxing you're only as great as the opponents you face in the ring. Let's take a closer look at some of Ali's greatest opponents!

CHARLES L. SONNY LISTON

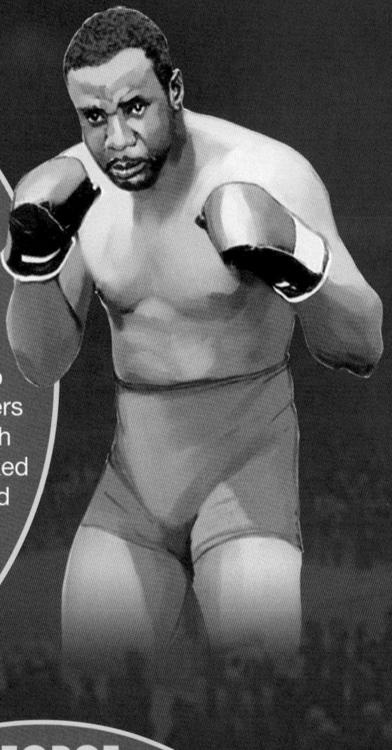

'Sonny' Liston was the twelfth of thirteen children. His early life is a bit of a mystery because there are no records of his birth. He claimed he was born on May 8, 1932, but it has been estimated that he was born in 1928. As a teenager, he fell foul of the law when he became involved in a series of robberies. He was eventually captured while robbing a gas station and sentenced to eight years in prison. He started boxing in prison and, on his early release for good behavior, he built up a fearsome reputation both in and out of the ring. Many boxers refused to fight him because of his alleged involvement with organized crime. However, on September 25,1962, he knocked Floyd Patterson out in the first round and became the world heavyweight champion. He lost the title to Ali in 1964. Sonny died young, at thirty-eight years of age, due to heart failure, on December 30, 1970.

SONNY'S PRO BOXING STATS!
WINS 50 • KNOCKOUTS 39
LOSSES 4 • DRAWS 0

GEORGE FOREMAN

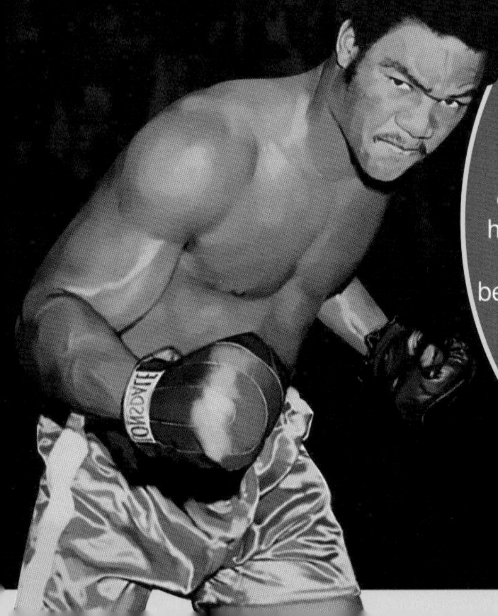

'Big George' was born in Texas in 1949. He was interested in football in his teens but gave it up for boxing. He had a troubled youth, but boxing gave him something to believe in. In 1968, he won the Olympic gold in Mexico City for boxing and turned professional the following year. In 1994, he entered the record books, when at the age of forty-five he knocked out the twenty-four-year-old Michael Moorer to retake the title and become the oldest man ever to become heavyweight champion of the world! After retiring from boxing, George became famous for promoting the 'George Foreman Grill', a fat-reducing grilling machine. He is also an ordained Christian minister who has his own church.

GEORGE'S PRO BOXING STATS!
WINS 76 • KNOCKOUTS 68
LOSSES 5 • DRAWS 0

JOE FRAZIER

'Smokin' Joe' was born on January 12, 1944 in South Carolina. He was stocky as a child, because of which his uncle predicted he would be a great fighter. In fact, smaller kids would often pay him a quarter to protect them from the school bullies. When Ali was stripped of his title in 1967, Joe refused to take part in the elimination tournament to find a successor. He even petitioned the President of the USA to reinstate Ali's boxing license. Frazier retired from boxing in 1976 and went on to make a small appearance in the movie Rocky. He made a comeback to boxing in 1981, but it lasted for just one fight which was a draw with Floyd 'Jumbo' Cummings. Joe and Ali have remained rivals even in retirement, although they have had brief moments of reconciliation.

JOE'S PRO BOXING STATS!
WINS 32 • KNOCKOUTS 27
LOSSES 4 • DRAWS 1

KEN NORTON

'The jaw breaker' Norton was born in Illinois in 1943. At high school he was an outstanding athlete, playing for the state football team and competing successfully in several track events. Norton took up boxing when he was in the U.S. Marine Corps, in the early 1960s. He remains most famous for breaking Ali's jaw in the first of the three clashes with him. He lost the other two fights, but both were very close matches. Norton's last fight was in 1981, following which he quit the ring to pursue a career in film and television, making over 20 movies. He continued making TV and public appearances until he was involved in a near fatal car crash in 1986, and withdrew from public life.

KEN'S PRO BOXING STATS!
WINS 42 • KNOCKOUTS 33
LOSSES 7 • DRAWS 1

LEON SPINKS

'Neon' Leon was born in Missouri, in 1953. In 1976 he won the Olympic gold medal in the light heavyweight division, while his brother, Michael, won gold as a middleweight boxer. Leon turned professional in 1977. After seven fights he challenged Ali for the world heavyweight title in February 1978. He is said to have partied so long and hard after defeating Ali that he never quite recovered from it. The rematch, however, was completely different, with Ali dominating the younger man. And so, on September 15, 1978, Ali reclaimed the title for the third time. Leon later challenged Larry Holmes for the world title in 1981, but was knocked out in the third round. He finally retired from boxing in 1995.

LEON'S PRO BOXING STATS!
WINS 26 • KNOCKOUTS 14
LOSSES 17 • DRAWS 3

LARRY HOLMES

'The Easton Assassin' was born in 1949 in Georgia. He grew up in Easton, Pennsylvania, which gave him his famous nickname. Larry was the fourth of twelve children and his family was very poor. He was forced to drop out of school to take a job in a car wash to help support his family. Holmes took up boxing in his late teens, and in the early days he worked as a sparring partner for Ali, Frazier and other boxers. He turned professional in 1973 and his left jab became one of the most lethal weapons in boxing. He beat Ken Norton to become champion in 1978, and defended his title twenty times before retiring in 1986. He returned in 1988 to fight Mike Tyson, but the fight was stopped in the fourth round after Tyson dropped Holmes three times. This was the only time Larry Holmes was ever knocked down!

LARRY'S PRO BOXING STATS!
WINS 69 • KNOCKOUTS 44
LOSSES 6 • DRAWS 0

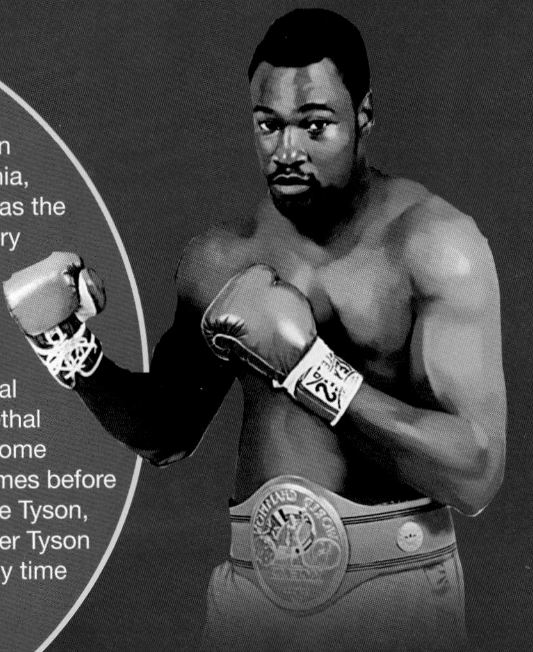

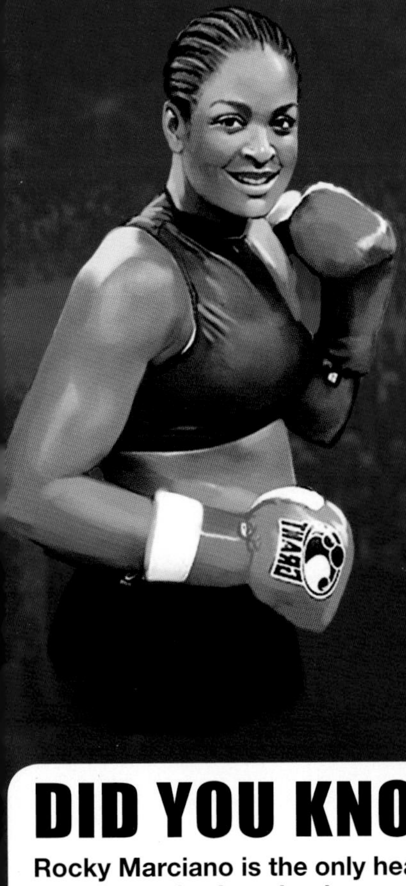

THE OTHER ALI

Ali's daughter, Laila Ali is a retired American professional boxer. On June 8, 2001, Laila fought Jackie Frazier-Lyde, Joe Frazier's daughter, in a fight that was dubbed by the media as a Ali/Frazier IV in reference to the famous trilogy of bouts between their fathers. Laila won by a majority judge's decision after eight rounds. She also became the women's super middleweight champion in 2002.

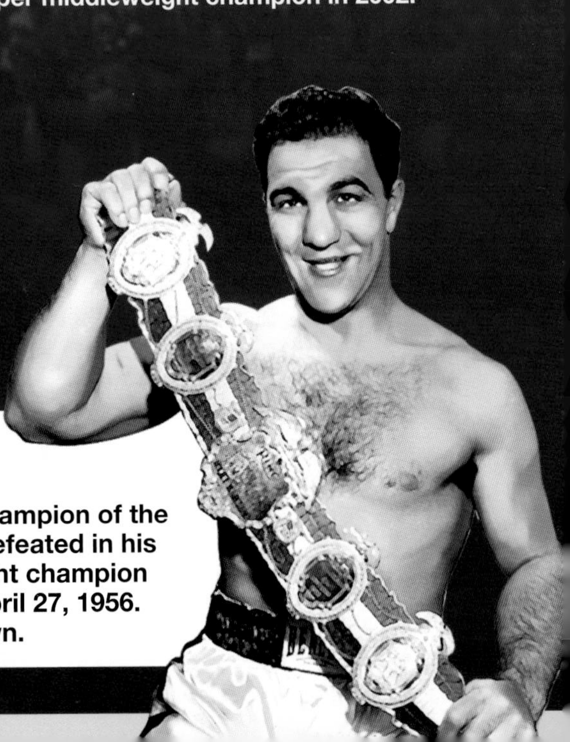

DID YOU KNOW?

Rocky Marciano is the only heavyweight champion of the world to retire from boxing completely undefeated in his professional career! He was the heavyweight champion of the world from September 23, 1952 to April 27, 1956. He fought 49 fights, and he never went down.

MUHAMMAD ALI

A LIFE OF AGONY - A LIFE OF ECSTASY

January 17, 1942: Born in Louisville, Kentucky.

1954: Starts learning boxing after his bicycle is stolen and he vows to take revenge upon those who stole it.

1954: Makes amateur boxing debut.

1960: Wins gold at Rome Olympics in the light heavyweight category.

1960: Makes professional debut.

1961: Attends his first Nation of Islam meeting.

1962: Meets Malcolm X, who was to become his spiritual mentor.

1964: Becomes world heavyweight champion after defeating Sonny Liston in seven rounds.

1964: Converts to Islam. Changes name to Muhammad Ali.

1965: Defeats Sonny Liston again in first round knockout.

1966: Objects to Vietnam War and refuses to be inducted into the armed forces. Stripped of his titles as a result.

1967-1970: Period of exile from boxing.

1971: Beaten by reigning world champion Joe Frazier. His first professional defeat.

1975: Defeats Joe Frazier.

1975: Converts to mainstream Sunni Islam.

1977: Marries Veronica Porsche. Their daughter Laila Ali was also to become a famous boxer.

1980: Beaten by Larry Holmes.

1996: Lights the Olympics flame at the Atlanta games.

June 3, 2016: Passes away in Scottsdale, Arizona.

Cultural Knockouts

Muhammad Ali's fights against Sonny Liston, George Foreman and Joe Frazier were massive sporting events. They are also considered to be major cultural landmarks of the 20th century. Ali screaming at a fallen Sonny Liston to get up after a first round knockout in 1965 is considered to be the most popular sports photograph ever. Coming at a time during the civil rights movement, this single photograph redefined African American power on the new stage to come.

Ali's bout with George Foreman for the heavyweight title took place in Kinshasa, Zaire (present day Democratic Republic of the Congo) in 1974. Nicknamed 'Rumble in the Jungle' by the press, this was the first major professional boxing bout to take place in Africa. Ali was hugely popular with the locals, who backed him throughout. One of the promoters of the bout was Don King, who later on became famous for his association with numerous other boxing legends such as Mike Tyson and Evander Holyfield.

Ali's 1975 bout against Joe Frazier took place in Manila, the Philippines. Nicknamed 'Thrilla in Manila' by the press, this bout was the culmination of the Ali-Frazier rivalry. Ali won the fight, and it quickly became known as one of the most important sporting events of the 20th century.

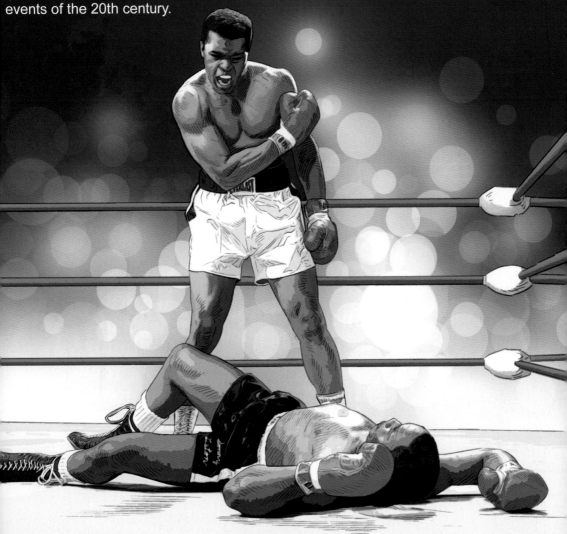

ALI'S WISDOM

I HATED EVERY MINUTE OF TRAINING, BUT I SAID, 'DON'T QUIT. SUFFER NOW AND LIVE THE REST OF YOUR LIFE AS A CHAMPION.'

A MAN WHO VIEWS THE WORLD THE SAME AT 50 AS HE DID AT 20 HAS WASTED 30 YEARS OF HIS LIFE

HEARTS AND SOULS HAVE NO COLOR

IT'S JUST A JOB. GRASS GROWS, BIRDS FLY, WAVES POUND THE SAND. I BEAT PEOPLE UP.

I am an ordinary man who worked hard to develop the talent I was given. I believed in myself and I believe in the goodness of others.

I done wrestled with an alligator, I done tussled with a whale; handcuffed lightning, thrown thunder in jail; only last week, I murdered a rock, injured a stone, hospitalised a brick; I'm so mean I make medicine sick.

Snippets

AS A BOY, CLAY LOVED COWBOY MOVIES AND HORROR FILMS.

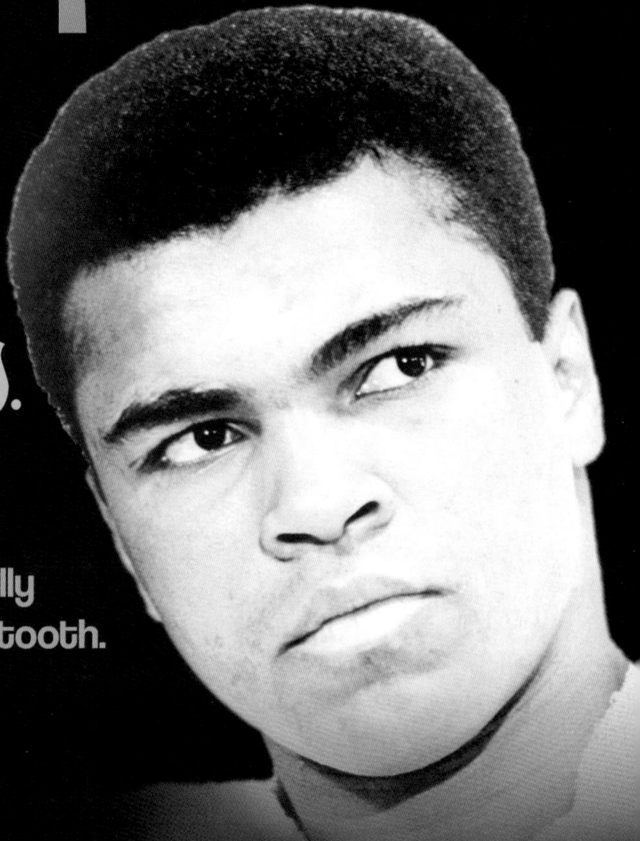

He threw his first 'punch' at six months when he swung his arm in bed and accidentally loosened his mother's front tooth.

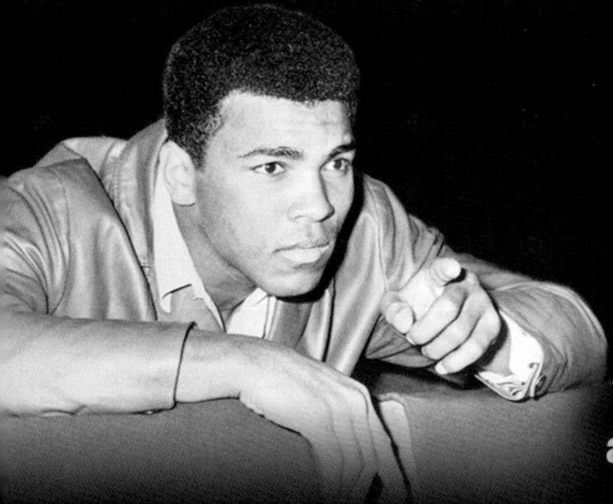

For his 1964 fight with Sonny Liston, Ali talked to everyone that knew Liston—trying to figure out how his mind worked as he searched for weaknesses.

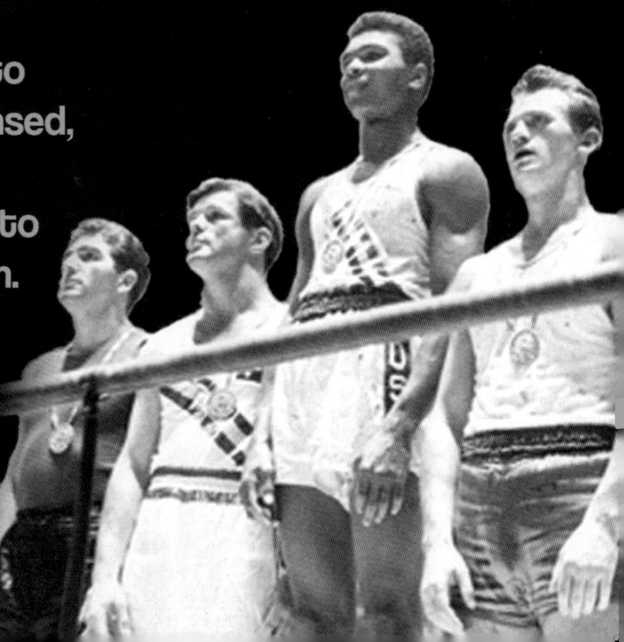
USA

In 1990, when Ali flew to Iraq to help get 15 US hostages released, the hostages turned down a faster flight home to be able to fly back with Ali and meet him.

Not only was Clay afraid of flying to the 1960 Olympics... he was also afraid of the water and couldn't swim.

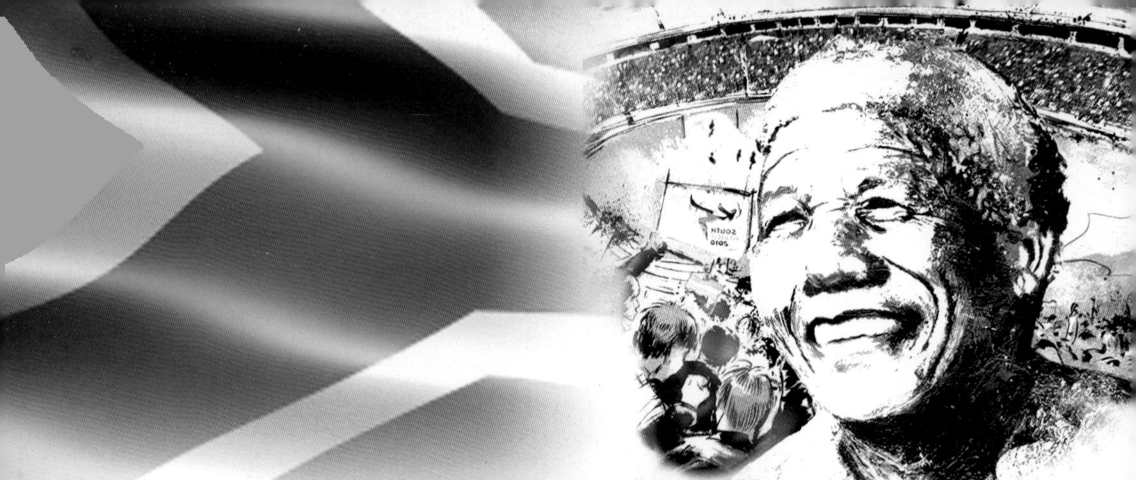

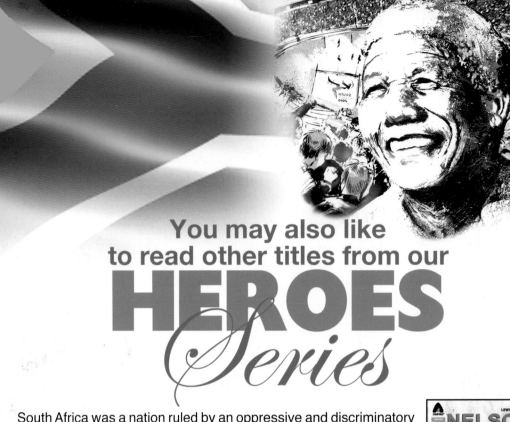

You may also like to read other titles from our

HEROES *Series*

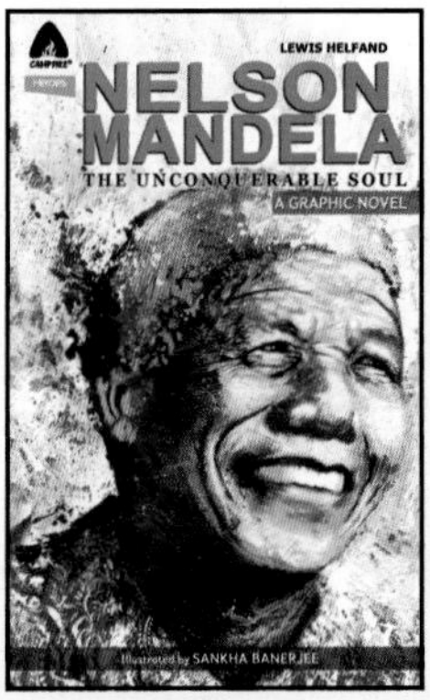
LEWIS HELFAND
NELSON MANDELA
THE UNCONQUERABLE SOUL
A GRAPHIC NOVEL
Illustrated by SANKHA BANERJEE

South Africa was a nation ruled by an oppressive and discriminatory set of laws known as apartheid. Black men and women could not have certain jobs or live in certain neighborhoods, or even walk down the street without being arrested or assaulted by the brutal police force. South Africans desperately needed their freedom and Nelson Mandela answered the call. He took the lead in the fight for the equality of all races. He was stripped of his rights, and sent to the harshest prison in all of South Africa to die. But his spirit could not be broken. From his tiny prison cell, Mandela managed to rally the entire world.

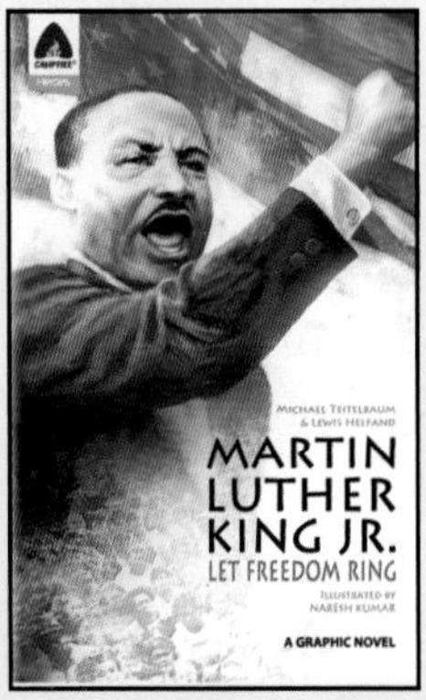
MICHAEL TEITELBAUM & LEWIS HELFAND
MARTIN LUTHER KING JR.
LET FREEDOM RING
ILLUSTRATED BY NARESH KUMAR
A GRAPHIC NOVEL

Son of a black preacher, King was taught from a young age that he was equal and deserved the same rights and freedoms as anyone else. He dreamed of a nation where people are not judged by the color of their skin but by their character. And he believed that this dream could one day become a reality.

Armed with only the non-violent teachings of Gandhi and a staunch belief that all men and women are created equal, Martin Luther King Jr. stepped to the forefront of the Civil Rights Movement. Through a series of peaceful protests and marches, King captured the attention of the world...and changed the lives of millions of Americans forever.

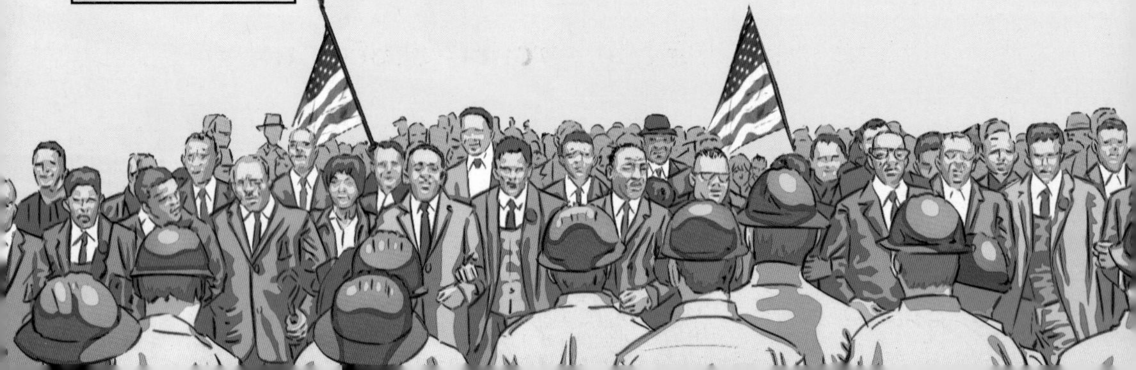